StarScope

StarScope

by

SARAH DELAMERE HURDING

POOLBEG

ABOUT THE AUTHOR

Sarah Delamere Hurding is a psychic, academic and intuitive spiritual healer. With degrees in English, philosophy and publishing (BA Hons, MSc, MPhil), she brings a unique approach to all things esoteric.

No fey New Ager, Sarah is practical, witty and down-to-earth – and her wisdom is accessible to many. So put aside your preconceived ideas and see where the StarScope journey takes you . . .

'Psychic Sarah' makes frequent media appearances and writes regularly for the *RTÉ Guide*, the *Irish Daily Star*, the *Sunday World*, the *Daily Express*, the *Daily Mail*, the *Irish Mirror*, the *Sunday People*, the *Evening Herald*, the *Irish Independent*, *Spirit* and *Destiny* magazine and *KISS* magazine.

Check out Sarah's fresh new angle on all things astrological and psychic . . .

Acknowledgements

MANY THANKS TO BONO,
MY FATHER, FAMILY AND
MANY DEAR FRIENDS FOR
THEIR ON-GOING LOVE
AND INSPIRATION

Published 2003
by Poolbeg Press Ltd
123 Grange Hill, Baldoyle
Dublin 13, Ireland
E-mail: poolbeg@poolbeg.com

Typesetting, layout, design © Poolbeg Group Services Ltd.

1 3 5 7 9 10 8 6 4 2

A catalogue record for this book is available from
the British Library.

ISBN 1-84223-174-X

Illustration by Magpie designs
Typeset by Magpie designs in Bembo and Trebuchet 11.5/15.2
Printed by Nørhaven Paperback A/S, Denmark

www.poolbeg.com

Dedicated to all those who enjoy
STAR gazing
– look heavenwards

INTRODUCTION

Hi, welcome to StarScope!

Colourful, bright and informative, this is one book that is sure to hit the spot. Prepare to be amazed, amused and entertained by the insights into your life, love, career and lots more.

StarScope will be an important reference book for years to come, containing information and guidance that is relevant and helpful.

Stay ahead of the game and look up your "nearest and dearest" and see what makes them tick. The knowledge and psychology of StarScope is invaluable.

People may be unnerved or spooked by your new-found wisdom. So do use it wisely and carefully!

Sarah

Contents

Chapter One:

Ruling Planets

• • • • • • • • • • • • • • • • • •

*This chapter identifies your Ruling Planet and the various
energies that influence your Sun Sign. Use this chapter for
added insight into 'the face' you present to the world. Check
out the forces that describe your emotional landscape and
reveal the uniqueness of your nature. Keep an open mind
and prepare to be surprised.*

ARIES
March 21st – April 20th

RULING PLANET: MARS

Aries is ruled by the fiery uncompromising planet Mars.
This glowing red explosive energy influences sex drive, our
competitive streak and physical activity. Mars inspires a
warrior-like mentality that fires up adrenaline levels and
takes no prisoners. Aries therefore possesses a determination
to win at all costs. This sign is well equipped to deal with
most crisis situations.

The energy of planet Mars inspires the Arian to swift action and the resolution of pressing issues. On the downside, Aries struggles with temper flares and a fierce unbending will – good in some situations, but don't rush in where angels fear to tread!

PERSONALITY: Technically Aries is the first sign of the Zodiac and its symbol is the Ram. The Ram represents the beginning of the birthing process – the Zodiac journey. It charges headlong into life with a big statement: I AM! The Arian determination to beat the pack is legendary. And because of this focus Aries makes an inspirational leader. Arians hate to lose at anything and their dynamic nature ensures that they rarely do.

Aries energy is able to adapt and cope with a great variety of stress and strain. The ability to do several things at once is also an enviable trait. However, the rot sets in when Aries starts to flounder or loses balance. If the Aries personal equilibrium is challenged, the fun begins.

Do be careful of your tendency to lash out verbally or even physically if you feel you are losing your grip, Aries. Stay calm, cool and be assured that you will win, even if it does not always look that way. You have the power and control to influence things in your favour, but only if you remain serene under pressure. Never show the opposition chinks in your armour. Patch them up and get on with the contest…

Watch that stubborn streak too! It would really benefit you to learn how to use charm, words and clever flattery to get your own way. Be careful not to kick and scream when things do not go as you wish. Aries also needs to keep busy and active. You have so much surplus exuberance that it can manifest as restlessness if you do not find an outlet.

Keep things moving and make sure that your vitality is expended on positive and constructive pursuits. Physical activity of any kind can help, be it sexual, sporty, or moving around in a busy job. Aries has a brilliant sense of humour too. Truly a fireball of energy, activity and fun – quite a combination!

FUTURE CAREER: In work the Arian enthusiasm must be fully engaged or focus gets scattered. Find a job that keeps you on your toes, as Arians love to quite literally think on their feet! Co-ordinating a team of people really suits the leadership qualities of Aries. You must feel valued, independent and indispensable. Not too much to ask for…

When challenged, Aries can be very inventive and is expert at defending territory and interests. Aries copes well under pressure. But if you are Aries be careful not to alienate people with your need to control events and circumstances.

Being a fire sign, quite literally a job as fire-fighter, metallurgist, or welder would suit. Aries is also brilliant at arts and crafts.

Aries energy links well to the professions of psychiatry, dentistry and psychology. As Aries does not beat about the bush, you can be guaranteed to give a fair and accurate assessment in whatever field you work in.

FUTURE HEALTH: To maintain optimum health, Aries must channel energy wisely. This fire sign is closely linked to the 'fight or flight' adrenal glands. Excess restlessness should therefore find a physical outlet. Competitive sports suit Aries, so attempt anything you can go out and win. If there is a trophy to bring home, then it suits you!

Aries may occasionally be troubled by headaches. Keep an eye out for persistent mild headaches that may indicate a secondary kidney problem. Aries is very connected to the head. So it would be a rare Arian who did not experience the odd bash, bump or bruise. Guard against clumsiness. But if you are sporty you can expect sprains and strains every now and again.

Aries is an intrinsically healthy sign. As long as you pay attention with a good, sensible routine not much will go wrong. Stick to savoury foods and eat plenty of protein. Be aware that spicy foods introduce too much fire to your system – you have quite enough already! Do the basics of eating, sleeping and exercising hard. Then overall you can look forward to years of good health.

FUTURE LOVE: Aries is a dynamo and falls in love very quickly . . . or should I say lust? Of all the signs Aries is not backwards about coming forwards! With a dynamic Arian things move quickly. They are quick to show interest when they fancy someone, but they tire just as quickly once the fun is over. Aries has a low tolerance level. And if their ferocious physical appetites are not satiated, there will be problems. Partners have to keep up – or else!

If you are Aries pay a little more attention to the finesse of romantic relationships. Some signs love to be wooed and want love to develop slowly but surely. Unless you can develop some grounding and patience, you are liable to miss out on the subtle nuances of seduction.

Also, be cautious re commitment. Make sure your feelings are going to last before you say 'I do'! However, if you have found someone who can match your lust, enthusiasm and appetite for life, therein is a lasting connection. Hold onto it for dear life. Rarely does such intensity and reciprocity come around twice. So be willing to put in the work and effort once you are settled. Build on equality in your relationships and all will be well. Singletons however should sow their wild oats and proceed with caution. Passion is a seductive feeling, of course. But more haste, less speed would not go amiss.

COMPATIBLE SIGNS: Fellow Aries understand your passionate nature, but guard against major rows when stubborn wills clash. Gemini is very suitable and compatible. And Leo is all heart. Sagittarius is a great match in the bedroom. But things could get boring quickly. Scorpio is a sexy sign but the Scorpion need to be in control could trouble Aries. Ideally, Aries should avoid Taurus 24/7. But it can work if independence is respected. Pisces is way too intense and overly romantic – the language of love is just too different.

BIRTHSTONE: Diamond, amethyst
COLOURS: Reds and gold
ZODIAC NUMBER: 5
FAMOUS SEXY ARIANS: Warren Beatty, Vic Reeves, Victoria Beckham, Chris Evans, Elton John, Russell Crowe, Mariah Carey, Eddie Murphy, Joan Crawford, Celine Dion, Charlie Chaplin, Marlon Brando, Vincent van Gogh, John Major, Quentin Tarantino, Vivienne Westwood

TAURUS
April 21st - May 21st

RULING PLANET: VENUS

Venus is the planet that engages our feelings. This emotional energy challenges the way we relate to each other socially and financially. Venus heightens the connection between our romantic and economic relationships. She demonstrates that everything is interlinked. According to this Ruling Planet, love, money, sex and material possessions are irretrievably married – for better or for worse!

Venus emphasises partnerships, professional and personal. If you are Taurus, notice how your attitudes concerning money are reflected in your attitudes re love and romance. This may sound particularly mercenary, but remember Taurus is a practical Zodiac sign that oozes common sense. Love comes at a price with Taurus...

PERSONALITY: Taurus is the second Zodiac sign. The keynote of the Bull is "I have". This methodical creature needs to roam the pastures, assess the landscape, graze and generally plod around. Taureans are loyal and respect their own. Eternally charming, they cover their tracks in the nicest possible way. Taurus is one of the Zodiac's nifty movers...

There is definitely an emphasis on material goods with this sign. Possessions represent stability and safety for Taurus. For when surrounded with the trappings of wealth, Taurus can take on the world. Material decadence amounts to self-confidence and pride for this earth sign.

Aside from an innate natural charm, Taurus is prone to possessiveness. With their need for security and surety, Bulls are sticklers for control. Taureans need to know where they stand. And that everything is going to be 'just so'. Shake their financial foundation or threaten the status quo, and you can expect short shrift . . .

Never corner a Taurean, if you know what is good for you. Ever heard of the 'red rag to a bull'? Once 'level head-ed' Taurus loses its temper, you can expect a stampede. So it is best to allow this fixed sign to rule the roost in a laid-back, easy manner . . .

Taureans are not the Zodiac's chief risk takers. They will gamble only on a sure thing and like to see proof of a return before an investment is made, be it emotional, financial or romantic.

Your Taurean birthright ensures oodles of patience, beauty and charisma. You can truly charm the birds from the trees. What you say is always interesting, for you have a natural intelligence and instinctual understanding of life. You are methodical, systematic and deliberate in your gestures. Just be careful not to take advantage of that seductive ability!

If you are Taurus, avoid unnecessary or prolonged stress by facing things as and when they arise. Do not buy into proverbial ostrich behaviour or hide your head in the sand when the going gets rough . . .

FUTURE CAREER: Taurus loves a steady routine with predictable hours and no upsets. The ability to organise a wide range of people, items, and functions means that many careers are suitable. If you are Taurus, never work with someone who wants to run the show or control the proceedings. For this will drive you quite mad, as you need to feel indispensable . . .

With the emphasis on all things material and financial, Taurus possesses a great propensity to make money. Being great bankers, the large corporations suit this methodical mentality. Taureans are disciplined and anxious to succeed, for the fulfilment of ambitions provides the necessary stability which Taurus holds so dear...

Naturals in the world of beauty or luxury, Taurus has aesthetic taste and a nose for classic items. And, since bulls are naturally linked to the earth, suitable careers are agriculture, farming and architecture.

Taureans are wonderfully musical. So expect chart success and major accolades when you express your creativity!

FUTURE HEALTH: Taureans have a natural grace and beauty that often inspires jealousy in others, but, your love of food makes you prone to weight gain if you are not careful. Rich foods are the 'bugbear' of your existence. So go easy on the sauces, chocolate and sweets. Plenty of fresh fruit and vegetables will keep your system revved up and working more efficiently. Lay off the gunk!

Exercise is crucial for Taurus, as your metabolism is rather slow. You also respond well to a regular gym routine. The repetitive movements of weight training suit you, and you can expect good results quite quickly. Taurus loves the afterglow of a sensuous massage and sauna, but the discipline of the workout must come first.

Taurus is connected to the voice and neck. So do guard against sore throats and voice problems. Also, keep an eye on thyroid function, especially if you notice weight gain you cannot account for – be honest about the cream buns whilst making your assessment!

FUTURE LOVE: Natural good looks and 'bucket loads' of charm enable the Bull to play the field, and have the pick of the crop, but Taurus is rarely in a hurry to connect. This earthy creature wants to be sure of a good thing first – those security issues again! Marriage brings the 'safe' feeling that loyalty and commitment provide, and, once committed, Taurus tends not to stray. Well, not when anyone is watching anyhow.

There is no escaping the compelling Taurean. Sounds ominous? Well, it can be, for when Taurus is off balance, there are issues of possession, and an obsessive tendency can ruin otherwise healthy relationships.

Taurus finds it difficult to let go and needs to express anger and frustration vocally, for if emotions become blocked the eventual explosion is not a pretty sight. Never treat loved ones and friends as possessions. Learn to respect their freedom and independence . . . your loyalty will be well rewarded. A great provider, and seriously dependable, you make an ideal partner for those who want security, safety and material stability.

Romantic gestures come easily to Taurus and you are the stuff dreams are made of. No Zodiac sign is as sensual, intense and romantic all at the same time . . . What's your number?

COMPATIBLE SIGNS: Earth signs Virgo and Capricorn are

true soul mates. They understand your need for reliability, grounding and sensual expression. Scorpio, your opposite, provides a powerful telepathic link - sexy too! Leo is good fun and looks great. And Pisces is something of a loose cannon ... Aries is not a good idea 24/7 – it could end in tears. Aquarius is detached and missing the TLC factor. And Sagittarius is too unpredictable and flighty. Cancer and Libra are good friends, but too different. And go easy with fellow Taurus – a potential clash of the Titans!

BIRTHSTONE: Emerald, moss agate

COLOURS: Pale blue and greens - also pink

ZODIAC NUMBER: 6

FAMOUS SEXY TAUREANS: Jack Nicolson, Al Pacino, Michael Palin, Shirley MacLaine, Bianca Jagger, Cher, Andrea Corr, Bono, Michelle Pfeiffer, Meryl Streep, Diana Ross, Priscilla Presley, Sigmund Freud, Pope John Paul II, Queen Elizabeth II, William Shakespeare, James Brown, Barbra Streisand, George Clooney, Karl Marx, Orson Welles, Salvador Dali, David Beckham, Tony Blair, Jean Paul Gaultier, André Agassi, Janet Jackson, Pierce Brosnan

---

GEMINI
May 22nd - June 22nd

RULING PLANET: MERCURY

Mercury's influence is cerebral and lively. This planet's position is the best indicator of the way a person's mind works.

Mercury is a small but potent planet that impacts on our intelligence and thought patterns. Mental agility may be instinctive, logical, slow and deliberate, or somewhat scattered. Whether we are intuitive or excruciatingly systematic in our thinking, Mercury provides the clue...

Mercury enhances our ability to make decisions. And it also determines how we communicate. It is no wonder that Geminis have such lively minds and original ways of thinking. Their interest in a great diversity of people, places and subjects also reflects Mercury's activity.

PERSONALITY: Gemini is the third Zodiac sign, represented by the Twins. The keynote of Gemini is "I think", consequently, the mental plane is the main domain of this cerebral sign. The Twins inhabit an 'airy' environment. So a certain amount of duality is inevitable. It goes with the territory and makes Gemini a challenging and stimulating sign to relate to.

Gemini can do several things at once – always useful! In fact the more external 'mental' activities this sign engages in, the better. Reading many books, thinking about diverse and varied subjects, and setting themselves mind-blowing tasks keeps Gemini amused.

Concentration is the 'bugbear' of Gemini existence. An innate restlessness combined with a predisposition to boredom means that Gemini is difficult to entertain. Living with such in-built duality is a job in itself. And Geminis need to utilise strengths and develop patience in order to retain sanity!

Gemini is likely to gloss over subjects and does not take kindly to dredging up emotive issues. This nifty avoidance inspires accusations of superficiality. And Gemini is inclined to be flippant when bored!

On the plus side, Gemini is eminently entertaining and guaranteed fun. Not much will destroy this determined sensibility that looks for the good in everything.

The Gemini destiny demands a lively lifestyle. But Gemini is inclined to live on frayed nerves. This expends a lot of energy and can spread Gemini – who wants to get everything done yesterday – a bit thinly. At its best the Gemini mind is constructive, optimistic and keen. However, Gemini is capable of deception, fraud and underhand behaviour in a bid to stay amused!

Gemini recognises the complexity of life and the human tendency to wriggle! So rarely does this sign trust implicitly. This, of course, puts the question mark permanently over their behaviour, if we are to believe the validity of projection.

FUTURE CAREER: Gemini is liable to go quietly insane unless permanently stimulated. A predictable routine is virtual suicide for a sign that needs endless entertainment. Something must hold Gemini's attention, or it is not worthy of that attention.

Never settle for tedious work that makes you feel ungrounded, or tired, Gemini. You must be energised by the task in hand, or expect copious amounts of hot air to be expended in frustration!

Many leading surgeons, counsellors and psychotherapists are Gemini. And for those who like to bounce ideas around, teaching and lecturing are perfect.

Communications, media work and publishing are tailor-made . . . and the Internet holds endless possibilities, as does the travel industry. The ideal career involves a laptop, travel and the requirement to speak on the phone several times a day . . .

Film work or creative work behind the camera is OK in theory. But Gemini has to be focused and determined to make it to Hollywood . . .

FUTURE HEALTH: Gemini is essentially a lithe, wiry, healthy person. But the tendency to get overstressed should be tempered. Correct channelling of energy is crucial to Gemini health. And any activity that expends excess or frantic stress is to be indulged . . .

Gemini tends to have a high metabolism, but can become slow and sluggish if bored, listless, or unfulfilled. A happy Gemini is a slim, fit and lively individual – a stimulating mind encapsulated in an 'airy' body. The Twin with the sulky face, however, can be overweight, overindulgent and very wasteful of time, food, and money!

Vigorous daily exercise keeps Gemini at the peak of fitness, for both mind and body benefit from a strict routine. Anything that enables Gemini to feel the wind in their hair is recommended. Cycling, hang-gliding, parachuting, running, and racquet sports offer the variety Gemini needs.

Gemini rules the lungs – so do not even think about smoking. And since Gemini influences the shoulders, arms and hands, the avoidance of broken limbs is also highly recommended . . .

FUTURE LOVE: It is relatively easy for Gemini to make the

moves when they are attracted to someone. These great communicators of the Zodiac possess a fine imagination. Charming, witty and creative, not much stands in the way of Gemini on the prowl . . .

Over time however, Gemini's dual nature is a potential spanner in the works. Along with their low boredom threshold . . . an immature Gemini finds the battle to settle down a constant struggle. Indeed, complete faithfulness is a rare achievement for those with lashings of Gemini energy.

Partners of Gemini have to understand their need to fulfil restless urges. At least permit a semblance of freedom. The looser the leash, the more likely it is Gemini will stay true, so it certainly does not pay to mistrust or nag Gemini!

With Gemini, the risks are worth it. For Gemini is great at expressions of heartfelt love. Gemini is not afraid to verbalise feelings, and indeed may astound many with the speed with which they fall madly in (and out) of love. Also, sexually, Geminis make for lively and imaginative bedfellows. So complaints in the 'boudoir' department are unlikely!

Gemini needs to avoid the 'slippers and sofas' syndrome at all costs . . .

COMPATIBLE SIGNS: Aries is a great match – these two can be best friends as well as lovers. Fellow Gemini understand. Whilst Aquarius has intelligence and detachment, which keeps the interest up, Cancer is far too emotional and needy. And there is a lot of game playing and potential deceit re Pisces. Virgo and Capricorn are way too staid, organised, and predictable for flighty Gemini. But Scorpio and Sagittarius present a challenge. Scorpio is the seducer and

Gemini will play along. And Sagittarius is playful, but too fiery.

BIRTHSTONE: Agate, beryl, aquamarine
COLOURS: Bright colours, yellow in particular
ZODIAC NUMBER: 7
FAMOUS SEXY GEMINIS: Julian Clary, Kylie Minogue, Nicole Kidman, Liz Hurley, Mark Wahlberg, Denise Van Outen, Tom Jones, Sir Paul McCartney, Mel B, Bob Dylan, Clint Eastwood, Brooke Shields, Marilyn Monroe, Judy Garland, Bob Hope, William Butler Yeats, Queen Victoria, Henry Kissinger, John F Kennedy, Naomi Campbell, Colin Farrell

---

CANCER
June 23rd - July 23rd

RULING PLANET: THE MOON

The Moon influences our lives at a profound level. Her powerful lunar energy has an amazing impact on our creativity. Both our psyche and energy are invariably affected, and depend upon her current phase and position.

The Moon connects us to the feminine aspect, regardless of our natal sex. The nurturing energies of the Moon define our parenting skills, and emotional impulses. Its gentle but relentless force shapes our familial and domestic arrangements.

Lunar inspiration affects intuition, instinctual reactions; and the ebb and flow of our feelings. Moon energy rules the changing tides of the sea. But she also governs the twists and turns of our behaviour patterns . . .

PERSONALITY: Cancer is the fourth Zodiac sign, represented by the Crab. The keynote of Cancer is "I feel". The personality of this Crustacean is difficult to describe. Defensive, at apparently illogical times, Cancer is still one of the most loving, open Zodiac signs. The innate 'Crabby' tendency at unpredictable moments only adds to the fun . . .

Cancer is a receptive and highly sensitive sign, capable of huge empathy. The Crab cuts to the chase, giving oodles of love, care and reassurance when required. Moody and unfathomable, maybe . . . but win Cancer's trust and you ensure a lifetime of friendship and support.

It is very easy to get on the wrong side of Cancer. Even casual, cutting remarks can have a devastating effect on the sensitised Crab. Be warned! Cancer is very black and white when someone wrongs them. There is no negotiation, and no reprieve. You are history . . .

When off balance, Cancer can be its own worst enemy. A born worrier, the Crab can get quite worked up about silly details and arrangements. This sign is not great at going with the flow. Worries can become quite irrational, and self-defeating.

Cancerians need to be nurtured, loved and treasured in order to flourish. Only when they feel secure do they reach peak form. Shake their foundation and surety? Cancer will beat a hasty retreat, ignoring you thereafter!

The contents of the Cancer brain are vivid, lively, and entertaining. Prepare to be greatly amused. The Crab possesses a wicked sense of humour. Plus an uncanny ability to see through pretence and deception.

There is a touch of genius about Cancer. Hence the temperamental nature. Cancer is creative with an incredible imagination, which often feeds unpredictable reactions. Obviously, Mr or Miss Crabby is liable to make a mountain out of a molehill, when under pressure.

If you are Cancer, learn to channel your imagination in constructive and positive ways. For, when you are inventive and focused, few can match your original, impressive demeanour ...

FUTURE CAREER: Cancer should emphasise career enjoyment rather than riches and wealth. When the correct life path is found, 'filthy lucre' inevitably rolls in. But Cancer comes unstuck when overly focused upon finances and security issues.

In work, the Crab's creativity requires an outlet. However, Cancerians also need routine and respond well to structure. Continuity is important, as well as variety and change. Cancer loves to be surprised and stimulated, but not unnerved or disarmed ...

Cancer is astute with a keen nose for business. This sign is shrewd, and can turn anything into a profit-making venture.

Since Cancer has a great connection to the past, and is the traditional 'hoarder' of the Zodiac, the Antique and Fine Art disciplines make sense too. The caring and pampering professions allow Cancer to nurture and inspire others. And Crabs are often great cooks, who love the whole 'foody' thing.

This creature's natural habitat is the open sea. So work on cruise ships, freight carriers and ferries fulfil the need for adventure combined with security of tenure ...

FUTURE HEALTH: Cancerians are healthy with a strong constitution. But stress and rumination are the scourge of this lunar creature. Ruled by the Moon, routines with an eastern or spiritual origin are particularly beneficial. Yoga, swimming, and aerobics help Cancer channel energy constructively ...

Do not panic about the connection between Zodiac Cancer and the disease of the same name – there isn't one! However, be responsible and keep up with routine checks of the breast and chest area...

When you are off-balance a stomach upset is the main event! So do monitor your reaction to different foods. For if your system is overstressed or sensitised you are more prone to intolerance. Rotate foods, and keep an eye on cravings.

Cancerian skin is particularly sensitive, and prone to itchiness or rashes of untraceable origin. A dietary approach plus attempts to de-stress will help you manage ...

For optimum health, Crabs should listen to heart, body, and soul at all times. Never doubt those 'inner rumblings'...

FUTURE LOVE: Cancer thrives on the nurturing possibilities of love connections. But strong and powerful emotions should be monitored, or the Crab risks overwhelming the object of their affection ...

Cancer is a true romantic who enjoys being wooed and

seduced. However, 'cosiness' may set in, if the urge to nurture and protect takes precedence. Crabs should maintain their independence, and so guarantee a lifetime of intensity and passion.

If you are Cancer, be flexible within your relationships, and allow for development and change. Protect yourself, or you may feel left behind and abandoned when love moves on. Respect freedom. There is no point drowning someone in kindness. Besides, your wonderfully warm sensuality and ability to 'tune in' will keep them coming back for more.

You are an expressive and brilliant lover. Guard your heart though, for you are quite sensitive and susceptible. Always make sure that your affections are reciprocated, before you get in too deep.

Temper the urge to be overly sentimental about the past, for this may hamper your progress in the present. Current relationships do not respond well to a persistent potted history of past encounters. For sanity's sake, discard those rose tinted spectacles . . .

COMPATIBLE SIGNS: Fellow Crab is a match made in heaven, whilst Virgo is a stabilising influence and support. Scorpio is a whirlwind in the bedroom. And Pisces is a lot of fun with a wicked sense of humour. Taurus is a compelling partner though there will be differences of opinion! Capricorn is reliable and steady, but on balance is probably too austere and cold. Leo will get distracted and not be able to give full-time attention. Gemini is too flirty, though shares a sense of humour. Air signs do not measure up . . .

BIRTHSTONE: Pearl, moonstone, emerald
COLOURS: Pale blue, silver, sea greens, greys and violet
ZODIAC NUMBER: 2
FAMOUS SEXY CANCERIANS: Pamela Anderson, James Cagney, George Michael, Neil Morrissey, Mike Tyson, Dani Behr, Courtney Love, Richard Branson, Harrison Ford, Robin Williams, Tom Cruise, Princess Diana, Nelson Mandela, Gareth Gates, Michael Flatley, Louis Walsh

---

LEO
July 24th - August 23rd

RULING PLANET: THE SUN

The Sun is the most luminous and obvious 'planet' in the sky. Down the aeons the Sun has been worshipped for its life-giving force. Without the Sun we would not exist and our lives would have no warmth, heat or sustenance. The Sun is the centre of our World, and the Universe. All the other Ruling Planets revolve around it.

The Sun enhances and emphasises our primal instincts. It heightens a person's power, and lends them an air of ultimate authority. Ego issues go hand in hand with those ruled by the Sun - it could be no other way! But the Sun also ensures great generosity and a magnanimous attitude. Along with an open heart and sunny disposition, those ruled by the Sun are difficult to resist.

PERSONALITY: Leo is the fifth Zodiac sign, represented by

the Lion. The keynote of the Lion is "I create". The Leo personality loves to be adored and is compelled to find a kingdom over which to rule. Leo is the performer of the Zodiac who needs a 'spot' in which to shine. It is inevitable that Leo will stumble into the limelight, for there is no place to run and hide once the Sun comes out!

Leo takes enormous pride in achievement. And the Lion is typically deserving of accolades and reverential treatment. Spells of depression last but a moment. For the Lion is eternally optimistic. Leo does not buy into negativity or toxic thinking, and is not prone to self-sabotage.

Natural serenity, dignity and regal grandeur identify Leo; who makes an entrance, even when incognito . . .

Life must be experienced to the MAX according to Leo. The Lion does not waste energy ruminating about the past, or feeding off regrets. Every moment is savoured and heightened for complete sensation. Leo is prone to hedonism and loves to luxuriate in comfortable surroundings indulging an inherent laziness!

Leo is a master at energising a team, task or situation. For it is difficult to feel downcast in the face of such a sunny, jolly disposition. But Leo must also be very careful not to antagonise. Unruly Leo can be quite argumentative. And there is certainly an air of natural authority that comes with the Leo buzz. Leo should watch out - mistakes are made when bloody-minded arrogance goes to the Leonine head!

If you are Leo it is advisable to develop some tolerance and flexibility. Leave things to unfold organically as much as possible, and bend others to your will with a softer approach.

A slightly understated Leo is going to go much further, than one who is in-your-face garish and bordering on the offensive. Basically, if Leo can keep the reins on over-the-top behaviour, gestures and statements, there is no competition!

FUTURE CAREER: Leo is the Zodiac showman/showwoman. Never mind the occupation, the Lion inevitably finds a way to make an impact. Leo is a creative sign with the potential for vast achievement. Leo combines beguiling maverick style with inspirational energy. Here is an ambitious sign that loves the thought of adulation, if not the experience . . .

Leo is prepared to put in Trojan effort to ensure success. But the Lion plays fair and will not sabotage the reputation of others for personal gain. The Universe acknowledges this honesty. And victory is sweeter for a genuine display of honour.

Work linking to stage, music, theatre or film is highly desirable. Leo makes a great TV presenter, and the occasional mad chef is known to be Leo. For controlled, disciplined Leo, a career in the army is appropriate.

The Lion who enters the ministry makes a very effective pastor or preacher, whilst natural charm and charisma render Leo a potent politician – of the performing variety of course.

FUTURE HEALTH: Leo needs warmth, whether from a log-fire, hot water bottle, or the Sun itself. The Zodiac Lion has a strong constitution and can weather most things, but must take care of circulation above all. Leo rules the heart, so

Lions must nurture this vital organ with the correct diet, exercise and emotional support.

Stretching exercises, swimming and yoga are all great exercises for the Lion who needs to guard against back problems in later life. Maintaining suppleness and flexibility will protect both the flow of energy and the posture of Leo.

Any form of movement that requires imagination and self-expression is great for Leo. Music and dance keep the heart in peak condition, along with a daily constitutional in the fresh air.

Leo is well advised to stay away from formal exercise or team sports unless it is possible to avoid the natural inclination to show off! Pumping iron is not for Leo either – for the same reason . . .

FUTURE LOVE: Leo is all heart, and should therefore guard against being hurt. The Zodiac Lion is easily wounded, and falls in love heavily and swiftly. If intense feelings are returned in full, Leo is destined for blissful happiness. But life can be unkind. And Leo will usually experience heartache, before peace and harmony finally descend.

Leo is a faithful creature, who is naturally loyal but open. The Lion loves social intercourse, and needs the stimulation of a variety of connections. Partners should understand that Leo is completely faithful when given free rein!

The Leo heart is slow to heal. For Leo feels everything deeply and intensely. If you are Leo be careful not to overwhelm your partner with your generous spirit. Less is definitely more when you are in love. You do need to make a heart connection, but hold back to protect yourself. Make

23

sure that your partner is up for it and committed before you let it all hang out!

Be careful not to be too dominant in your relationships or you will scare everyone off, never mind the love interest. Accept that sometimes people will say 'no'. Leo needs an enthusiastic and responsive partner - someone who can occasionally give 'what for!'

COMPATIBLE SIGNS: Fellow fire signs suit Leo. Passions fly, and there is understanding without tedium. Taurus is 'low key', but provides the quality romance which Leo desires. Gemini is lively and interesting. However, loyalty issues could send it all pear-shaped. Water signs are generally too broody and intense for Leo. Pisces is liable to outwit the Lion, which will not go down well. And Scorpio is a match for any Leo - These conflicting egos will fight it out incessantly! Virgo sees through Leonine traits in an instant. And Capricorn is just not up for the permanent party . . .

BIRTHSTONE: Ruby, amber, chrysolite
COLOURS: All the colours of the sun from sunrise to sunset
ZODIAC NUMBER: 19
FAMOUS SEXY LEOS: Bill Clinton, Mick Jagger, J. Lo, Arnold Schwarzenegger, Madonna, Alfred Hitchcock, Fidel Castro, Napoleon Bonaparte, Mussolini, Jacqueline Kennedy Onassis, Robert Redford, Geri Halliwell, Neil Armstrong, Princess Anne, Roy Keane

VIRGO
August 24th-September 23rd

RULING PLANET: MERCURY

Mercury enhances mind power, empowering both intuition and logical thought. Sun signs ruled by this energy usually have staggering intellectual capacity. Mercury enables its people to see around corners, and to cover all aspects of an argument. This planet is thorough, brilliant, and leaves no stone unturned.

Mercury facilitates the decision-making progress, propelling us towards conclusions. Whether by logic or intuition, Mercury allows for optimum mind function. Those ruled by Mercury possess the inside track to swift resolution. Some situations need the clear, sharp discipline of logic, or lateral thought, whilst others cut to the chase with a searing and impressive intuition. Mercury wins either way . . .

PERSONALITY: Virgo is the sixth sign of the Zodiac. The keynote of this Earth Goddess is "I serve". Supposedly modest, shy and prudish, Virgo has a reputation for being the cool, aloof Zodiac Virgin. Nothing could be further from the truth. Virgo's links to harvest, fertility, and female goddess energy conjure up a suitably prolific image.

Virgo is perhaps the Zodiac's best-kept secret. This sign is right about most things, much to the infuriation of those who think they know best. Many little oracles are born under Virgo! The combination of intuition, logic, and grounded sensibility make Virgo a formidable opponent indeed.

Virgo has tunnel vision when focused and is inclined to get caught up in the intricacies of an argument. Virgo is innately intelligent, but an overcautious attitude to life is a potential problem. Virgo waits for life to happen. Or rather, life happens whilst Virgo sits there, observes, takes note and probably writes about it!

Typically, Virgo finds it difficult to engage in the fray. The Zodiac Virgin is not inclined to 'put it out there' and consequently gets overlooked much of the time. But given a chance to shine by being ASKED, Virgo quickly outwits the competition.

Virgo is a practical earth sign with an answer for everything. Virgo pays attention to detail and gets results. However this little worrier is inclined to miss the bigger picture fretting about inconsequential nonsense.

Virgo is no great chatterbox, but she can knock the socks off anyone in an argument. When the Virgin speaks, it means something. There is a purpose to every Virgo action, thought, word and deed. Here we have the Zodiac workaholic who makes every second count . . .

If you are Virgo, be mindful of your intimidating intelligence. You have the ability to 'blind with science', and few can match you. Because you are usually right, you may inspire jealousy. So stay silent rather than alienate the world. One thing is for sure . . . your searing intuition ensures your impact as a weapon of massive distraction!

FUTURE CAREER: To flourish, Virgo needs a secure, safe

environment. Any work that diverts negative rumination into positive output is to be encouraged. It is very difficult to pick holes in Virgo's work, for they have already spent hours doing just that. Virgo makes a great publisher, writer, secretary, or personal assistant. Anything left to Virgo will be done efficiently and brilliantly in next to no time!

Group activities and teamwork do not always suit. Virgo tends to get overlooked, or may become annoyed with everyone else's incompetence.

Virgo makes a brilliant teacher, as ruler Mercury ensures the delivery of clear, accurate, information. Investigative journalism is also suitable, for Virgo can write effectively and has an original way of putting things.

Because Virgo tends to ruminate about health issues, careers in medicine and alternative healing are ideal.

Finally any career that connects Virgo to Mother Nature is restorative and calming. Opportunities to empty and de-stress that busy mind should be welcomed!

FUTURE HEALTH: Virgo has impressive levels of physical and mental energy, but any excess is liable to find an outlet in worry and stress. Virgo needs to sublimate wayward ener-gies and enhance connections to Mother Earth.

Virgo rules the nervous system and stomach. So when things go wrong, stomach complaints and frayed nerves sur-face. Whole foods and simple recipes form the best fodder for Virgo. And the avoidance of additives is advisable.

Alternative approaches to healing suit Virgo's disposi-tion. Treatments such as reiki, yoga, crystals and homeopathy knock 'niggles' on the head . . .

An aerobic exercise such as yoga is much better for Virgo than a rigorous gym workout. But a regular routine is crucial to ongoing health. Variation will nip the scourge of boredom in the bud . . .

FUTURE LOVE: Virgo finds it difficult to believe that anyone would fall for them. Highly self-critical, Virgo likes to offer perfection only. So if they feel inadequate in any area – not slim, tall or cute enough – they will take some persuading! The irony is that Virgo is often quite stunning. And others fail to understand where the reluctance to engage comes from.

Virgo often gets called aloof, snobby or unattainable. But a smug Virgo is a rare creature indeed. If you want to woo and win a Virgo, plenty of reassurance about your genuine intentions will be needed.

Virgo modesty can be a problem in the bedroom, but what is rarely reported is that when the Virgin gets into gear, he/she is earthy and passionate. Once committed, Virgo is loyal and faithful. Even if the physical aspect of a relationship has diminished, Virgo will not stray.

If you are a Virgo, be careful not to project your issues onto your partners and loved ones. Modify your expectations of people, places and things for sanity's sake. Learn to accept others on their own merit and appreciate the positive aspect of doing things differently. You can not expect to realistically control the proceedings from dawn to dusk, so chill…

COMPATIBLE SIGNS: Taurus and Virgo fulfil each other's wildest dreams! And Cancer has the full-on sensuality Virgo needs. Virgo and Virgo are liable to drive each other wild with desire, but mad with frustration. Pisces is highly charged with oodles of sex appeal, whilst Scorpio is suitably sexy, minus the control issues. Aries is a loose cannon, without stability. Similarly, Gemini is exciting company, but as for lifelong commitment, forget it! Aquarius understands, but gets exasperated when Virgo is right. Libra is funny, irresistible and hard work. Leo and Sagittarius are OK for a fling.

BIRTHSTONE: Sardonyx, jasper, cobblestone, emerald
COLOURS: Browns, dark grey and navy blue
ZODIAC NUMBER: 7
FAMOUS SEXY VIRGOS: Hugh Grant, Michael Jackson, Pink, Claudia Schiffer, Cameron Diaz, Liam Gallagher, Keanu Reeves, Harry Connick Jnr, Guy Ritchie, Stella McCartney, Barry Gibb, Sophia Loren, Gloria Estafan, D H Lawrence, Leo Tolstoy, H G Wells, Queen Elizabeth I, Lauren Bacall, Ingrid Bergman, Beyonce Knowles

---

LIBRA
September 24th - October 23rd

RULING PLANET: VENUS

Venus heightens our feelings. This emotional energy challenges the way we relate to each other socially and financially. Venus points out the connection between our romantic and economic relationships. According to this Ruling Planet love, money, sex and material possessions are irretrievably married – for better or for worse!

Venus's activity in Libra emphasises the importance of equilibrium and balance. Libra needs and thrives on positive partnerships. This sign flourishes when there are impartial judgements and merciful decisions to be made. Libra is characterised by the gracious and fair demeanour that Venus bestows. Merciful and magnanimous when in balance, Venus heightens Libra's ability to live compassionately and considerately.

PERSONALITY: Libra is the seventh Zodiac sign, which is symbolised by the karmic weighing scales. The keynote of these Libran Scales of Justice is "I balance". Libra needs to relate, for this sign feels incomplete and inferior when not making meaningful connections. Establishing harmony is the *raison d'être* of Libra.

Music expands Libran consciousness. It is both inspirational and healing for this sign to expose its psyche to a wall of sound.

Libra is elegant from the inside out. Along with a great image and eye for what looks right, Libra always makes an impression.

Librans are not happy unless they are sharing something. They need to express their souls interdependently. Equilibrium holds the key to success, for when off balance, Libra is prone to getting caught up in relationships that are too cloying or claustrophobic.

Gregarious Libra desires nurturing company. These souls thrive wherever they are valued and appreciated. With a wicked sense of humour, Libra is invaluable socially. The

Scales do not actively interfere, but they do need to feel indispensable. This sign loves to define status and boundaries, and gets mightily distressed when disorder descends.

Libra incarnates with inherent wisdom, and is well able to offer impartial judgements which help others. However, Libra is not so skilled at unravelling personal dilemmas. Indecisiveness is the traditional Libran challenge. If you are Libra, discern what will work for you, and discard what has no hope of coming to fruition. Any decision is a good one when you feel stuck.

Be sure not to sit on the fence too often, or you will miss out on many of life's golden opportunities. It is actually better to take a leap of faith and go for something, rather than sit back and see what happens. Begin to notice that when you do this generally NOTHING happens! Life will NOT fall into your lap, Libra. So learn to go after things and do not be afraid to take the initiative...

FUTURE CAREER: Getting to the top of the career ladder is a potentially isolating experience for Libra. Libra requires company and needs a team situation as a foil for self-expression. Working as the proverbial lone ranger or lighthouse keeper does not suit!

Libra loves glamour. So careers in hairdressing, styling, makeup and costume fit the bill. Many creative artists and musicians are born under the sign of Libra. Glitzy professions like theatre, media and television bring the injection buzz Libra needs . . .

This sign is tailor-made for a small fashion boutique, or design house. Libra is skilled at one-to-one encounters, and makes a good sales person.

Careers in the army, police or even a secret agency are all suitable for Librans who respond well to discipline and structure.

With their natural gregarious and humorous disposition, Libra has a nose for PR. They also make good personal assistants, and may satiate their taste for the limelight by steering others towards fame and fortune.

FUTURE HEALTH: Balance holds the key to optimum health for Libra. Librans have good energy, but can be a bit frantic if not manic at times! Exercise is an important 'grounding' experience. And energy should be expended in a measured way. Gentle but determined long-haul exercise that tests stamina and durability is ideal.

The Planet Venus ensures the beauty and desirability of Libra, but Libra is inclined to put on weight if the sweet tooth is indulged. Balance and moderation in diet will ensure that alluring looks are maintained!

Libra rules the kidneys. So it is important to boost hydration levels by drinking lots of water. Venus presides over the parathyroid gland, which also indicates that bodily fluids must be balanced for optimum health. Headaches should be checked out if they are persistent.

Libra is inclined to have a slow metabolism. Aerobic exercise keeps everything ticking over, but discipline is not usually a Libran strong point. Efforts will be visible and worthwhile . . . persist!

FUTURE LOVE: Librans love the thought of being in love.

They thrive on the anticipation as much as the event itself. Libra tends to fall in love very easily, and should make a concerted effort to choose wisely. A trail of broken hearts does not a pretty picture make. Librans must be careful with their emotions. Being aware that they may be more vulnerable than they realise, it is imperative for Libra to exercise discrimination and protect their interests.

If you are Libra, learn to accept people on their own merit. And try to watch what you expect from them in return. Honour the freedom and independence of partners and family members, then your expectations will be repaid tenfold . . . The looser the grip, the more you will receive. Unconditional love, painful though it may be, also guarantees big rewards.

Libra is a born romantic, so needs to keep its feet on the ground. Start to be realistic about love. Don't just plan the wedding ceremony. Work out first what a lifetime together actually means.

Romantic thoughts are all very well. Indeed they will feed your imagination for hours on end. But do remember you have to relate to human beings not knights in shining armour, or princesses from the fairy tales.

COMPATIBLE SIGNS: Aries, Libra's polar opposite, is highly compatible. Gemini is a master of delivery. And the Aquarian's sense of humour wins every time. Taurus is a great provider. Libra wants for nothing . . . until the boredom sets in. Cancer is highly seductive and permanently interesting. Leo has instant appeal – the fireworks fly when these two hit the sack. Libra with Libra makes a good team.

But expect a clash eventually. Pisces is too emotionally clever, and tends to manipulate to get a reaction. Capricorn is too tame and tedious, while Scorpio is totally unfathomable!

BIRTHSTONE: Sapphire, diamond, opal
COLOURS: Indigo, pale blue, green, pink
ZODIAC NUMBER: 3
FAMOUS SEXY LIBRANS: Brigitte Bardot, Will Smith, Gwyneth Paltrow, Sting, Luciano Pavarotti, Eminem, Danii Minogue, Sir Bob Geldof, Simon Cowell, Sarah Keating (SIX), Kate Winslet, Donna Karan, Mahatma Ghandi, John Lennon, Heather Locklear, Groucho Marx, Pele, Michael Douglas, Catherine Zeta Jones, Julie Andrews, Bruce Springsteen

---

SCORPIO
October 24th - November 22nd

RULING PLANET: PLUTO (and Mars - *see Aries*)

Pluto highlights personal obstacles and our ability to overcome them. This planet has a strong influence on our hidden secrets. Life's mystery and dark side loves Pluto energy. Its terrain is the skeleton in the closet, and the subterranean depths of the unconscious.

Pluto is the ancient god of the Underworld. This energy dances in the shadows, and is not afraid to stare death in the face. An intrepid fearlessness attaches to this Planet's vibration. Pluto is resilient, determined and will not take defeat lying down. Therefore, Pluto inspires transformation. But Pluto can be dark, dangerous and cruel. When off balance resist and avoid this energy at all costs . . .

PERSONALITY: Scorpio is the eighth sign of the Zodiac, signified by the Scorpion. The key phrase for this sign is "I transform". Scorpio can turn negative situations around and thrives on a challenge. When determined and focused, this energy has the power to succeed.

Scorpio is a deep and passionate soul that dislikes laziness. This intense nature is inclined to feel the blues. And personal storms are an important part of the Scorpio legacy. Difficult times enable a deep understanding of life. Superficiality is not an option!

Privacy is very important for Scorpio who needs to feel in control of people and situations. Personal space is at a premium for this profound water sign. This energy hates to feel crowded and anyone who invades the Scorpion's nest had better beware . . . The Scorpio 'sting in the tail' has real 'ouch' factor.

Scorpio is a reserved but abundantly blessed Sun sign with tremendous energy, commitment and resolve. Mental, emotional and physical excess needs to be channelled constructively, as the capacity for disaster is quite high. And a wrong turn can send this Sun sign into quick decline. But with transformation as the main drive of Scorpio, it is inevitable that the Scorpion comes back for more, like the proverbial phoenix rising from the ashes...

Because Scorpio rules the reproductive system and genital organs, many people assume this Sun sign is sexually driven. This is, of course, the case, but it is certainly not the sole motivation of Scorpio. Scorpio is actually quite straight-laced, cautious, and old-fashioned about commitment, and is very loyal even when temptation strikes.

If you are Scorpio, find positive ways to express yourself and engage in activities that sublimate your energy. The negative traits of jealousy, suspicion and obsessive ruminating are by no means ingrained. You have an incredible energy that is able to experience life in all its glory (and all its depravity as well!). With Scorpio around, there is certainly no shortage of drama, passion and intensity...

FUTURE CAREER: Scorpio is very ambitious and has great energy to bring to their chosen career. All that sexual excess and drive is very readily channelled into public pursuits. Work and personal development are crucial to the survival of Scorpio, for if boredom, listlessness or disappointment kick-in, the dark side comes out to play.

Whatever life path Scorpio chooses, there is an accompanying ability to make money. This sign knows about financial management and how to transform small amounts into major investments. The imaginative skills of Scorpio may be applied to any tedious task with staggering results.

With an eye for detail and acquired patience, Scorpio makes a good surgeon. And with their grip on the human psyche, many specialist psychiatrists are Scorpions.

Careers in the army or policing suit the Scorpio ability to get to the bottom of things, and exercises those control issues. In the reverse, Scorpio makes a brilliant criminal. But

I am not about to recommend a life of crime!

FUTURE HEALTH: Scorpio has boundless excess energy, so physical exercise is crucial to the Scorpion's health. Sports that expend a lot of effort and have a high aggressive factor are ideal. Also any link with water-based activities puts Scorpio right in their element. Scorpio should choose any exercise that stretches endurance and channels energy.

Scorpio rules the reproductive system. So Scorpio must take care of sexual organs with regular checks. There is no cause for alarm; however, it is better to be safe than sorry. The Scorpion is prone to constipation, but should be careful not to become obsessed with assimilation problems . . .

Scorpio can be prone to ill health when 'blocked'. So it is important for Scorpio to clear emotional issues with plain talking. Psychological issues are part of Scorpio's legacy. At times the Scorpion may be challenged by depression or obsessive problems. Exercise de-stresses the mind, of course, but psychotherapy or the occasional 'heart-to-heart' will knock most things on the head!

FUTURE LOVE: Scorpio is both plagued and blessed by deep emotion. This renders the Scorpion a great catch indeed, but it also signifies that there are deep-seated issues to be processed in matters of the heart. Scorpio rises to the challenge, but needs to temper obsessive and possessive tendencies in relationships. Scorpio loves to control the proceedings and feels uncomfortable when out of its depth...

It takes the Scorpion time to trust and feel comfortable one-on-one. Indeed, it is this fear of commitment and heartache that is responsible for the Scorpion's rampant reputation. Scorpio would rather have a string of affairs than commit to anticipated heartbreak . . .

Love needs to find its feet before Scorpio relaxes enough to enjoy deep connections. The Scorpion needs to guard against jealousy, suspicion, and resentfulness. When insecure, Scorpio is aggressive and prone to picking fights. There is inevitably intense drama when Scorpio does not feel loved.

If you are Scorpio, learn to cope with your deep feelings and be patient with yourself. When you find your soul mate, you will realise what a gift these emotions really are. You are loyal and committed once in love. So recognise that mischievous secret grin which manifests when Scorpio loves someone . . .

COMPATIBLE SIGNS: Fellow Scorpio is a true soul mate, while Taurus and Virgo really suit. These seductive earth signs provide the missing link. Cancer and Pisces connect emotionally, but there may be game playing and blackmail when things get intense. Leo and Scorpio are powerfully attracted – a very physical relationship. Aries connects well with Scorpio, but this is more friendship than intense passion. Sagittarius has to be willing to compromise, or forget it over the long term. Avoid dominant Capricorn and flighty Gemini. Libra is a bit bland, whilst Aquarius is too busy and distracted.

BIRTHSTONE: Opal
COLOURS: Maroon, dark reds, black and purple
ZODIAC NUMBER: 4

FAMOUS SEXY SCORPIOS: Joaquin Phoenix, Larry Mullen Jnr, Liam McKenna of SIX, Jodie Foster, Prince Charles, Katharine Hepburn, Winona Ryder, Theodore Roosevelt, Marie Antoinette, Marie Curie, Bill Gates, Vivien Leigh, Pablo Picasso, Julia Roberts, Hillary Rodham Clinton, Sam Sheppard, Louis Nurding, Jonathan Ross, Leonardo DiCaprio, Demi Moore, Meg Ryan

---

SAGITTARIUS
November 23rd - December 21st

RULING PLANET: JUPITER

Jupiter is the largest planet in the solar system. It is associated with expansiveness and development, both intellectual and physical. Jupiter was the king of all the gods, akin to the Roman god Zeus. This regal energy of kingship blesses those born under Jupiter with dignity and composure. Along with inherent spirituality and the ability to philosophise, Jupiter bestows abundance and wealth, whilst the inherent cosmic link to ancient gods ensures great luck.

Positive mental energies direct those born under this sign. Knowledge, vision and optimism are all gifts from Jupiter. However, caution is needed, for Jupiter can inspire over-confidence and stubborn behaviour. Watch out for extravagance and histrionic 'drama queen' behaviour!

PERSONALITY: Sagittarius is the ninth sign of the Zodiac. This fire sign is symbolised by the Archer who shoots his arrow heavenwards. The keynote of Sagittarius is "I believe". Predictably, the fiery, assertive energy of Sagittarius is not easily confined. This Sun sign is identified by a great enthusiasm for life, along with a sense that anything is possible . . .

Sagittarius is hugely self-confident, which is all very well until this exuberant fireball goes too far, and trips itself up. No task is too lofty, and no ambition too mighty for Jupiter energy. Commendable indeed! But Sagittarius does need to temper enthusiasm with caution and common sense once in a while.

To avoid major frustration and defeat, the Archer needs to inject some realism into the proceedings. Although well able to cope with challenging situations, Sagittarius should be mindful of human frailty once in a while. Even while cooking up grandiose plans, this dynamo character would do well to have plan B and C in place . . .

The ability to think expansively makes Sagittarius an extraordinary visionary. Dreams have a habit of coming true, simply because the wish fulfilment factor is so heightened. When grounded, Sagittarius is destined to achieve great things, so long as flexibility amidst adversity is maintained.

Freedom is so important to Sagittarius. This natural philosopher needs the option of possibilities. The 'grass is always greener' for Sagittarius. When stifled or restricted the Archer can be difficult company indeed. Sagittarius loves to be kept guessing, and lives life close to the edge. Security, comfort and predictability bore the Archer rigid!

Sagittarius is a brave and heroic sign that is both eccentric and exasperating. The Archer aims true, and his flaming arrow hits the spot more often than not.

With a delicious sense of humour, Sagittarius is invaluable socially. This joker is guaranteed to be centre stage in any prank. Here is a live wire determined to get its way . . . attempt to capture one if you dare!

FUTURE CAREER: Tedious, routine jobs are anathema to Sagittarius. This free spirit needs to be permanently stimulated, or it shrivels up and crumples in a heap! The Archer must find ample opportunity for self-expression and strive to be challenged at every turn. Work that tests skills of anticipation or predictive ability is ideal...

Sagittarius has a healthy competitive streak, so needs an environment that gives just enough containment and discipline, without being threatening. Any job that is all-embracing suits. The Archer's gift of vision is desirable, for the creativity of this fire sign must be respected.

Employment that requires attention to fine detail is not right for Sagittarius. But having said that the Archer can turn its hand to most things for a limited stretch of time. Travel, sports and languages are natural talents, so should be developed where possible.

Gifts of charm, humour and a winning demeanour make Sagittarius a great sales person. The inevitable 'high jinks' ensures endless fun . . . and a whistle while we work!

FUTURE HEALTH: Sagittarius needs to get sufficient exercise in as many and varied ways as possible. The Archer has a lot of nervous energy, and is quite susceptible to bouts of depression and sluggishness when unfit. Attention must therefore be paid to physical activity that both entertains and maintains fitness.

Sagittarius should avoid becoming fired up by stress. So Eastern methods of channelling surplus energy are recommended. Tai chi, yoga and martial arts fulfil the Archer's philosophical bent, even whilst calming the system . . .

A sensible diet is crucial to Sagittarian equilibrium. The hips and the thighs are the Archer's domain. So the consumption of junk will inevitably show in these areas. Fresh fruit is good for this fire sign that needs to watch the waistline. Extra vitamins and minerals are often necessary to avoid the high likelihood of burn-out. Sagittarius should avoid sugar, and aim to eat high protein energy foods.

Sagittarius can be clumsy, so do guard against tears and sprains during any kind of physical activity . . .

FUTURE LOVE: Sagittarius has boundless energy for love and life. This freewheeling nature needs variety and diversity, which can of course herald trouble when it comes to commitment. Sagittarius has wild oats to sow, and is not ashamed to say so! Strong passionate feelings and natural urges often get the better of the Archer, who is not intentionally unfaithful, but simply finds that 'things happen', now and again . . .

Sagittarius is never backwards about coming forwards! But as the mature Sagittarian values companionship and conversation, there is an option on the mellow route. So long as the Archer is free to roam and consider endless possibilities, fidelity is not a problem. This may be unnerving for loved ones. But if Sagittarius is respected and unconfined, no harm is done. One whiff of possessiveness, and this fire sign will find ways to wander, come what may . . .

If you are Sagittarius, you may at times be too casual about love and sex. Jealousy is not in your vocabulary, which can be both liberating and disconcerting for loved ones. However, once you connect with your soul mate, nothing will persuade you to stray. When you truly fall for someone you will know all about it . . . and so will everyone else!

COMPATIBLE SIGNS: Aries has a lot of passion to share with Sagittarius, whilst Leo is ideal mentally and physically – a fulfilling connection. Libra is up for it – just about anywhere! And Aquarius is quirky but adventurous. Gemini fills in the gaps, with endless chatter guaranteed. Cancer is an intriguing and mysterious partner, who keeps Sagittarius guessing. Virgo is interesting, and captivates for a certain amount of time, where Pisces is very compelling and drives Sagittarius to distraction, for good or bad! Possessive Scorpio and the plodding earth signs Taurus and Capricorn should be avoided . . .

BIRTHSTONE: Topaz, turquoise
COLOURS: Dark blue and purple, regal colours, light blue
ZODIAC NUMBER: 6
FAMOUS SEXY SAGITTARIANS: Brad Pitt, Ralph Fiennes, Warren Beatty, Eddie Murphy, Joan Crawford, Celine Dion, Marlon Brando, Winston Churchill, Frank Sinatra, Tina Turner, Mark Twain, Walt Disney, Jane Fonda, Bette Midler, Andrew Carnegie, Zoe Ball, Uri Geller, Steven Spielberg, John Galliano, Mel Smith, Lorraine Kelly, Woody Allen

CAPRICORN
December 22nd - January 20th

RULING PLANET: SATURN

Saturn's authority puts a restraining order on excess. This Planet holds the Universe in check. Not an easy energy, Saturn challenges recklessness. Saturn is our conscience warning against foolhardiness. Intimidating to the free spirited, Saturn may undermine weak self-esteem, heightening self-doubt and confusion.

Saturn's buzzword is 'don't', which may repress, depress, or comfort, according to disposition. Like an autocratic parent, this Ruling Planet is good to have around in a crisis, but debilitating when we need to muster self-confidence. Balance is crucial in the face of Saturn's warning flag. It is advisable to take the hint and put the breaks on questionable behaviour, but equally important to resist Saturn's bullying . . .

PERSONALITY: Capricorn is the tenth sign of the Zodiac. Represented by the Goat with the fishy tail. Capricorn's keynote is "I use". The sure-footed Goat is able to traverse treacherous mountains, whilst keeping its feet firmly on terra firma. The fishy tail represents the ocean emphasising the ability to swim free without constraint – the spiritual nature of being.

Traditionally Capricorn is depicted as a rigid, unbending and inflexible sign. And very stubborn with it! This is not the complete picture, of course, but Capricorns do love to get their way, and are expert at finding the chinks in people's armour. The Goat is brilliant at subtle manipulation, and well able to 'plant the seed' months in advance to ensure a specific outcome.

The Capricorn legacy combines material savvy and survival skills with spiritual expression. Practical, financial and business ventures provide the Goat with the opportunity to express their true essence. For this sign has the potential to integrate life's material and spiritual dimensions – powerful indeed . . .

Focus gets Capricorn absolutely everywhere. And a fully integrated Goat may achieve great things. The development of self-confidence is crucial to Capricorn's success. But it is important that the Goat does not abuse their natural authority, or things could get ugly. If Capricorn maintains spiritual balance all will be well. However, many of the world's control freaks are Capricorn, who sacrifice kindness to serve their ambitions . . .

If you are Capricorn, learn to adapt and survive, rather than seek to control at all costs. Maintaining devious levels of manipulation is very self-defeating, as you will no doubt realise. So never use a string of lies to get you to where you want to be. Your stories may captivate an audience, but in time your exposure as a fraud may be too much to bear.

Your brilliant mind brings many temptations. Ambition is very important to Capricorn. Learn to delegate and ask for favours on your way to the top. Remember that with enough determination you can conquer any mountain you wish to climb . . .

FUTURE CAREER: Capricorn is very skilled and reliable. The Goat has a great head for facts and figures. So all business ventures suit this ambitious energy. Capricorn is guaranteed to cope well with routine, and thrives on structure and discipline. This Saturn-influenced sign loves security and seeks to control the proceedings wherever possible.

The Goat has an instinct for the route to the top. So any chance to stay ahead of the game is closely monitored. The concept of failure does not exist in Capricorn's rarefied environment. And whatever this earth sign attempts is sure to make an impact.

By definition Capricorn is a winner. There is little the Goat is not capable of. However, avoidance of equal partnerships is advisable, for Capricorn needs to 'stand alone'. This sign makes an ideal company director, principal, or business representative . . .

Many self-made people are Capricorn. The Goat is willing to tolerate 'spartan' conditions, and will do what it takes to be a success . . .

FUTURE HEALTH: Mobility is crucial for Capricorns. Goats need to keep active and on-the-move. So that those creaking joints work well into old age! Knees and shins are vulnerable to scrapes and sprains and must be protected at all times. Running and swift walking are good exercise for Capricorn, who should maintain supple limbs.

Capricorn skin has to be looked after, for it is prone to dehydration, never mind the weather. This organ can dry out wind, rain, or shine. So skin care should be a permanent part of the Goat's routine . . .

Since Capricorn rules the teeth and bones, a healthy calcium intake is important, as well as regular visits to the dentist!

Tedious gym visits are best avoided. But it is important for Capricorn to keep warm at all times to boost flexibility, even though the Goat may prefer to feel cool. Warmth is crucial for the prevention of rheumatic pain later in life. Capricorn can expect to trot effortlessly into the twilight years. So long as these basic rules are adhered to . . .

FUTURE LOVE: Capricorn is cautious in matters of the heart. The Goat needs to find its feet, and tends to warm up slowly. Once committed, Capricorn remains steadfast and true, since few can match the Goat's devotion and loyalty. It is advisable for Capricorn to ditch the control issues, for when Capricorn develops an open attitude to feelings and emotions, anything can happen . . .

Capricorn often holds back for fear of rejection. Trust is the key, plus a willingness to make mistakes occasionally. When the Goat falls in love it is usually for keeps. For, when this earth sign surrenders, their amour is already won over. Capricorn is not a great risk taker and does not act on impulse. This is good protection of course but can mean that Capricorn misses out on all the fun!

The Goat is a sure thing, who expects as much in return. Fair enough! But if you are Capricorn, do unwind. Also, watch that tendency to penny pinch. You do not wish to come across mean-spirited. It is not a crime to spend money, but missing out on romantic dinners, presents and gestures of affection is!

Down-to-earth as you are, let go. Loosen purse and heart strings, just a little . . .

COMPATIBLE SIGNS: Fellow earth signs Taurus and Virgo bring passion and practicality . . . the ideal mix for Capricorn. Pisces is adoring and malleable – very useful, but Cancer may be overly emotional. Aries is simply too hot to handle – great for a fling, if you dare have one! Scorpio likes to be in control, as does fellow Capricorn - an inevitable clash waiting to happen. Libra is simply too different. And Aquarius has to get its way – a recipe for disaster…Gemini is way too wild and challenging for Capricorn. And Sagittarius is dangerously impulsive. Opportunistic signs need not apply!

BIRTHSTONE: Amethyst, turquoise
COLOURS: Black, dark greys, greens, browns
ZODIAC NUMBER: 33
FAMOUS SEXY CAPRICORNS: Mel Gibson, Pete Waterman, Jim Carrey, Rod Stewart, Nicholas Cage, Kate Moss, Christie Turlington, Helena Christiansen, David Bowie, Benjamin Franklin, Elvis Presley, Joan of Arc, Richard Nixon, Edgar Allen Poe, Martin Luther King, Joseph Stalin, Henri Matisse, Paul Cézanne, Mao Tse-tung, Noel Edmunds, Denzel Washington, Rowan Atkinson, Mel C

AQUARIUS
January 21st - February 19th

RULING PLANET: URANUS

(and Saturn - *see Capricorn*)

Uranus is the planet of personal transformation. Inspirational for the individual, this Ruling Planet also blesses generations. Uranus challenges the status quo, and constitutes a challenging, difficult energy. Independent and radical, this planet moves slowly, heralding profound drawn-out change . . .

To be born under Uranus is an honour indeed and one which needs to be treated with healthy respect. This planet inspires altruism but also signifies self-importance and eccentricity. Uranus allows for detachment as well as the ability to be all things to all people. This mode of being is a law unto itself. In true maverick style Aquarius knows best. A perverted rebellious streak gives Uranus the edge.

PERSONALITY: Aquarius is the eleventh sign of the Zodiac, symbolised by the Water Carrier, and described by the key phrase "All for one and one for all". This mind-set connects to group consciousness. Altruistic and humanitarian, Aquarius looks outwards . . .

With the buzzword "I know", Aquarius is invaluable when the going gets rough. On a deep inner level Aquarius carries the full knowledge of the Universe. The Water Carrier who learns to access the unconscious is truly a walking oracle!

Aquarius is the true philanthropist of the Zodiac, with the Wisdom of Ages resting on its shoulders. This sign imparts logical and objective advice. Second-to-none in a crisis, Aquarius keeps a cool head. This air sign has sympathy, wisdom, and practical help to share. Aquarius is someone the whole world can turn to in an emergency!

Glamorous, cool and aloof, Aquarius knows how to present an elegant face to the world. At times unapproachable and distant, the Water Carrier is intensely private. Far from being deliberately unfriendly, Aquarius is simply guarded.

With an inherent understanding of human nature this sign is no fool. Rarely one to let down defences, Aquarius values loyalty whilst honesty and integrity are extremely important; Aquarius is kind-hearted and will not judge too quickly.

As a great visionary, the Aquarian intellect takes some beating. But the Water Carrier can be quite inflexible. Once Aquarius has made up its mind, this sign is fixed and rigid with plenty to prove. The Water Carrier acquires a unique way of being, and precious little will budge this. Aquarius should guard against appearing old fashioned by being open to the changing times. However, Aquarian quirkiness is always charming. Never mind out-of-touch!

If you are Aquarian, always follow your eccentric heart. But learn some adaptability too. Keep up with current trends. And be prepared to modify the game plan. Be aware that although you are usually right, you are NOT always so. So reserve judgement on issues you are unsure about. Pride comes before a fall . . .

FUTURE CAREER: There is a touch of brilliance about

Aquarius. This original mind, which borders on kookiness, means that Aquarius gets the best results when left alone. Aquarius does not like to be dictated to, and needs to find a unique way through life's challenges . . .

With a natural affinity for science and detail, the Water Carrier borders on genius. Being a natural humanitarian, Aquarius is tailor-made for caring professions with substance. The medical and healing professions beckon . . .

Aquarius is liable to feel stifled in a noisy office situation. Although the Water Carrier is able to work as part of a team, much leeway is important. Aquarius loves to take responsibility and express creativity. This air sign thrives on rescuing others, whatever the context. So any career that combines communications with altruistic gestures is ideal.

Aquarius loves to fly and spread wings. The Mile High brigade is full of Aquarians who like to get their feet off the ground!

FUTURE HEALTH: Both Aquarius and Uranus are associated with the circulatory system, which makes Aquarius susceptible to varicose veins, pulmonary problems, and hardened arteries. This potential can be avoided with sensible diet and a regular fitness routine. Forewarned is forearmed!

The polar opposite of Aquarius is Leo, ruler of the heart. The link between circulation and heart is immediately obvious. So Aquarians must adopt a healthy heart regime and stick to it.

Aquarians should not even think about smoking, and must take regular cardiovascular exercise. Sports like swimming, tennis, and squash allow Aquarius to shine whilst providing that crucial work-out.

A low fat diet high in fruit and vegetables is fundamentally important. Be aware that porridge is brilliant for lowering cholesterol and boosting general health . . .

Also, Aquarius must watch their back! The spine and muscles are vulnerable to aches, pains and sprains. So, even though Aquarius likes to be cool, this air sign needs to stay warm . . .

FUTURE LOVE: Aquarius is a private person who does not readily make deep, intense connections. The Water Carrier acts similarly to cautious Capricorn, but for different reasons. Aquarius is alluring, charismatic, and rarely spoiled for choice. However, Aquarius does not fall in love easily. Interested in a whole range of options. Aquarius flits in and out of possibilities until surety descends.

Aquarius has a magnetic pull, which may attract and repel in equal measure. On the one hand enticing and curious, Aquarius disconnects quickly when uneasy. Of course there is nothing wrong with being careful, but Aquarius should guard against missing out on the love of their life. Too much detachment and preservation of privacy can render the Water Carrier isolated and alone. It is important that Aquarius opens up from the heart to make lasting links . . .

If you are Aquarius, learn to show your emotions more fully and be honest with love's expression. Once you fall for someone, you fall heavily. Your choice of partner may be unusual. But your loyalty ensures that they have you for life.

Find a partner who respects your maverick nature and

unique disposition. Prepare for an exciting and fulfilling relationship. And certainly don't allow anyone to sway your choices . . . as if!

COMPATIBLE SIGNS: Fellow Aquarius is compatible and entertaining, while Gemini offers everything, and has a great sense of humour to boot! Libra brings a lasting and lustful connection. Aries is a great idea when the balance is right. And Leo is fun for a moment or two. Virgo annoys Aquarius by being right once too often! But Sagittarius is unusually devoted. Expect a clash of the Titans with Capricorn. And watch Pisces who will get under your skin and invade your space. Taurus is too cosy and home orientated for Aquarius who wants to party.

BIRTHSTONE: Amethyst, aquamarine, opal
COLOURS: Electric blues, turquoise, sea greens
ZODIAC NUMBER: 22
SEXY AQUARIANS: Robbie Williams, John Travolta, Frank Skinner, Elijah Woods, Oprah Winfrey, Ronald Reagan, Vanessa Redgrave, Virginia Woolf, James Joyce, Charles Dickens, Garth Brooks, Charles Darwin, Wolfgang Amadeus Mozart, Galileo, Prince Naseem Hamed, Cindy Crawford, Eddie Izzard, Jennifer Jason Leigh, Jennifer Aniston Pitt

PISCES
February 20th - March 20th

RULING PLANET: NEPTUNE
(and Jupiter - *see Sagittarius*)

Neptune, ruler of the oceans, has energy enough to transform the masses. The processes inspired by Neptune are laborious but profound. Ideologies, beliefs and social norms come under the jurisdiction of Neptune. But commendable spiritual tendencies may become off-the-wall fanaticism. The downside of Jupiter involves escapism, indecisiveness, and elaboration of the truth.

Neptune off balance muddles the vision. So discernment is important. Those ruled by Neptune should guard against self-deception, for wild fantasy and wish fulfilment tendencies need to be monitored. With Neptune in the frame, dreams and visions are loaded with significance. This depth, wisdom and imagination may be expressed as a great gift...

PERSONALITY: Pisces is the twelfth and final Zodiac sign. The keynote of Pisces is "I understand". This sentiment signifies the end of the Zodiac Journey. Represented by two fish swimming in opposite directions but connected by a cord, the Pisces habitat is the deep oceans, seas and waterways of the Spirit world.

Pisces possesses inner knowing and profound vision, making them the most psychic of all our StarScope signs. Life is expansive and exciting for the Zodiac Fishes. So to swim free must be the Pisces goal, bar none . . .

To fully embrace their birthright, Fishes are advised to dive into a voyage of self-discovery. This is nothing to be alarmed about, but is certainly a challenge as it unfolds. Pisces should embrace the leaps of faith along the way, and always pay attention to hopes, dreams, and wishes . . .

Pisces must learn to discern the truth of their visions, and not be afraid of a profound ability to read situations and people. Boundaries are an issue for Pisces. This water sign needs to preserve privacy and personal space at all times, but must also be mindful of a tendency to invade the lives of others uninvited . . .

Pisces is a courageous and insightful friend, but should realise it is impossible to sort everyone out. The Fish needs to look after itself first and foremost.

If you are Pisces, make the most of your creativity, cleverness and poetic vision. Stay awake, and keep your feet (fins) on the ground! Your tendency to dream and think profound thoughts is second-to-none, but be sure not to traipse down elaborate scenic routes in your imagination, which really have no bearing on reality.

Don't beat yourself up over your inherent indecisiveness. It is part of your Piscean legacy. So learn to 'go with the flow' of your changing emotions. And remember that any decision is a good one if you follow it through. Discipline the changeable dreamer and you will always be a truthful incisive force to be reckoned with!

FUTURE CAREER: Pisces works well as part of a team, plugging away discreetly in the background. Fishes are not comfortable centre stage, but they greatly dislike being over-looked. Reflecting the myriad fish in the sea, the Pisces per-sonality is diverse! Many careers are suitable depending entirely on personal choice. When Pisces feels valued and finds a niche – anything goes . . .

Any career that allows Pisces room to breathe, function and express creativity is valid. Pisces likes to hide behind masks and deflect attention. So comedy and humour suit the fishy disposition . . .

Pisces is instinctively caring. Work that combines the expression of feeling and intuition is ideal. Nursing, coun-selling, social work and psychic work fit the bill.

A flexible routine containing a wide variety of tasks is best for Pisces. Versatility is a gift received at birth, but, when the boredom sets in, it's off to the next challenge fairly live-ly! Discipline is needed for Pisces to stay around long enough to make an impression . . .

FUTURE HEALTH: Pisceans have an extremely sensitive con-stitution. Alternative medicine is often a gentler more effec-tive approach for delicate Fish. Pisces should always liaise closely with health professionals, since they can react quite badly to prescription drugs.

Neptune connects to the nervous system which renders Pisces highly suggestible. Someone innocently asking the Fish if they feel OK, can send them off to the doctor in a mild panic! Like Virgo, Pisces gets overly stressed by worry and health matters . . .

Pisces has a tendency towards addiction which acts as a buffer for suppressed issues. The development of healing and psychic ability helps Pisces manage this uncomfortable disposition. Spiritual understanding allows Pisces to arm against attack from the environment, toxic people, and dubious energies . . .

Pisces rules the feet. So Fish must wear shoes that fit properly or, in time, they can expect an interesting range of foot ailments! Reflexology (which massages the feet and supports a sensitive system) is an absolute 'godsend' . . .

FUTURE LOVE: Pisces loves to display a whole range of emotions with passion and gusto! Love delights in the Fishes' openness, but is also embarrassed by that tendency to be over-eager in public places! Pisces must learn to define boundaries. And should be careful not to chase love away in an eagerness to please . . .

Pisces is liable to be overly intense, a little sentimental, and highly idealistic. These honest qualities echo the naïve child attempting to make a dream come true! So, Pisces must be mindful that adult relationships inspire a mixed bag of emotions, requiring adjustment and compromise along the way . . .

It is all very well holding onto romantic notions of happiness for as long as possible, but life has a way of delivering harsh and insightful lessons to help us grow up. Pisces is quite vulnerable to a heartache, or two, whilst this 'education' takes place.

If you are Pisces, enjoy the intensity of your passions, but learn to curb your enthusiasm! There is no one to match you romantically and your 'performance' is always honest. Do access the lighter side of love, life, and happiness. And do not take things quite so seriously . . .

You may always find refuge in the fantasies revolving around your head, but will this substitute for an experience of the real thing? I think not!

COMPATIBLE SIGNS: Cancer and Scorpio speak the Pisces language of love. Virgo is highly compelling, but once attraction fades the arguments could be interesting! Fellow Pisces either repels or attracts. Follow your instincts. Avoid Sagittarius except for an exciting fling. Taurus is up for it but will tire of Piscean mutability. Leo goes along for the ride – up to a point. And Capricorn is too staid and not impulsive enough. Gemini is untrustworthy – surprise! And Libra is a nitpicker! Aquarius gets down and dirty, but this is potential war, not fun at all . . .

BIRTHSTONE: Moonstone, chrysolite
COLOURS: Sea greens, shades of blue, lilac
ZODIAC NUMBER: 11
FAMOUS SEXY PISCEANS: Jon BonJovi, Billy Crystal, Michael Caine, Rachel Weisz, Patsy Kensit, Sharon Stone, Melinda Messinger, Zane Bowers, Chelsea Clinton, Liza Minnelli, Sidney Poitier, John Steinbeck, Johnny Cash, Jerry Lewis, George Washington, Elizabeth Taylor, Nat King Cole, Mikhail Gorbachev, Caroline Corr, Ronan Keating, Eva Herzigova, Ja Rule, Thora Birch, Tea Leoni, Kristin Davis

Chapter Two:

Decans

....

This subject of Decans tends to be glossed over in Astrology books. Here is an added insight into the specific week of your birth. There are subdivisions (Decans) within each Sun sign, which reflect the great diversity inherent within each of the Zodiac signs. Check the chapter on Ruling Planets for more detail about the planets that energise your personal Decan.

ARIES March 21st – April 20th
Ruled by Mars

FIRST DECAN March 21st – March 30th
Planetary Influence: Mars

You are a natural leader who can be forceful and convincing. Others find you annoying but inspiring. So curb that determination to get your own way. You have boundless energy and get things done, but there is no need to be too pushy when you want victory. Simply stating your case in no uncertain terms should do it. With focus, you can achieve great things, for you are destined to win or else go down fighting! Watch that tendency to be overly stubborn though. Feisty as you are, a mellow demeanour will usually be more potent and effective than a confrontational one. You are a Zodiac crusader: a pioneer. With a head full of ideas, you are ever ready to spring into action.

SECOND DECAN March 31st – April 9th
Planetary Influence: The Sun

Being influenced by the Sun your charisma is formidable! You are guaranteed to turn heads and get people's attention. And your mere presence in a room is enough to convince us of your magnetism and power. You do not even have to open your mouth to make an impact, for you have star quality! If you have aspirations of fame, there is every chance you will be successful. A potent mix of drive and energy gives you staying power when focused. And your instant appeal will bring inevitable recognition. You are magnificent! Who would dare to turn you down? Persistence and a big smile are about all you need to clinch a deal . . .

THIRD DECAN April 10th – April 20th
Planetary Influence: Jupiter

You are a truly unique individual, and possess dynamic Arian traits combined with strong moral fibre. Respectful of people and responsibilities you do not give into temptation easily. Your fiery energy inspires and motivates. A strong sense of right and wrong makes you a great politician, preacher or healer. However, when it all goes pear-shaped, you are one of the world's worst hellraisers. Your ability to stir emotions is intense and somewhat scary. So deal with bitterness or frustration in a level-headed way. Loved ones should respect your privacy, for you cannot abide to be stifled or dictated to. Personal freedom gives you leeway to love and support those you choose.

 TAURUS April 21st – May 21st
Ruled by Venus

FIRST DECAN April 21st – April 30th
Planetary Influence: Venus
The rulership of Venus renders you rock solid and dependable with a romantic sensibility. Rarely will you risk or jeopardise a sure thing. Patient, methodical, and persevering, your slow steady energy may not win the race, but you are sure to finish with a commendation. You are a force to be reckoned with, for nothing phases you! Your grounded character ensures that you are the most loyal and loving friend or lover. Being an earthy creature, you delight in sensual pleasures of the flesh, or indeed anything that affirms your life force. Nature nurtures you, whilst beauty and serenity inspire your soul. You are centred and focused, with unshakeable foundations!

SECOND DECAN May 1st – May 10th
Planetary Influence: Mercury
Highly creative, you possess a rare artistic sensibility. Your

intuition is sensitised which ensures that you do not miss a trick. With refined taste and high expectations, you can be unexpectedly shy. Even though you are easily wounded, you have an unbending, unswerving will that triumphs at every turn. As a born survivor, you feel things deeply but can move on when required. Your complex character is both earthy and perfectionist, but you are inclined to bury your head in the sand rather than deal with something tricky. Stay real and monitor unrealistic expectations. Your high ideals and sense of purpose guarantee that you will find what you are looking for – eventually!

THIRD DECAN May 11th – May 21st
Planetary Influence: Saturn

Your staying power is impressive! Slow-moving you may be, but you always find your way through a maze of difficulty. Life's challenges inspire you, as well as test your patience. Logical, grounded and practical, you have an answer for everything. Flights of fancy are not an option. So do not be seduced by those who sell dreams! You are pragmatic and eminently sensible. Let common sense prevail - however mysterious life gets. Your innate resilience ensures that you bounce back from the brink every time. But watch out for that lazy streak. Walk permanently in a well-defined groove, and not much will veer you off track. You attract loving friends and family connections that last a lifetime.

GEMINI May 22nd – June 22nd
Ruled by Mercury

FIRST DECAN May 22nd – May 31st
Planetary Influence: Mercury

Mercury bestows on you a quick wit and lively mind. Your thought processes change like the wind, and it is impossible to pin you down. This makes for an edgy exciting personality that keeps us both interested and exasperated! You are versatile and multitalented. Little is beyond your remit. Your willingness to tackle most things ensures results, so remain focused. Well able to keep the rest of us guessing, you are a resourceful character who lives by wit alone. You love to keep your options open and play the field, or at least appear to be so doing. Success is a surety for your ambidextrous disposition. You are eminently loveable, mischievous and forgiven a lot!

SECOND DECAN June 1st – June 10th
Planetary Influence: Venus

You are blessed with a rapier wit, and lively mind. Venus and Mercury help you to seduce whomever you set your sights on. Whether for business or pleasure, you are a dab hand at getting your own way. Gentle charm ensures your success. And your cutting sense of humour makes you irresistible. You are popular and shrewd with great focus. So whatever you set your heart upon can be yours, as long as concentration is maintained. You do not have it in you to be actively devious in a damaging way, but you can be pretty nifty, when push comes to shove! Expect a fun-filled life of humour, joy, love and understanding.

THIRD DECAN June 11th – June 22nd
Planetary Influence: Uranus

You are quite 'out there' and always on the look out for new experiences. For you, reality is one big joy-ride that occasionally becomes the ghost train! As an eternal optimist, you have visions and dream dreams, each one more magnificent than the last. Your natural intensity means that you experience life by the minute. You are a law unto your self in true maverick style. Your upbeat groove does not have to indicate immaturity, but there is a part of you that will never grow up! Uncompromising as ever, you will stick your neck out, rather than damage your personal integrity. You are a powerful figure with the Midas touch, who can quite literally run the show without being there!

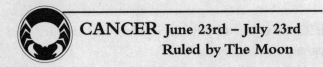

CANCER June 23rd – July 23rd
Ruled by The Moon

FIRST DECAN June 23rd – July 1st
Planetary Influence: The Moon

You are highly intuitive and emotional: a lunar creature who is responsive, empathetic, and sensitised. Nothing passes you by, for you are profoundly psychic. Relationships come easy and you are tailor-made for human interaction. Always engage in the full flight of your emotions. Never mind the climb up the career ladder. Home is where the heart is, and you will not rest until you find your soul mate. Your dedication and likeability ensure your success. You are not the most 'pushy' sign, but you are inherently lucky. It is impossible not to love you! You have a unique perception, and view the world in a matter-of-fact but astute way. There are no flies on you . . .

SECOND DECAN July 2nd – July 12th
Planetary Influence: Pluto

You are a mysterious and enigmatic personality: a passionate and deep individual who feels everything on an intense level. Life is exhausting but exhilarating for those connected to you. Certainly, there is never a dull moment! At times you feel like an alien in a strange land. You are highly psychic with many overwhelming perceptions and intuitions. For sanity's sake, find an outlet so that your incredible imagination can express itself! You are liable to implode and beat yourself up when things go wrong. But to an extent you thrive on hardship and respond well to a challenge. Resilient and defiant, you are fiercely independent and treasure your privacy.

THIRD DECAN July 13th – July 23rd
Planetary Influence: Neptune

You are very sensitive with a lovely gentle energy. As you have an innate ability to understand and empathise, you make a great confidant. With your personal, intimate relationships you can be clingy. You love to be loved, and need to be needed! Reassurance is important, but displays of affection are always repaid in kind. You can be intense and demanding, but you also have a lot to offer. Watch out for irrational reactions and guard against moodiness. You are artistic, creative, with a definite eye for beauty. Expend your energy positively for maximum fulfilment. Let your intuition be your guide, and you will end up better off than those who follow the logical route.

LEO July 24th–August 23rd
Ruled by the Sun

FIRST DECAN July 24th – August 1st
Planetary Influence: The Sun

You are a powerful compelling character, possessing great charisma and appeal. With incredible magnetism, you know how to command attention, and you are skilled at getting your own way. You are never likely to be ignored, even when incognito! Ego is an issue. But you automatically instil respect in both loved ones and opponents. Using humour and witty rhetoric you manoeuvre situations to maximum effect. Loyalty, generosity, and restraint make you a regal creature that never stints on affection and support. Your warmth of character and skills of performance attract the limelight. Express yourself on the stage of life. And expect the spotlight to shine upon you.

SECOND DECAN August 2nd – August 12th
Planetary Influence: Jupiter

You have extra determination and expansive vision: truly, a master who can see the bigger picture. Somewhat idealistic, you are a pioneer who wants to save the World. Never mind laziness, you need to maintain a sense of purpose. You have a wicked humour and know where to find the fun! Jupiter's influence renders you brave and optimistic. Very little demoralises or defeats you. You are kind, open-hearted, and destined to be successful – without even trying. You inspire friendship and treasure your intimate relationships. It is very difficult to dislike or begrudge you anything. Your Midas touch makes you perhaps the luckiest sign in the Zodiac. It is your destiny to win big, in some respect.

THIRD DECAN August 13th – August 23rd
Planetary Influence: Mars

As one of life's true survivors, adversity brings out the best in you. You are a dynamic character, who is willing and able to take on challenges. Indeed you are powerful! Whatever you set your heart on, can be yours. But stay on track and avoid confrontation. You possess rare grace and charm. So there is no need for masterstrokes or manipulation. Acknowledge your gifts, and develop self-confidence. You are able to achieve great things through faith and belief alone. As a true entrepreneur, you can seal the deal with the full force of your personality. Few distrust or doubt you. Your reassuring presence instils confidence in the rest of the world. You understand life and the people therein.

VIRGO   August 24th–September 23rd
Ruled by Mercury

FIRST DECAN August 24th – September 3rd
Planetary Influence: Mercury

Failure is not in your vocabulary! You set very high standards and are extremely self-critical. As someone who can objectify and assess situations at the drop of a hat, you are flexible and adaptable. A born survivor, you can turn disappointing events into a real gift. You are a cerebral Sign, adept at both logical and intuitive thinking. A natural student, you transport the wisdom of ages into the present. Hard-working and studious, very few subjects are beyond the remit of your lively mind. You can tackle most things standing on your head, but your creativity needs to be permanently stimulated or you get bored. Love has to be heart, soul and passion, or you will not bother!

SECOND DECAN September 4th – September 13th
Planetary Influence: Saturn

You are a veritable force to be reckoned with! There is no point trying to pull the wool over your eyes…you can see around corners! With your exacting standards and strong ambition, you are inclined to take life quite seriously. As well as being determined and focused, your organisational skills are second-to-none. It is virtually impossible to fault you! You are a master of discernment, with an innate understanding of human nature. And since you never take 'no' for an answer, your success is guaranteed. You are reliable, honest, and not in the least bit ruthless. There is an on-going sense that anything can happen in your life, and probably will . . . You carry infinite possibilities!

THIRD DECAN September 14th – September 23rd
Planetary Influence: Venus

Venus introduces a warm, loving and tolerant quality to your personality. You are content with simple pleasures and do not aspire to the giddy heights! You are warm, affectionate, and respond to plenty of TLC. Because you are all heart, you give freely with no strings attached. But you are no push over! Your natural intelligence renders you canny, witty and wise. And you are so self-assured that you feel no need to control people. In love you are earthy, sensuous, and 'in it for keeps', but with no tedium or boredom factor. And you make an exceptionally caring and considerate lover. Loving and patient, you forgive and tolerate a lot without damaging your self-esteem. Are you human?

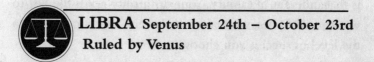

LIBRA **September 24th – October 23rd**
Ruled by Venus

FIRST DECAN September 24th – October 3rd
Planetary Influence: Venus

The very core of your being yearns for harmony. Finding peace is the sole motivation of your body and soul. You are gentle and companionable, making a genuine and reliable friend. Beautiful from the inside out, you are pure with oodles of integrity. Even though you are stoic and determined, you will usually put others first, for your loyalty and generosity are beyond question. What you may lack in terms of ambition and determination, you make up for with charm and skills of diplomacy. You have enviable social talents! With skilful self-expression you will 'tell it like it is' in the nicest possible way. An endless imagination, creativity and ability to put things into words guarantee your success.

SECOND DECAN October 4th – October 13th
Planetary Influence: Uranus

As a cool customer, you are willing to calculate your moves. You are nobody's fool. Independent and candid, you are not afraid to tackle things head-on. Not much is beyond you. You keep a cool head in a crisis, and know when to act for maximum impact. Logically minded, you are not liable to get carried away. You are free spirited. But, you do not compromise readily. Things have to be on your terms, or they tend not to happen! Outgoing, popular and approachable, you never want for company. And your in-built protection is that inherent likeability. Your originality holds the key to wealth and riches, whilst honed instincts will propel you to the level of success you choose.

THIRD DECAN October 14th – October 23rd
Planetary Influence: Mercury

Lively, witty, versatile, with an imagination second-to-none, you are an enthusiastic chatterbox! And great company to boot. Boredom is not a word in your vocabulary. You are the Zodiac 'wild child' guaranteeing eternal high jinks and endless fun! There is the touch of the Maverick about you, for you will not be dictated to, or 'told'. Entertaining, mad and hilarious company, the rest of us cannot expect to get a word in edgeways. Communications and conversation stimulate you and your social calendar is always busy. You are attractive to many, and, boy, don't you just know it! You love to be IN love, and feel less than complete without it. Get the next round in.

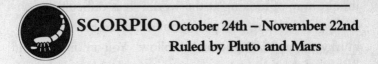

SCORPIO October 24th – November 22nd
Ruled by Pluto and Mars

FIRST DECAN October 24th – November 2nd
Planetary Influence: Pluto

Your dynamo personality is captivating and compelling, and your powers of persuasion are irresistible. Not one to give up easily, you are the master seducer/seductress of the Zodiac! Nothing will defeat you, whilst your heart is open and compassionate. You bring warmth, discipline and passion to your relationships, whilst your magnetic charisma means there is no need for words – one look from those soulful eyes does the trick! Insightful, but non-judgemental, you get straight to the point, and are great to have around in a crisis. Your level head and sensible demeanour sort things out, and you are able to wriggle out of compromising situations in a most charming way! Complex, but utterly adorable, nothing escapes your eagle eye.

SECOND DECAN November 3rd – November 12th
Planetary Influence: Neptune

Laid-back Neptune makes you less intense and driven than

fellow Scorpio. You are charitable, giving, and maintaining the 'status quo' is a priority. Being family-orientated you make sacrifices for the sake of peace and quiet! Getting ahead is not so important. Job satisfaction is crucial, but prestige and status are not. You are stimulating, interesting company, somewhat offbeat, but eminently charming. Mystery emanates from your very pores. And you have a unique way of looking at the world. It is difficult to fathom your thinking and perceptions, but wherever you go, quirky fun and intrigue surely follow! You are intense and meaningful without being intrusive - delicious company, altogether . . .

THIRD DECAN November 13th – November 22nd
Planetary Influence: The Moon

The Moon enhances your mystery and powers of seduction. You are guaranteed to be compelling and alluring, even first thing in the morning! Truly magical, you have the ability to captivate anyone you care to mention. All things to all people, you are very feminine and powerful, never mind your gender. Enticing in the extreme, you are also very domesticated. Tender, loving, and caring, you give priority to security and comfort in the home. Silence is golden when you are around, for your presence is simply enchanting. Your allure is transmitted with a gaze, touch or meaningful gesture. You are subtle, canny and adaptable. If any person is capable of casting a spell, it is you!

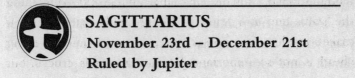

SAGITTARIUS
November 23rd – December 21st
Ruled by Jupiter

FIRST DECAN November 23rd – December 2nd
Planetary Influence: Jupiter

Jupiter guarantees you eternal optimism and an indomitable spirit. You are endless fun with a serious side that surfaces intermittently. Love of life and the acquirement of knowledge are your strong motivations, for you are an intelligent philosopher who likes to get to the bottom of things. You crave freedom and cannot stand any form of restriction. Restless as you are, you can be exhausting but stimulating company. Life must be a continual exploration and journey, as you do not respond well to the idea of 'arriving' somewhere. Books, literature and philosophy expand your horizons if you cannot literally travel, but you are destined to go far, one way or another!

SECOND DECAN December 3rd – December 12th
Planetary Influence: Mars

Oh boy! You are a handful! With more than your fair share of energy and zest, you are entertaining but tiring. Once you have decided something, there is no stopping you. You possess an indomitable will. And you WILL make things happen, come what may. Quite compulsive, your determination to succeed is a wonder to behold. But you are generous spirited, and will not intentionally tread on toes. Truly you are a force to be reckoned with. You like to be stimulated, unsettled, and amused – all at the same time! But you are endlessly entertaining and rarely cause offence. With your sense of fun, stamina levels and passion power…you should come with a government health warning!

THIRD DECAN December 13th – December 21st
Planetary Influence: The Sun

What a regular dynamo! With clarity of purpose and extra energy, you get things done. The Sun bestows on you an open, generous spirit. And not much stands in your way. You are inherently lucky. Even when challenged, something will surely happen to 'save the day'. Optimism is a way of life. Rarely does your will get crushed beyond repair. You look for the good in everything and everybody. And often the leap of faith is repaid in full. People love your 'off the wall' madness and wicked sense of humour! Variety is the spice of life, and you thrive on a bit of scandal or gossip. You need endless stimulation, and were not created to be ignored…the craic sure is mighty!

CAPRICORN
December 22nd – January 20th
Ruled by Saturn

FIRST DECAN December 22nd – December 31st
Planetary Influence: Saturn

Determination will see you through – but life is hard work! So expect character-forming challenges to occur regularly. A true survivor, your achievements are precious indeed.

Stoic qualities serve you well. And much effort goes into the attainment of your dreams. With grounded equilibrium, you are a formidable force when focused. Your tenacity and discipline win every time. When up against it, keep your head down. Expect to reach the dizzy heights of success, but first prove your durability. Fame awaits you if you are patient and do NOT give up. You are sensual and practical: a skilful, considerate friend and lover. Appreciate the view along the way, and learn to value the 'little things' in life…

SECOND DECAN January 1st – January 10th
Planetary Influence: Venus

Your artistic temperament and diverse talents ensure that you do not miss a trick! Less the drama queen, more the Queen Bee, you are compelling and seductive. A photographic-style memory serves you well, but watch you do not lose perspective. Even superhumans need to keep a grip on reality! That high intelligence may tempt you to take advantage – 'lesser mortals' beware! An aesthetically appealing environment is very important to you, and you do have impeccable taste. Domestic and material bliss travel hand in hand. You make a reliable and committed partner, but only when you have reached a respectable position. First things first… You ARE romantic, just not before it is appropriate to be so!

THIRD DECAN January 11th – January 20th
Planetary Influence: Mercury

Mercury gives you the edge! You are highly motivated and

disciplined. Nothing blocks your route to the top of the tree. And you possess a ruthless streak that comes into play if someone attempts to sabotage or undo your good work – understandable! You do not respond kindly to competition – you HAVE to be the best – or else! A true perfectionist, you have a brilliant mind. There is indeed a touch of genius when you are in full flow. An exceptionally creative and powerful personality, you cast a spell. And who can say 'no'? With a computer's memory for detail, you take some beating. Facts and figures trip off your tongue. When you want to impress, you surely will.

 AQUARIUS January 21st–February 19th
Ruled by Uranus

FIRST DECAN January 21st – January 29th
Planetary Influence: Uranus

A truly free-spirited being, you are not afraid to follow your heart. One of life's philanthropists; there is not a selfish bone in your body when you are balanced and stable. Your destiny is to serve humanity with discernment and wisdom, speak the truth as you see it, and always be willing to help. Life is a trip! There is always something to think about, and to be getting on with. No problem is insurmountable. Your great instincts and innate wisdom mean that you are a walking oracle, with enviable skills of detachment. You know how to isolate and intercept dilemmas even as they arise. Pearls of wisdom trip from your tongue ... So focus on what counts!

SECOND DECAN January 30th – February 8th
Planetary Influence: Mercury

Lively and quick-witted, your mental agility is impressive. Liable to be academic and highly intelligent, you happily grapple with most topics. With great eloquence, you are rarely lost for words. You hate to admit mistakes so will store up excuses just in case, but that perfectionist streak makes you your own worst critic. A true Renaissance man or woman, you need a lot of stimulation or boredom sets in. Very sociable but intensely private, you are complex. Adaptable and willing to work in unusual conditions and in unusual ways, you will try anything once! Flexibility is your middle name whilst you amuse and amaze. You respect life, humanity and see the best in everyone, without being wet...

THIRD DECAN February 9th – February 19th
Planetary Influence: Venus

You house an interesting blend of energies. Less cerebral and intellectually driven than the previous two Decans, objectivity is not the strong point of your feeling-based personality. Compassionate in the extreme, and beautiful with it, you do not possess the ability to detach and consider! With a tendency to get in too deep, you get involved with other people's problems far too readily. Out of the goodness of your heart, you want the world and its aunt to 'be OK!' Altruistic in the extreme, you must guard against a tendency towards self-sacrifice for the benefit of loved ones. Toughen up a bit . . . Your creativity is second-to-none. So channel positive energy into yourself, and do not disperse your life force . . .

PISCES February 20th–March 20th
Ruled by Neptune

FIRST DECAN February 19th – February 29th
Planetary Influence: Neptune

Neptune governs transcendence, spirituality, illusion, and suffering. So you are one interesting, compelling human being! Inspirational and creative, it is nigh on impossible to fathom your murky depths. Even your silence is loaded and fascinating. Quiet and unassuming, no one is bored in your company, for your mere presence ensures an element of mystery. Generous-spirited, you are willing to give without guarantee of a return. A true romantic with a poetic soul, you are naturally psychic, wise, and profound. Your sensitivity and compassion make you highly desirable, but your spirituality ensures that you are not impressed by anything superficial. Natural ease, combined with a romantic, dreamy and sexy spirit, makes you a great catch indeed!

SECOND DECAN March 1st – March 10th
Planetary Influence: The Moon

The feminine energy of the Moon heightens your sensibilities. You are a gentle, nurturing soul. Above all you are caring, sharing and kind. A beautiful person indeed, the finer feelings of love, romance and perception encapsulate your *raison d'être*. There is no active deception or nastiness hidden away. In fact the very idea of you having hidden secrets is quite a joke! OK, so everyone has a shadow side, but it is difficult to find it in your case. With a talented and unusual disposition, you possess a refined, artistic nature. You are a creative and poetic personality, skilled enough to make a fortune by not doing very much at all! The art of living excites you . . .

THIRD DECAN March 11th – March 20th
Planetary Influence: Pluto

You are positively spooky! The energy of Pluto ensures that you miss nothing. Being very psychic and intuitive, it is impossible to lie to you. And with your great intensity and heightened sensitivity you are exceptionally powerful. Not much stands in your way, once you are committed to a plan of action. Your great intelligence identifies you. With a lively mind and definite vision there is no stopping your Pluto driven character. Natural flexibility and versatility make you a winner every time... You are not held back by negative or corrupt ideas and thoughts. Life flows for you. And you are truly blessed with access to phenomenal opportunities. Live and let live.

Chapter Three:

Yearly Motivational Message

. . . .

The more things change, the more they stay the same

ARIES: When planetary activity puts you under pressure, you will find yourself trying to please everyone but yourself. STOP! Take back the reins of your life and resume control. It's not like you to give your power away. So DON'T! Give yourself the respect and attention you have been giving others. There are many challenges winging your way, and you need all your reserves on stand-by.

At certain points in your life the dynamic planets will have paved the way for growth and change. Keep your eyes peeled and sense the moments when you need to act, and the times when you need to simply reflect. Anything that no longer fits your scheme will have to go out the window! New projects will surface and stimulate you with an alternative challenge. Be open to new developments and reach your fullest potential. An experimental mood can serve you well and stretch your creativity in an impressive way.

Use recreational time to find out who your friends are. Long-term connections will shift and change for Aries. You must adapt to the shifting energy or else let go. Many tests of loyalty will arise as your circumstances develop, but your confidence and optimism can be accessed. So decide to keep positive rather than buy into defeat or introspection.

Let 'ever onwards and upwards' be your motto. Take special note of new ideas and visions. Do pay particular attention to your dreams when looking for inspiration. Learn to access your unconscious and make it work for you. Tough changes and decisions are likely at certain points. Try to be excited rather than daunted by the shape of things to come. You are one of life's survivors. Whatever you put in motion will come good for you, and will have a direct bearing on your life in the future. Clear up existing problems, and do the pruning you have long delayed . . . Out with the old!

TAURUS: Whether you want it or not, your psychic ability will develop. Your instincts are at a premium. A different thing, I know, but think how formidable you will be with both gifts at your disposal. You would certainly regret it if you ignore your powerful hunches. Listen to your soul and what it tells you. You won't go far wrong. But if you hesitate and feel obliged to think and behave in particular ways . . . expect to be undermined. It serves you well to be courageous and brave.

Stand up for yourself and if necessary lay down the law in no uncertain terms. You must make profound statements and allow your actions to count for something. Never be tempted to bury your head in the sand and always be prepared to move forward in very unexpected directions. Nothing will ever be the same again if you are courageous enough to act. Change that has been hovering for quite some time will manifest finally, much to everyone's annoyance and shock! But it's all good, and inevitable to boot...

It's important to get rid of negativity in the form of stagnant energy, clutter and people who no longer offer you an equal deal. Do not keep your life clogged up with things that never worked in the first place. Detox at a deep level early, whenever necessary. If you are brave and radical, there will come a time when you look back and won't recognise yourself! Get rid of all your 'stuff' and consequently move forward lighter and brighter than ever before.

Embrace your potential and the numerous opportunities for expansive change. There will be potential loved ones of all shapes and sizes. Variety is the spice of life, of course – don't you forget it! Enjoy all your connections new and old, for changes in your status are inevitable. Always follow through your big ideas and bring realistic plans to fruition.

I know that you hate everything that threatens your status quo, but do ditch anything past its sell by date. Spring clean your life when required . . . resistance to change is futile.

GEMINI: Lively fun and action through-out your life is your birthright, Gemini! Expect your outlook to expand. This will greatly enhance your connections. Partnerships of all kinds will benefit if you remain open. Love commitments, business deals and friend-ships improve if you allow the inevitable to unfold, but you do have to remain open to the shifts and changes of your circumstances. Not everything can be neatly mapped out and planned. So suspend judgement and prepare for some surprises. Success will be written all over your face if you go with the flow and make room for the unusual! It is down to you to turn things around when the opportunities arise. Any venture you embark upon is destined to succeed. Put the full force of your conviction behind it, so! Take the leap of faith and follow through with lifelong ambitions.

It is continually important to question yourself, Gemini. Who are you? Where are you heading? And what do you want from life? You need to find clarity in order to bring form and shape to the future. Remember that up to a point you are the creator of your destiny. And you certainly have a responsibility to make intelligent and truthful decisions. So stop buying into the belief that life is something that happens to you. There is more to play for than you realise and life has dealt you a respectable hand. Be confident and happy with where you have got to, but be determined and focused enough to take a different road if you have to. Flexibility is the key and leads to luck and inspiration.

Spring-clean your thinking even while you de-clutter and reshuffle your environment. Differences in opinion are inevitable in your relationships at times. So you need to be sure of your terrain and the standards you wish to maintain! Tension will occur in your personal and working life if you don't hold to definite principles. Others need to know where they are. So I suggest you work out the answer. Leaving anything dangling could prove to be mighty embarrassing.

Keep your cool and don't lose your head when you get overly stressed. Deep breathing will be most useful to calm the jitters. Watch your levels of expectation and don't raise your aim too high just yet. Better to stay grounded than to overshoot the mark completely. The Universe will provide what you need. So remain open to what you want…that will come later!

 CANCER: Expect to make important career 'moves', and learn to sense when the time is right. Any opportunity for self-enhancement should be embraced with open arms. Take innovative action based on renewed self-confidence. And lose negative patterns of thinking, which de-value your abilities. Keep your spirits up and celebrate in style. You need to look after yourself better, so introduce a fitness regime that you can maintain. Never be afraid to stand up for yourself and fight for your 'right to party'…amongst other things! Great change is an eternal possibility if you are Cancer. It's down to you! So be brave and decisive when push comes to shove.

Allow for self-expansion and trust the Universe to assist you with new projects. Boost your chances by remaining open to life's ebb and flow. There's no point in getting frustrated when things don't work. Learn detachment and attempt to reserve judgement. Prepare to give something a second chance if appropriate. Things are usually better and more successful the next time around! Be careful financially, but don't be afraid to experiment with your career and creativity. You always deserve more fulfilment and recognition. So go out there and get you some!

Go with the flow in your relationships and don't shut down when the going gets rough. It's not really fair to close ranks and detach from those who have been loyal and true over many years, although you will never be 100% sure what's going on with your love life. Don't panic! Your circumstances may at times shift dramatically, but always for the best. Your unconscious attracts the right conditions for change towards you. So learn to read these intuitively and do not be afraid to go for gold, when you know it's the right thing.

Reserve judgement but do follow through your intense feelings. It's very important that you don't ignore your powerful urges or hunches. If you do, it's highly likely a missed opportunity will return to haunt you. Take charge of your life and the bull by the horns! Others will admire a determined formidable you. So strengthen yourself by making big decisions which you then adhere to.

LEO: Physically and mentally you always benefit from inspirational change. A dynamic Leo always attracts lots of attention. The way you think and perceive life will radically alter as you develop along the way. Follow through with your strong ideas. Pinning down your definite ambitions is always a good place to start.

Once you kick yourself and those around you into touch, there will be no stopping you! Loved ones, friends and acquaintances will have to adjust to your newly revived strength. Anyone who is not ready to meet you on equal terms or willing to accept the formidable you can move on. This will always be a test of loyalty and true feelings. Start to run the show and take charge of your future. Your image is set to flourish and blossom in unexpected ways.

Be in control of your destiny, and expect to thrive in ways you had only dreamed of to date! Your social ambitions will be realised and you will get the recognition you have long deserved. Get back into the driving seat and accelerate at full throttle! The race is on and you are streets ahead of the competition. Be aware that personality clashes are inevitable as your tough streak emerges.

Be more organised. Clear up residue clutter from your life and release the mistakes of the past. For a clear leap into the unknown you need to be liberated and unburdened. So ditch anything that holds you back or seeks to drag you down…be it animal, vegetable or mineral! Learn your lessons and move on. Never be afraid to tie up your loose ends. Be quite ruthless and disciplined about what no longer fits. Always watch that your heart is respected. Sometimes you fall prey to a battering because you are so open. This is no criticism but do protect yourself a little more.

VIRGO: It is as if someone has turned the headlights on full beam. Suddenly you see clearly! You are emerging from a long, dark tunnel. And you have successfully passed through many trials and tribulations. Parade your flying colours, as you certainly deserve an esoteric pat on the back. Condition normal, Virgo!

Situations that defeat lesser mortals can actually strengthen you, and make you into a real contender. Not much will ever stand in your way if you remain focused. Always draw on the full flow of your creativity to build on the effect. Accentuate the artistic and refined aspects of your nature. Combine these with good business sense and there will be no stopping you!

Personal freedom is permanently within your grasp. If you reach for the stars, you can expect to be propelled straight to the top. There is no reason why you shouldn't make the end of the game without even trying. You always get through the worst challenges with full marks. Believe that the best is yet to come and it surely WILL!

Do occasionally expect tension and frustration in a family situation. A look to the past will provide clues and a way out of the mess. It is important to integrate your many experiences for the new you to emerge. Not everyone will feel comfortable with the changes – the phrase 'no more Mr Nice Guy' comes to mind'. Resistance from those who rely on you is likely. Commitments will be challenged. So take note . . . those who can keep up with you are truly for you.

Equality is crucial to the shape of your future relationships. Decide to have no time for those who hold you back or sabotage your attempts to get ahead, or have a life! Be clear with your feelings and don't mislead anyone…least of all yourself.

 LIBRA: Planetary activity may place your system under some stress at times, Libra. Guard against this and make your health a priority. Tie up important business, and stay ahead of your commitments for optimum stress management. It is fundamental that you always listen to your changing emotions. Your instincts will develop, as will your willingness to listen to them! Pay attention to the whisperings of your heart. You need to keep your wits about you, especially if you intend to wander down avenues never before broached.

You will probably find that a rethink is forced upon you from time to time. The way you communicate and display your affections will always be subject to change. New honesty and daring humour may consequently emerge, which can only spice up your love life. At such times look back over your shoulder temporarily to learn from the past. But then wrap it up in a box and return to sender. Don't allow nostalgia to fuzz up your ability to make intelligent decisions. Planetary alignments will always support you with any new venture. Let the expansive horizons of Jupiter inspire you – and learn to discern when the genuine opportunities manifest. Be realistic and keep your feet on the ground. It is important not to overstretch yourself or to make unreasonable demands on loved ones.

Your luck is in! The rollercoaster ride of life will get turbulent but interesting. Success is yours if you choose to access it. So keep your eyes peeled and your wits about you.

SCORPIO: Your personal strength will be as impressive as you want it to be. Keep things consistent and always aim to build on the great strides you have already made. The more dynamic you become, the easier previously impossible moves will get. Follow through all your potent ideas. Never mind what others think. Your mental attitude is expansive and your energy formidable. Always give priority to major growth: personal, professional and spiritual. Your inner resilience will mount daily!

At times things will, of course, get a bit chaotic, if not 'shambolic'. This will test your need for order and control. Be aware that certain circumstances are beyond your capabilities. Things happen! Be philosophical and don't allow your soul to be shaken, or stirred. The uncertainty may put you under some stress. So pace yourself and know when to stop…detachment will preserve your sanity. Your workaholic tendencies sometimes get the better of you. Do watch that candle and don't burn it at both ends.

Loved ones might be quite intimidated by your determination and resolve when you are focused. Good for you! Important career decisions will intermittently emerge but don't expect everything to go according to plan. Your ambitions are strong and people may sometimes think you have changed beyond recognition…you know different. You are there for those who count and can't be bothered with those who don't!

SAGITTARIUS: Your life can be expansive if you allow things to simply happen. Your ruler, the planet Jupiter, is always very busy on your behalf. New ways of interacting and connecting with others will be forthcoming. You will have lots of fun and your humour is guaranteed to keep everyone amused even when the going gets tough. Be willing to experiment with your career and long-term plans, but stay realistic at the same time. Watch that you don't get too pushy with loved ones. It is especially important to think before you speak. The capacity to put your foot in it will be quite high!

Expect your luck to change in direct proportion to the risks you take. Jupiter will be supporting you and challenging you to push the boat out. Don't undersell yourself. You are capable of a lot more than you appreciate. So go for it in career matters and follow your heart in love. Decide to be all you can be . . . choose life, it's the only one you have (not strictly true but it works to make a point!). Get busy and creative. Do not be tempted to put things on hold . . . If it works it works; if it doesn't, well at least you have found out at last!

Finances will improve, usually if you switch off and forget about them. Always be open to new knowledge professionally acquired, for it will add another string to your bow. Organise your priorities and the rest will follow. If you take all the opportunities that arise, life will change organically. That stagnant feeling will shift and you won't feel held in one place for much longer. Remember this is not a dress rehearsal, so be all you can be!

CAPRICORN: Focus is highly important as always, Capricorn. Make the most of your contacts and channel your ambitions effectively. Expect a stimulating and challenging time. Not everything will go your way, but most things will! It all depends to what extent you can maintain positive thought and action.

Every New Year gives us a chance to project healing and good vibes into the ether. What we put out there will reflect back to us like a boomerang. So make sure it's all good – you don't want bad feeling, frustration and bitterness coming back to haunt you, now do you!

Watch that personal restlessness does not mess up your relationships. Take as much independent time as you need. But do learn to be more communicative of your deeper feelings. If you do this you will find that loved ones know where they stand and are consequently more secure and easier to live with. Altruistic behaviour does not always come easy. So content yourself with the knowledge that giving love leeway and room to develop will bring you much fulfilment – if only you will allow it. Unselfish expression could become the most selfish thing you ever do!

Lap up the good vibes, great attention and favours galore that accompany the full expression of your heart. Don't be afraid of hurt any longer. Step into a brighter, freer and lighter Universe. Lose that stubborn streak and channel the energy into ambition and progress. That way you will have more privacy, as well as deeper love links. The irony is that being more open will allow you to preserve the boundaries of privacy that are so important. Give out so that you may receive.

AQUARIUS: Sound vision is yours to access in an on-going arrangement with the Universe! Expect your horizons to expand and new visions to manifest. Communication is fundamentally important. So keep a clear track of your feelings and don't be afraid of heartfelt expression. If you focus and concentrate on your goals, daily life will become more comfortable and manageable.

You may often find the early part of the summer a challenging time. But the 'hiccups' will make you even more determined to build on the progress you have already made. You will pass all the tests the Universe plonks in front of you. Be courageous and aware that a higher plan is in place. You can expect things to look very different if you take them on and are not defeated by mere circumstances.

Paint a picture you like! Keep your perspective bright and light and your bravery will astound you and those who love you. Everyone else might be a little jealous of the strides you make at times, but let bad feeling be 'water off a duck's back'. Don't buy into the competitive nature of others who throw you off balance. Be your own counsel and get through things under your own steam. As a self-sufficient unit you are second-to-none. Few can match your independence, wisdom and tenacity. So be assured of your superiority; just don't tell the whole world about it!

Let love be the beacon that guides you through the storm. Mutual sharing and caring with loved ones will light your way. Be clear and honest with yourself. And don't let unrealistic expectations muddy the waters. Hold on tight when the ride gets bumpy, but enjoy the view nonetheless. As long as you know where you're heading you will reach your destination.

 PISCES: Watch how you drift along, Pisces. Try to be disciplined and stick to your plan of action, rather than be swept along. You may have to swim across or against the tide, just until you know you're in the correct flow. Once you are hooked up with the Gulf Stream of your destiny, there will be no stopping you!

Be aware that some fish are predatory, others just go along with the shoal. You need to combine the two elements and be independent, ambitious and amenable all at the same time. Don't be afraid of teamwork as you thrive in an environment where you pull your weight, but be formidable in your single-minded determination as well. There will be those who jolt your equilibrium . . . or try to. Don't buy into their nonsense. Keep focused, move on and ignore all attempts to scupper your cunning resolve.

Invite the spotlight to shine on you, when you are ready. Until then juggle all your balls to good effect, as long as they fit in with the game plan. Lots of new friends and acquaintances will surface along the way. Be on your guard for their agendas, but also be aware they may NOT have ulterior motives. So give all takers the benefit of the doubt until you know different!

Let the goal of self-expansion be your inspiration. No, I don't mean your waistline! Expect to be creatively inspired. Your success is guaranteed and abundance is yours. But you must follow through contracts and commitments. Avoid tedium and routine as much as possible. But don't waver in your resolve to make dynamic changes. Never allow the sceptical reactions of others to defeat you. Remain focused and you can expect major developments in all areas of your life. Muster all the self-confidence and self-belief at your disposal. All will be well.

Chapter Four:

Zodiac Times

· · · · · · · · · · · · · · · · · · · ·

This chapter offers quick, practical advice that can be applied to most situations. Check out your best qualities but be warned about the things that may trip you up.

ARIES

Ruling Planet: *Mars*
Gender/Duality: *Masculine - Positive*
Element/Triplicity: *Fire - Inspirational Level*
Quality/Quadruplicity: *Cardinal – Enterprise, Ambition*
Primal Desire/Planetary Principle: *Leadership/Action*
Day of the Week: *Sunday*
Zodiac Angel: *MACHIDIEL – Self-esteem, Assertiveness, Individuality*

Arians are very determined and will win at all costs. Anyone up against you in the race for a lover/job/recognition will be doomed to fail (unless they are also Aries, of course!). You are a born survivor and have the energy to achieve great things. Always busy, you can appear to be quite self-absorbed. However when you fall in love (or lust) you are quick to pounce! Be careful that this passionate drive within you does not land you in trouble. Aries can burn out quickly, which is fine if you want to love 'em and leave 'em. In the long run though you should think of your reputation and go for someone who can handle your sense of mischief and fun.

Try to develop your tolerance levels. You do hate people to disagree with you, and are well able to find ways to convince them to change their minds. Watch out for this tendency to manipulate just because you want your own way. Learn to live and let live! There is a whole diversity of expression in the big wide world. Your mantra is very much 'I am' and that's that. This is admirable, as we have to take it or leave it where you are concerned, but don't be in such a rush, or you stand to miss out on many of life's experiences. You see things always on your own terms and tend to gloss over the complexity of situations. But at least you know where you are with this philosophy – what you see is what you get!

Aries loves to take life as it comes, but you get further if you plan and think ahead. Do not be afraid to take action with someone you are unsure about and see where you get to with each other. The partner who looks uneasy is just overwhelmed by you, not repulsed! If your love has problems or a broken heart, give them a chance as they are worth the effort. You will be duly rewarded.

In the long term: try to stop jumping in with two big feet. Curb your natural energy. Channel it into positive creativity rather than lose patience if the rest of the world does not match your enthusiasm. Vitality and determination are your gifts, but you have to learn that not everyone shares the same qualities. Learn to be cool to attract and keep a mate. Your bedroom antics will tell a different story, but that is your secret for the moment!

Arian colour: Red and gold
Birthstone: Diamond, amethyst
Magical Numbers: 5. 40.

TAURUS

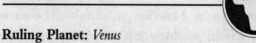

Ruling Planet: *Venus*
Gender/Duality: *Feminine - Negative*
Element/Triplicity: *Earth - Practical Level*
Quality/Quadruplicity: *Fixed – Strength, Willpower*
Primal Desire/Planetary Principle: *Stability/Production*
Day of the Week: *Friday*
Zodiac Angel: *TUAL – Patience, Stability, Security*

Taureans are charming, sensual beings who love to feel secure and in control. If you are Taurus, you will have to watch that possessive streak with partners, and lose the tendency to assume ownership of your conquests. With your tender touch it is unlikely that lovers will complain too much. But be careful not to shoot yourself in the foot with double standards.

The Taurean destiny is to accumulate material goods and many possessions. Taurus loves the trappings of wealth and has minimalist, subtle taste. Sometimes a lapse of judgement is displayed when Taurus adheres too rigidly to the past. Gaudy, ostentatious items can make their way into collections simply because they derive from a credible heritage.

Taureans are spontaneous even though they value their 'safety net' almost to the point of paranoia. Never be the one to rock the Taurean status quo – you will surely regret your misdemeanour. Taurus is not a risk taker. But with a steady flow of energy their capacity to cope with a phenomenal workload is legendary.

Taurus is a fixed earth sign that plods (sorry- strolls!) through life with a steady, easy stride. Little phases you when you are in your element. However, we should all be warned, when you do lose it, you blow BIG TIME! Angry Taurus does not a pretty picture make. Remember the proverbial bull in a china shop?

As a Taurus, keep an eye on your need to feel in control of everything and everybody. However, a surprising aspect of your nature is your shyness when it comes to making connections sexually. You are quite passive and need the 'opposition' to take the initiative – well, you prefer it! Taurus does not like to put itself on the line for love. If you're not a sure thing- forget it, Taurus won't even come close!

Taurean good looks and natural charm open many doors. And your innate intelligence means you have a witty answer for any affront to your sensibilities. When you are afraid or alarmed you tend to fall asleep! Be careful not to accumulate a string of flirtations that come to nothing. Keep your options many and varied, but remember to decide eventually!

Fix up a hot date or several with that cute one you have your eye on, but don't spoil things with insecurity. Good-looking they may be but so are you! Unwind and do not be intimidated by each other. If you have a partner, take a breather and make sure they don't cramp your style. You can't change the one you love, but you can have a damn good try!

In the long term: do not allow jealousy to mess up important relationships. You are caring, considerate and love sex. What more could a lover wish for? If you do not treat your partner as a possession there is every chance you will walk them down the aisle eventually – and keep them for an eternity!

Taurus colour: Pale blue, green and pink
Birthstone: Emerald, moss agate
Magical Numbers: 6. 10.

GEMINI

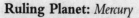

Ruling Planet: *Mercury*
Gender/Duality: *Masculine - Positive*
Element/Triplicity: *Air - Mental Level*
Quality/Quadruplicity: *Mutable – Flexibility, Versatility*
Primal Desire/Planetary Principle: *Communication, Versatility*
Day of the Week: *Wednesday*
Zodiac Angel: *AMBRIEL – Adaptability, Communication, Relationships*

Gemini can do and think several things at once- always useful! You have boundless nervous energy and need variety and stimulation to keep you sparkling. Your nature is naturally flirtatious and lively which puts you streets ahead when it comes to scoring with the opposite sex. Watch out for superficiality and try not to flit around quite so much. Commitment is an alien concept for Gemini, and future lovers and friends will have your dual personality to contend with. An outlet is needed for that logical positive mind and its accompanying nervous tension. Deception and fraud are a highly likely if you don't nip questionable behaviour in the bud .

Be careful you don't let an important secret out. Your silver tongue has a habit of running away with itself. Plenty of social gatherings will liven up your love life if single. Get in tune with the boy/girl you have your eye on and the rest will be easy! If you have a boy/girlfriend do not tolerate cheating ways. It's OK for you, but not them – right? However do not mistake natural flirtatious fun for infidelity.

In the long term: master your personality and learn to relax. Avoid predictable routine like the plague. You need plenty of communication opportunities. How does a guy/gal know he/she has won you? There are the e-mails, text messages, phone calls and notes! Media work, teaching older pupils or even the medical profession will suit you. Try to avoid deceit in your important relationships. You don't want to lose him/her, do you?

Gemini colour: Yellow and any bright colour
Birth stone: Agate, beryl, aquamarine
Magical Numbers: 2. 7.

CANCER

Ruling Planet: *The Moon*
Gender/Duality: *Feminine - Negative*
Element/Triplicity: *Water – Emotional Level*
Quality/Quadruplicity: *Cardinal – Enterprise, Ambition*
Primal Desire/Planetary Principle: *Security/Love*
Day of the Week: *Monday*
Zodiac Angel: *MURIEL – Reticence, Self-reliance, Contentment*

Cancerians can be like the changeable sea – calm and tranquil one minute, brooding and threatening the next. 'Crabby' is an apt nickname for you when you hide under that shell, silent and scowling. But to those you love, you are kind, receptive, caring and protective. Your imagination is second-to-none. Just be careful it doesn't invent worries and dilemmas that don't exist! Use it positively and your natural psychic ability will blossom and never let you down. You are a true romantic, and lovers are in for a treat when you get going. But love needs to be equal and returned or things will get ugly. Don't waste your time on losers!

Make moves to be reconciled with a friend. Why not be the one to heal the rift? You must be looking hot, as you are a magnet for the opposite sex at the moment. Don't let it go to your head. Friends may be jealous of the attention you get. Never mind his/her reputation –have some fun! If you have a boyfriend or girlfriend, hang in there and don't run away if things get messy. He/she may not always be around so don't confuse him/her too much.

In the long term: claustrophobia in relationships is not good. You don't want to chase people away with too much love and kindness. Your big heart gets over-enthusiastic at times so watch the tendency to smother. Those 'crabby' pincers can puncture holes in things if you hold on too tight. Give people room to breathe and all the love in the world is yours to play with.

Cancer colour: Pale blue, silver, smoky greys, violet
Birthstone: Pearl, emerald, moonstone
Magical Numbers: 2. 7.

LEO

Ruling Planet: *The Sun*
Gender/Duality: *Masculine - Positive*
Element/Triplicity: *Fire – Inspirational Level*
Quality/Quadruplicity: *Fixed – Strength, Willpower*
Primal Desire/Planetary Principle: *Power/Creativity*
Day of the Week: *Saturday*
Zodiac Angel: *VERCHIEL – Courage, Leadership, Loyalty*

Leo expects lots of attention and loves being centre stage. You are generous-hearted and a great friend. Be careful you don't choose mates and lovers who always agree with you. Variety is the spice of life! Leos are the performers of the universe - a little proud and arrogant perhaps, but charming and full of life at the same time. You need people around you who can match your enthusiasm and exuberance. If the love you give is not returned, you get deeply wounded, so choose wisely. For lesser mortals (other zodiac signs), your passion for life can be overwhelming. Go for the guy/gal who gives you the eye, then follows it through with definite action. The 'wishy-washy' approach won't do it for you. So if he/she doesn't match you 100%, back off – only real men/women need apply!

The stars are all set to stir up your emotions. Guard your tongue – both with what you say and whom you snog! Expect a crossroads and choose carefully between two lovers. Biggest is best in this case but take his/her personality into account as well. Use plenty of fake tan and summery clothes to attract attention – never mind the weather. Take the advice of friends if your boyfriend/girlfriend is doing your head in. Cut him/her some slack and chill out.

In the long term: try to put money aside for driving lessons or further training. Save towards a travel plan. Be very wise in love – you do not want little surprises too early in life! Computer skills will be important for your future advancement. A happy marriage is your destiny so do not give the lads/lasses who fool around too much time or energy.

Leo colour: Any shade that reflects the sun in all its
glory – red, orange, gold, yellow
Birthstone: Ruby, amber, chrysolite
Magical Numbers: 5. 19.

VIRGO

Ruling Planet: *Mercury*
Gender/Duality: *Feminine - Negative*
Element/Triplicity: *Earth – Practical Level*
Quality/Quadruplicity: *Mutable – Flexibility, Versatility*
Primal Desire/Planetary Principle: *Crystallisation/Purity*
Day of the Week: *Wednesday*
Zodiac Angel: *HAMALIEL – Physical Health, Social and Administrative Skills*

It seems hardly respectful to call you a babe or dude, Virgo. Strangers would call you aloof and cool, but those who know you will vouch for your warm loving nature. You are practical and intelligent and very little escapes your attention. Try not to be so self-critical. Develop your self-confidence, as this will serve you well in years to come. You are much better looking than you appreciate. Believe the compliments and then you won't waste time doubting or undermining your boyfriends/girlfriends. Modesty is attractive but not when it gets in the way of love action! You are faithful and kind. Any guy/gal lucky enough to bed you will surely wed you!

Enjoy the company of your mates by all means. But do focus on the work when you have to. Virgos are fussy in love so if there is a lack of available talent, hang in there. You are older and wiser than your peers and need to be wooed. Do not be tempted by the serial seducer! In matters of the heart, intensity is your middle name. If you are in love remember it is cool to be cool - let your man/woman do the running.

In the long term: I would recommend further training to develop your talents. College courses and practical personal study are important to further career opportunities. Virgos are usually right but don't let it go to your head! Learn to listen to your intuition and trust it. When in doubt about a decision or action, hold back until you are sure. Never be persuaded against your better judgement.

Virgo colour: Dark blues, greys and browns
Birth stone: Sardonyx, jasper, cobblestone, emerald
Magical Numbers: 7. 11.

LIBRA

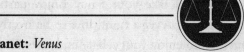

Ruling Planet: *Venus*
Gender/Duality: *Masculine - Positive*
Element/Triplicity: *Air – Mental Level*
Quality/Quadruplicity: *Cardinal – Enterprise, Ambition*
Primal Desire/Planetary Principle: *Union/Balance*
Day of the Week: *Friday*
Zodiac Angel: *ZURIEL – Straightforwardness, Balance,
Conformity*

Librans love company and your gregarious nature thrives on social activity. Do not be afraid to be lonely as you never will be, but do learn to be alone and content in your own space. Be careful to make gestures of love and friendship from the heart without expecting a return. Love is freely given and it will find you if you give up the frantic search. You fall in love easily so do not mistake flirtation for a declaration of devotion. Romance is heaven-sent for Librans and you give everything when you love someone. Make good decisions and follow them through. Be prepared for surprises in love and do not believe all the clichés – it could be 'Mr Nice Guy' who strings you along and forgets your birthday, whilst 'Jack the lad' turns up on the doorstep with bouquet and sheepish grin! Alternatively the flirtatious lady could turn out to be just right for you, while the shy girl is tedium personified! Reserve judgement and follow your gut instinct in matters of the heart. Let the hormones do the talking for once. And ignore the endless chatter in your head…

In the long term: be open to new experiences. You never know what will take your fancy. Enjoy parties and social events. There is never a right time to be overly shy, so learn to flourish and enjoy your self-confidence. Expect to attract a lot of glances, as you are looking good. Just relax and do not try too hard. One slow easy smile should reel them in! If you already have a boyfriend/girlfriend don't be quite so available to him/her. OK, so this is a game, but you will enjoy the prize if you give it a whirl!

Do not stress yourself with major decisions. Learn to objectify your situation and imagine you are giving advice to a good friend. This will help you when the indecisive Libran comes out to play. Do not allow him/her to do your head in and remember any decision is a good one if you follow it through.

Libran colour: Pale blue, green, pink and indigo
Birth stone: Sapphire, diamond, opal
Magical Numbers: 3. 18.

SCORPIO

Ruling Planet: *Pluto/Mars*
Gender/Duality: *Feminine - Negative*
Element/Triplicity: *Water – Emotional Level*
Quality/Quadruplicity: *Fixed – Strength, Willpower*
Primal Desire/Planetary Principle: *Control/Power*
Day of the Week: *Tuesday*
Zodiac Angel: *BARAKIEL – Risk taking, Opportunity and Self-development*

You have probably heard it before, Scorpio – you have a reputation as a sexy mamma or beast! Nothing wrong with that except you should close your ears to most of it if you are under-age…or too old! There will be plenty of time in years to come to play the temptress or seducer (unless you're over-the-hill as we speak). In the meantime think about all that excess energy you have for your studies or work! Only kidding. If anyone can look after themselves you can, Scorpio. Do be careful with friendships though and don't let moodiness spoil good times. You can be a bit impatient and intense, especially if you do not get your own way. So do ease up on the control and security issues. There are some things you can't change. Don't shoot yourself in the foot and miss a good romantic opportunity…you can be too cautious at times. Certainly don't ignore a potential liaison. And be careful not to avoid someone because of shyness. Although it shows you're seriously interested, it might also send them running. You're meant to be the demon love god, remember – do not hold back! Watch out for jealousy and trust your boyfriends, girlfriends and partners a little bit more.

In the long term: leave behind relationships that do your head in. A fresh start is always a good idea for you, so do not be afraid to wipe the slate clean and begin again. Lose your nervousness if you want to attract that person – a sense of humour and a nice smile should do the trick. Fix them with those eyes of yours and hypnotise to full effect. If you have a partner, do not be too pushy. They may not be able to put what is bothering them into words, so lighten up and enjoy the fun.

Communication is much more important than sulking, so be grown up and lose the mood swings. I know it is part of your Scorpio legacy, but learn to work with it. Mystery is fine and attractive: intense negative behaviour is not. Expect stormy times and make the most of passion. Scorpio must ride a rollercoaster of emotion, but it can be fun!

Scorpio colour: Maroon, dark reds, berry colours, black, purple
Birthstone: Opal, amethyst, topaz
Magical Numbers: 4. 6. 11. 78.

SAGITTARIUS

Ruling Planet: *Jupiter*
Gender/Duality: *Masculine - Positive*
Element/Triplicity: *Fire – Inspirational Level*
Quality/Quadruplicity: *Mutable – Flexibility, Versatility*
Primal Desire/Planetary Principle: *Liberty/Expansion*
Day of the Week: *Thursday*
Zodiac Angel: *ADNACHIEL – Optimism, Power of Vision, Expansion*

Freedom is so important to Sagittarius that any form of confinement could drive you quite mad. You need to feel there are endless options and possibilities open to you. Versatility is a key word and there is very little you cannot turn your hand to. Make sure you don't break too many hearts in your quest for greener pastures. You can be quite difficult to pin down, so someone to keep you on your toes is the best option for long-term happiness. If you can find the partner you can't quite understand, all the better, for as sure as 'eggs is eggs' if you work him/her out, you will be off! Your exuberant sexiness will win many admirers so enjoy the ride as you have the pick of the field.

If your boyfriend, girlfriend or partner is playing hard to get, just return the favour and do your own thing. Enjoy the company of family and friends so they think you have better fish to fry. If you don't panic, they will pay you lots of attention soon enough. Keep your options open and Jupiter, your ruler, will guide you in the right direction. Others might be watching you hoping that you trip up. Not a chance! Plan your strategy and the game, set and match is all yours.

In the long term: guard against boredom, as this is the one thing that can undo all your good intentions. Endless stimulation is a pressing need for Sagittarius, so if you have found what you are looking for don't blow it. Single Saggis should go with the flow and trust the Universe to deliver.

Sagittarian colour: Dark blue, purple, light blue
Birthstone: Topaz, turquoise
Magical Numbers: 6. 27. 32.

CAPRICORN

Ruling Planet: *Saturn*
Gender/Duality: *Feminine - Negative*
Element/Triplicity: *Earth – Practical Level*
Quality/Quadruplicity: *Cardinal – Enterprise, Ambition*
Primal Desire/Planetary Principle:
                                        Attainment/Crystallisation
Day of the Week: *Wednesday*
Zodiac Angel: *NADIEL – Confidence, Thoroughness,*
                                        Determination

A highly competent being is Capricorn! Be careful that you remain approachable and friendly as your unbending nature can put people off. Self-confidence is your birthright but this can be daunting for those with insecurities or silly agendas. You may experience your fair share of bitchiness until your peers catch up and realise you are a reliable useful friend. Use your humour to win others over if you can be bothered. Slow to fall in love, you savour the flowering of your emotions. This can be lost on younger males and females. So do not be surprised if you attract mature mates. There is plenty of fun when you relax, but you need to know where you are headed first!

Freedom of expression is crucial to Capricorn. You love to feel you are running the show. And there's an air of panic about you if someone else takes over! Chill out a bit, or your ambitious, controlling streak may be your downfall. Sometimes you can be too proud for your own good. Be prepared to admit mistakes and move on.

Adapt and survive rather than control at all costs in order to survive. Maintaining a devious level of manipulation is very self-defeating, as you will no doubt realise. Never use a string of lies to get you to where you want to be. Your stories may captivate an audience, but in time your exposure as a fraud may be too much to bear. Your brilliant mind brings many temptations!

Ambition is very important to Capricorn. Learn to delegate and ask for favours on your way to the top. Remember that with enough determination you can conquer any mountain you wish to climb. Focus gets Capricorn absolutely everywhere. Once you have found your full self-confidence you will realise how powerful you are! Don't abuse this position or your natural authority, as things could get ugly. Remember to balance your spirituality and all will be well. Many of the world's control freaks are Capricorn, so make sure you stay confident and kind.

Try not to adopt the same caution and control in your love life as you do elsewhere, Capricorn! It is important to learn to express your feelings and emotions from the heart. At times you will hold back for fear of rejection. Dare to be brave and wear your heart on your sleeve - the rewards will be huge. When you fall in love it is usually for keeps, for, by the time you agree to let go, it is more than clear that your partner is smitten. You are not a great risk taker and won't give your heart away to strangers. A sure thing is what you both offer and expect. Fair enough! Just make sure that you don't miss out on all the fun. Once you have found your soul mate, unwind and chill out. Watch that your tendency to penny pinch does not come across as mean-spirited. OK, so you're sensible with money, that's not a crime. But missing out on romantic dinners, presents and gestures of affection is!

Speak your mind and keep communication clear and honest. Make your peace with parents or friends that you have fallen out with. Use your surplus energy to good effect. Lots of social activity can lead to love interest. Keep your eyes peeled for the handsome sibling of a new friend! Do not let your partner take you for granted, but don't get too 'school marmy' or dictatorial with them! If you find you are bossing your partner around too much, it's time to move on.

In the long term: make time for fun as this will balance your serious minded nature. Success is important for Capricorn and with it your self-esteem increases. Dutiful and single-minded as you are, make sure that you find time for life's simple pleasures. Never let your competitiveness become the only thing that matters. Keep a sense of perspective.

Capricorn colour: Black, dark brown and green
Birth stone: Amethyst and turquoise
Magical Numbers: 4. 12. 33.

AQUARIUS

Ruling Planet: *Uranus*
Gender/Duality: *Masculine - Positive*
Element/Triplicity: *Air – Mental Level*
Quality/Quadruplicity: *Fixed – Strength, Willpower*
Primal Desire/Planetary Principle: *To Know and*
Understand/Truth

Day of the Week: *Saturday*

Zodiac Angel: *Cambiel – Ambition, Principles, Ideals*

Aquarians love to live life on their own terms and guard their privacy fiercely. Because of this you can be difficult to get up close and personal to, never mind dangerous with! The advice and support you give friends is legendary. You are older than your years and always have been. Be careful of sending mixed signals to the opposite sex. You don't want Mr or Miss Right to pass you by! Always compelling and charismatic as you are, certain people may find you unapproachable. Be aware that like a magnet you can repel and attract in equal measure. So smile extra sweetly and spell out your interest to a loved one.

Glamorous as you are, some people find you inaccessible or, even worse assume you are easy! Reassure a partner that you are 100% present or they may get insecure. Chat away with friends and acquaintance to boost connections or you risk becoming isolated. Playing hard to get will actually help you win the heart of Mr or Miss Popular. They will see you as a mysterious challenge so make them work hard before they get a reward!

In the long term: be aware that you will always need a certain amount of freedom. So stay away from partners, friends and careers that cramp your style. You have a kind, loving nature and work well with people. However too much structure or authority in a work situation will have to be avoided if you are to remain sane! Guard against a tendency to come across as obnoxious. You often ARE right, but others won't thank you if you live as if you are ALWAYS so! You like to keep tabs on people and events and love to feel as if you can control and manoeuvre people, (entirely for their own good, of course). You mean well and have a loving, compassionate heart, but feel as if you can always sort things out when push comes to shove. This personal confidence is sometimes overbearing, so learn when to keep shtum!

Aquarian colour: Electric blue, sea green, all the colours of the spectrum!
Birthstone: Amethyst, aquamarine, opal
Magical Numbers: 9. 22.

PISCES

Ruling Planet: *Neptune / Jupiter*
Gender/Duality: *Feminine - Negative*
Element/Triplicity: *Water – Emotional Level*
Quality/Quadruplicity: *Mutable – Flexibility, Versatility*
Primal Desire/Planetary Principle: *Unification / Sacrifice*
Day of the Week: *Thursday*
Zodiac Angel: *BARAKIEL – Sensitivity, Imagination, Thoughtfulness*

Pisceans are the dreamers of the Zodiac. You are clever, visionary and creative and tend to put the needs of others before your own. This will make you a loving parent and provider. Be careful not to tax your mind with needless worry as you have the tendency to conjure up many scenarios with that vivid imagination. Certainly avoid sending the opposite sex running for the hills with unfounded accusations. Try to relax and giggle a bit more! You are sensual and loving, but put the brakes on if you sense that your partner is getting claustrophobic.

Fortune smiles on you and there should be many good mates and exciting times. Give that person a chance and allow a relationship to take off. It will surprise you. If you have a partner who is rather selfish and not giving you much of a look in – think again. Put a limit on this bad behaviour and see do they pull their socks up! It might be time to make an important decision.

In the long term: it will suit you to work away discreetly in the background as part of a team. Attract lovers that let you act out your fantasies and who respond to your warm attention. Learn to laugh at some of your visions for if you don't the rest of the world will! Explore your mutable nature and learn to live with your changeable mind.

Make the most of your creativity, cleverness and poetic vision. But try to stay awake and keep your feet on the ground . . . if you can find them! Your tendency to dream and think profound thoughts is second-to-none, but if you are not careful you could find yourself traipsing down elaborate scenic routes in your imagination, which really have no bearing on reality. Don't beat yourself up over your inherent indecisiveness. It is part of your Piscean legacy and you will need to 'go with the flow' of your changing emotions. Remember that any decision is a good one if you follow it through. So learn to discipline the changeable dreamer and you will be a truthful incisive force to be reckoned with!

Pisces colours: Sea green, heliotrope
Birthstone: Moonstone, chrysolite
Magical Numbers: 11. 23.

Chapter Five:

Zodiac Cities and Countries
· ·

PLANNING TO TRAVEL?

Use this information to identify a suitable holiday resort or place to live. You should find that the energy of these places particularly suits your energy according to your Zodiac sign.

ARIES:
Countries and Regions: Denmark . France . Germany . Poland . Syria Japan . England
Cities: Brunswick . Birmingham(UK) . Naples . Marseilles . Krakow . Verona . Utrecht . Florence . Capua

TAURUS:
Countries and Regions: Cyprus . Ireland . Switzerland Egypt . Iran Capri . Greek Islands.
Cities: Dublin . Bologna . Mantua . Hastings(UK) Eastbourne(UK) . Palermo . Lucerne . Leipzig

GEMINI:

Countries and regions: Belgium . South Egypt . Wales
Sardinia . Armenia . United States of America
Cities: Cardiff . Bruges . Plymouth . London
San Francisco . Versailles . Nuremberg . Cordoba
Melbourne . New York.

CANCER:

Countries and Regions : The Netherlands
New Zealand . Africa (North and West) . Scotland
Paraguay . Algeria
Cities: Amsterdam . York . Manchester . Milan . Genoa
Venice . Tunis . Stockholm . Magdeburg . Cadiz . Algiers
Istanbul . New York

LEO:

Countries and Regions: Italy . France (South)
Iraq (South) . Sicily . The Alps (France) . Romania
The Lebanon
Cities: Bristol . Portsmouth (UK) . Chicago
Philadelphia Damascus . Madrid . Los Angeles . Bombay .
Bath . Rome Syracuse . Prague

VIRGO:

Countries and regions: Brazil . Crete . Turkey
Virgin Islands . Mesopotamia . Greece . Iraq
Cities: Boston . Corinth . Heidelberg . Athens
Jerusalem . Paris . Lyons . Reading

LIBRA:

Countries and Regions: Austria . Burma . Tibet . China
. Indo-China South Pacific Islands . Egypt (North) . Japan
Cities: Frankfurt . Vienna . Freiburg . Leeds
Nottingham Lisbon . Antwerp . Copenhagen.

SCORPIO:

Countries and Regions: Morocco . Norway . Uruguay
Transvaal . Syria . Korea . Bavaria
Cities: Dover . Fez . Halifax . New Orleans
Washington DC . Newcastle (UK) . Liverpool . Hull
Cincinnati . Baltimore . Valencia . Stockport . Milwaukee

SAGITTARIUS:

Countries and Regions: Australia . Hungary . Arabia
Spain
Cities: Bradford . Cologne . Toledo (Spain and USA)
Sheffield . Nottingham . Naples . Toronto . Stuttgart

CAPRICORN:

Countries and Regions: UK (Shetlands, Orkneys) .
India . Albania . Bulgaria Mexico . Macedonia . Lithuania
Cities: Delhi . Oxford . Mexico City . Brussels . Ghent
Port Said

AQUARIUS:

Countries and Regions: Ethiopia . Iran . Israel . Sweden
Russia . Poland . Abyssinia
Cities: Moscow . Salzburg . St Petersburg . Hamburg
Bremen

PISCES:

Countries and Regions: Portugal . Scandinavia
Mediterranean area (particularly small islands) . Sahara
Cities: Alexandria . Seville . Santiago

Chapter Six:

Eternal Horoscope

• •

The only Zodiac reading you'll ever need

This following chapter is designed to provide weekly inspirational comments for the Star Signs. Its relevance will not fade, for it is written psychically and is channelled information specific to your Zodiac sign. You may never need to fumble in your newspaper for your horoscope again! Along with metaphors and riddles to tease your mind, this unusual presentation offers guidance on healing, colour and pertinent numerology relevant to the week's vibration.

You may wonder how this idea of an eternal horoscope can possibly work, but try it and see. You will be astounded at the uncanny patterns, insights and points that are phrased to be always accurate. Look on this as an oracle, if you will, which provides personal guidance on a weekly basis as we head into the future. NB: I frequently get 3,4 and 5 numbers on the Lotto, so pay special attention to the lucky numbers at the foot of each Zodiac prediction!

CAPRICORN Time:
December 22nd – January 20th

WEEK ONE
January 1st - January 7th

Capricorn: Happy New Year to you! I do hope your waistband is not too uncomfortable at this stage of the proceedings. Watch out for a sense of constriction and work out why you feel stifled. It could be one mince pie too many, or else someone is getting your goat! I know I sometimes sound like a Christmas cracker . . . but do get to the bottom of that stodgy feeling. An energy drain needs to be de-clogged. So get cracking yourself!
Green for freshness and heart peace.
Pisces is interesting.
Lucky Numbers: 3.16.29.42.34.12.

Aquarius: May you reel in the New Year with good cheer! If you manage to achieve even half of what you aim to, the world will be a better place. You and yours should knuckle down and enjoy the remaining festivities. Equality counts for everything. So give others the same respect you give yourself. Be gentle and resourceful on your way to the top. It's very important not to shoot yourself in the foot. Your

resolutions are commendable, but keep them realistic!
Pale Blue for Divine Guidance.
Leo hits the spot.
Lucky Numbers: 19.27.25.21.33.5.

Pisces: God speed you into the New Year, Pisces! Swim free
and plunge into the rapids of the year ahead . . . expect
excitement and turbulence in equal measure. Simmer in the
nearest Jacuzzi if at all possible. You need to be invigorated,
refreshed and titillated. Let effervescence be the key to a new
bubbly approach to life. You can add your own sparkle and
lift dreary proceedings if you just decide to get busy!
Pop the cork in celebration . . .
Silver for shimmering promise.
Gemini is flattering . . . of course.
Lucky Numbers: 22.12.33.15.32.7.

Aries: The sentiments of Auld Lang Syne will have weighty
significance this year, Aries. Nostalgia fills the air like a fra-
grant but musty clove-filled orange! Work that one out . . .
something once juicy and sweet that you have kept spiced
up for a long time needs your attention! Don't slice it open,
as you won't like what you see. And certainly don't eat it or
attempt to digest it. In fact any rough treatment and it will
simply disintegrate into a ball of dust. The sell-by date is
long past . . . know when to let go.
Red and pink to let go of the old and bring in the new.
Taurus is hot and sweaty.
Lucky Numbers: 31.18.27.26.14.2.

Taurus: 'Go on, ya good thing!' To quote a certain turkey . . . let's hope you didn't get too stuffed over Christmas. Dustin has a native wit and wicked sense of humour but can he take it? It's all very well dishing up the dirt, but what happens when things get turned around? Watch yourself, Taurus. Don't get too confident and cocksure. Events are hovering in the ether that will trip you up if you're not careful. Lingering glances and chances put a different slant on your priorities. A fresh start takes on new meaning and you dare to stick your neck out. Just watch you're not garrotted . . . it's a nerve-wracking time of year for turkeys!

Gold and silver boost riches.

Aries is a challenge.

Lucky Numbers: 15.5.23.41.6.17.

Gemini: Merry New Year! You must be experiencing a time warp or jet–lag type sensation. One glass too many perhaps! Catch up with yourself and get your head together, or there will be a lot more on your plate than just cold ham. Don't settle for leftovers and if you find there's too much going down be selective. No, that does not mean dip into the Selection boxes, but it does mean choose Quality. Watch your step! The potential for a seasonal slip-up is quite high. Life changing events set you reeling . . . so do the Highland jig for good measure! Nifty footwork will make a difference. Red helps grounding.

Fellow air signs understand.

Lucky Numbers: 21.35.40.19.28.3.

Cancer: Expect a festive snog fest. So if you can't handle the heat, leave the mistletoe out of the kitchen! Lots of hugs and snuggles will keep you grounded. You need human contact and reassurance. And why not! Adapt to changing circumstances and don't scramble to hold onto the past. Be careful you don't smother people in your bid for attention, but do make the most of the love vibes coming your way. Keep your spirits up and follow through anything that grabs your vivid imagination.

Sea green for the heart of the matter.

Gemini is hilarious.

Lucky Numbers: 14.17.19.32.36.21.

Leo: High jinks guarantees a humdinger of a New Year! So have a riotous, joyous, noisy time and generally let your hair down. Live a little bit dangerously within the bounds of good sense. Let no stone go unturned, nor any invite unattended. Romantically raise the stakes in your game plan to spark interest. Plenty of attention leaves you purring like a pussycat, never mind a lion! Bend the rules a little bit if you feel you can get away with it. Then at least the scrabble will lose its sense of tedium. 'No dice!'

Red and green help separation.

Virgo is your alter ego.

Lucky Numbers: 20.18.8.34.6.25.

Virgo: Top of the New Year to ya! When you play with the big boys . . . expect to push the boat out. Leave a way home for yourself though and make sure the waves don't get too high and treacherous. We don't want to be sending out the lifeguard if you need to be rescued. The spotlight will shine upon you. So get comfortable and psyche yourself up. To be on the outside looking in is your normal state of affairs, but roles will be reversed. YOU will be under scrutiny. Be clear and focused and you will be dealt your finest hand. You get lucky with a big risk!

Black for protection.

Libra is off the rails.

Lucky Numbers: 19.8.17.23.4.12.

Libra: Gobble gobble! Too much turkey can have a strange effect on the best of us. Especially if it's over-cooked, dried out and going stale. Give up on whatever has lost its nutritional value in your life. And don't tread the old worn out paths simply for the sake of it. Habits die hard but now is the time to show willing and break them. A last splash won't go amiss. Just don't prevent the New by fixating on the OLD. Leave sentiment in the bucket and give nostalgia a run for its money. A gamble will pay off . . . but be bright and bold about it!

Purple for healing.

Knock the socks off Gemini.

Lucky Numbers: 24.15.22.13.5.41.

Scorpio: Make way for the love supreme! Happy New Leaf . . . Turn it over and begin writing at the top of a new page. You are the scribe of your life. So put pen to paper and go with the flow. Make it as risky, dynamic or conventional as you like, but take responsibility for the action. Stop passing the buck. And cast a plot Shakespeare would have been proud of. No need to resort to tragedy or farce though. Strike a balance using humour, common interest and spicy scenario. Remember the pen is mightier than the sword. You can create and have an impact!

Turquoise inspires creativity.

Taurus opposes you.

Lucky Numbers: 33.12.11.9.18.27.

Sagittarius: Trip the light fantastic! Glitter balls at the ready ... Prepare for a camp New Year! 'Put on the Ritz' as they say, and use all the extravagance at your disposal. If you can't indulge with a clear conscience at this point, then when? Glide around without a care in the world. If you put on a convincing performance you can expect reality to reflect your conviction. Your life is a tape playing in your head. So change the reel if it's getting you down. Put on a different hat and redirect the action.

Yellow for vibrancy.

Leo is fun.

Lucky Numbers: 2.16.31.3.18.24.

WEEK TWO
January 8th - January 14th

Capricorn: Hot foot it into the New Year, Capricorn! You may feel like you're dancing on hot coals, but it's just an illusion. Stop trying so hard to impress us. It's already clear that your agility, mental and otherwise, is second-to-none. So forget the eggshell crunching, and use your innate self-confidence to make great strides. Generally calm down – there's no need to dance at all. Wait for life to provide you with a genuine leap of joy…the rest is just fancy footwork!

Blue for peace.

Stop projecting onto fellow earth signs.

Lucky Numbers: 14.29.34.23.1.37.

Aquarius: So we have crossed the threshold into a New Year! Are you happy? Content? Fulfilled? Abundant? At this stage you should have every reason to be grateful. Count your many blessings and stop striving for the impossible. There comes a time when you have to find your feet, place them firmly on the ground and start walking. Fancy visions are all very well. And your dreams are exciting. But you also have to live in the real world. Wish upon a star or several by all means, but don't hold your breath or you just might asphyxiate!

Silver for moon madness and profound dreams.

Keep your eye on Aries.

Lucky Numbers: 25.19.3.14.19.17.

Pisces: As we go into the New Year, do you feel as if you're out on the high seas or in the safe waters of tranquil lake? It's all about perspective. Fish spend their lives swimming beneath the surface. So in a sense it matters not how deep and treacherous the waves are above your head. If you need to find a place of calm . . . go deeper. Explore the depths of your nature. A still small voice within you holds the key to many an adventure. Follow through and go where you will. Be confident in your ability to swim – it comes naturally.

Sea green for support.

Scorpio plays hard.

Lucky Numbers: 33.11.21.35.22.19.

Aries: Rev up your engines, Aries. You're going to need plenty of gas. But make sure precious fuel and energy are not expended wastefully. And keep yourself ecologically sound. Don't spend precious time driving up a cul-de-sac, however pretty the view. Sometimes the urge to have a look gets the better of you. Pause for thought or you really will set the cat among the pigeons! Watch out for unseen leakage and keep an eye on your Achilles heel. You mustn't overestimate your ability to hold onto the past. What's done is done . . . Yellow to de-stress.

Cancer has answers.

Lucky Numbers: 15.27.35.19.38.2.

Taurus: The urge to splurge will be high, Taurus – perhaps in the January sales or more likely on luxury items. It's not really your style to look at labels. So never mind the discount! When you set your mind, heart, body and soul on something or someone there's no escape (for the rest of us!). Be sure you go after the REAL thing this year. Stop falling short of your promises to yourself. It's right to honour commitments, but not at the expense of your sanity. There's nothing better than the real thing. It's just a matter of working out what the real thing IS!

Green for finances and heart.

Fellow earth gets down and dirty.

Lucky Numbers: 6.31.10.26.23.33.

Gemini: Wuthering Heights and tempestuous storms give your emotions the Heathcliff vibe! Watch out for desperation and don't be haunted by the passing of something that got a grip of you. Obsession and possession may be literary romantic notions, but they don't make for dignified behaviour in the here and now. Stay cool, Gemini! Press on across the moors if you have to, but I'm sure your landscape isn't that bleak. Take a closer look. There's fragrance in the air, blossom in the trees, and the heather's in bloom. See the bright side!

Lavender aids protection.

Leo is fun.

Lucky Numbers: 42.27.18.22.19.1.

Cancer: When will you feel better, Cancer? When you have the mortgage sorted? The pension, savings plan or deposit account at a 'safe' level? Have you ever wondered why security issues are so important to you? It's time to realise that you will never reach Havana. And that it's pointless hankering for what you don't have. What you may perceive as the state of 'having arrived' brings a different set of burdens. It's relative! The millionaire up the road has something bugging him. Even more significantly it's something you have that he wants . . . Let that be your one-upmanship!

Turquoise boosts creativity.

Virgo is sexier than you realise.

Lucky Numbers: 41.2.31.40.4.26.

Leo: Try to adjust to the things you can do nothing about. Certain things are beyond your control. And the sooner you accept this the better. Being Leo can be a challenge. You are destined for greatness and won't be able to escape. Whether you like it or not, your Leo legacy means that you will rule the world in some shape or form. Issues of attention will always preoccupy you. Are you getting enough? Do you have too much? What will finally satisfy you? Tap into your creativity and be all you can be! There's no point skulking in the shadows . . . the spotlight will find you.

Orange boosts vitality.

Capricorn is a nuisance.

Lucky Numbers: 23.18.19.29.30.34.

Virgo: Do you feel you need to solve a riddle or get to the bottom of something, Virgo? Let me give you a clue. Don't bother! How boring would it be to have all the answers? You come close anyway so be content and leave life a little mystery. Reserve judgement with big decisions. The answers will unfold organically just when you need them. Synchronicity delivers perfectly. And the timing will be spot-on too. So TRUST is all you need. It's the biggest little word there is . . . but go get you some!

Purple for healing.

Taurus tantalises.

Lucky Numbers: 14.19.31.42.3.25.

Libra: Perhaps you feel a time machine would be the answer to all your problems? And if you could rewind the clock, or go back to the future, what then? Oscillating between events is a juggling act few can maintain. So if you're trying to keep all your balls airborne prepare for deflation. There comes a time when the here and now takes precedence. So focus on the present and give life a whirl. You don't want to be looking back over your shoulder at this moment. Seize opportunities as and when they appear.

Violet for head stuff.

Cancer is a chancer!

Lucky Numbers: 25.14.30.24.31.6.

Scorpio: Even the most gorgeous, tasty, delicious dish can go flat and lose its oomph! Delectable as you are, watch you don't get too complacent. Your bubble may be about to burst through no fault of your own. Destiny has a completely different plan. And you will have to adapt and be more flexible. Take it on board as a life lesson. At least you won't go down like the Titanic. You have rescue measures in place. Just open your eyes and think on your feet. You're a born survivor; never mind that sinking feeling!

Deep blue brings calm.

Virgo is worth a go!

Lucky Numbers: 19.28.17.26.7.2.

Sagittarius: You need to be nimble-footed across the quicksand! Keep moving and think fast. Lively steps should keep you dancing. Just don't trip or get tangled up by intricate moves. The entertainment is purely for those watching. Frustrating this may be but for the moment the focus is on YOU! Use your humour as a diversion. And lighten the stress by not thinking. Simply do the next thing…and quickly. Decisive action will keep you sane and lead you away from danger . . . real or imagined.

Red boosts energy.

Leo inspires fun.

Lucky Numbers: 18.3.27.16.15.14.

WEEK THREE
January 15th – January 21st

Capricorn: I hope you have lost the decorations at this stage and embarked on a detox plan. You need to find some order amidst chaos. And the time was yesterday! Wrap up everything that no longer works for you. Have you made your bed? Don't feel you have to lie in it! Be the master of your destiny and make the necessary changes. If you don't, circumstances will begin to dictate a rather tedious sentence. Purple for dignity with a regal flavour.

Aquarius makes a link.

Lucky Numbers: 3.14.16.29.34.1.

Aquarius: The tide is high, are you holding on? You're still number 1 in the hearts and minds of the people who count. Panic not! A handsome display will attract your attention. Monitor your spending though. Not everything can be bought with money. Pay your way and bide your time. Do express your intention in matters of the spirit. The Universe has ordained a colourful statement. Be open to the plan and accept your lot. You will find that abundance comes when you least expect it. The source of your good fortune is known but unpredictable.

Blue for peace.

Pisces is fishy!
Lucky Numbers: 24.32.17.19.40.33.

Pisces: Submarines are useful for navigating or scanning the ocean deep. But you don't need that kind of mechanism. Subterranean voyages come naturally and are all part of your in-built survival kit. Do come up for some air at this point, not too quickly though; you don't want a bad case of the bends (nasty turn!). In all things take your time. What's the rush? Although you thrive on emotional intrigue and drama, keep it simple. Stop looking for evidence on the (sea) bed. Enjoy a good old 'snorkle' at the surface and take a breather. Leave deep (sea) diving to the big boys!
Sea green, but don't go too deep.
Scorpio lurks in pots...avoid the trap.
Lucky Numbers: 16.31.6.17.29.34.

Aries: The heat is full on, Aries. Are you up for all the attention? Expect the intense glare of full-beam, but don't act like a rabbit caught in the headlights. Keep your dignity at all times. Rampant though your reactions may be, please 'contain' yourself! Road rage is not attractive. Stay with it and on track. There is no room to manoeuvre. And you can't turn back just because the going got rough . . . it's not an option! Sunglasses will shield you from the outside world, so make full use of their protection. They will be the only 'mask' you can afford to wear. Prepare for over-exposure!
Deep red boosts protection.
Taurus is trying.
Lucky Numbers: 23.14.15.27.33.12.

Taurus: The proverbial red rag to a bull will be verily on display. You may feel simultaneously baited and excited. The blood will be fairly pumping through your veins anyway! Try to keep your finger on the pulse and monitor the heart rate, as an angry or passionate explosion would not be a pretty sight! On the other hand you need to get real and address a problem. A challenging situation will come back to haunt you. Admit your responsibility and redress the balance. Love finds a way through the maze.

Green for heart action.

Scorpio won't forget.

Lucky Numbers: 24.30.19.28.37.4.

Gemini: Get the jump leads out and kick-start the New Year! You don't seem to have even turned the engine on, never mind got into gear. Show willing at least and display some signs of life! Did someone leave your battery flat? Deflated you may feel, but get out the demister, humidifier, and antifreeze . . . there's life in the old boy yet! Possibly someone fogged your goggles. Or hot-wired your soul? Get over it . . . summon new vision and embrace a fresh start. The wide, open road awaits. So cruise on down the big highway – interesting diversions lie ahead.

Red for energy drive.

Aquarius doesn't seem to care.

Lucky Numbers: 40.3.22.11.39.33.

Cancer: Disentangle or disengage yourself from an emotional coil. You can't scuttle away this time. Your protective shell has worn thin, so fortify yourself. Battling against the elements is pointless and there is no place to hide. Try to look as if you don't give a damn. A nonchalant whistle should do the trick. Once clear of danger, breathe a sigh of relief and resolve to look after yourself. The time is now! Develop a tougher exterior, but leave a ruthless streak on the shelf. It pays to keep your wits about you.

Lilac for healing.

Leo is supportive.

Lucky Numbers: 31.6.16.27.34.4.

Leo: A rip-roaring time is the prediction for all Leonine creatures. Just preserve your energy and remember the 'cold light of day' is an imminent factor. Don't make promises you can't keep. And watch that you don't get carried away in the heat of the moment. Tomorrow's another day, and there's only one of you . . . at the last count! Unfortunately cloning has not gone mainstream yet. So work within the confines of your limitations. Boundaries are in place for good reason. They prevent you losing the run of yourself and help you to keep a grip on reality. Well that's the general idea . . .

Gold assists wisdom.

Virgo is beautiful inside and out.

Lucky Numbers: 32.15.16.17.33.41.

Virgo: I hope you don't feel 'picked on' by life, the Universe, or the annoying neighbour next door! Don't buy into blue thoughts. If you look around, you will see how far you have come. You're just not quite where you want to be yet. Be patient and don't allow the long wait to mar present enjoyment. Stress about nothing in particular will drain your energy. So leave the vampire force of negativity in the closet. Time is like quicksand . . . move quickly, don't sink and watch out for the incoming tide. The sun will light your way and dry out your path (Remember footprints in the sand?). Look for clues and directions.

Pale blue for Divine Will.

Taurus is a nuisance.

Lucky Numbers: 13.42.25.16.17.28.

Libra: A bit of rock 'n' roll will liven your step! Leave cheesy behaviour in the corner and lose all corny comments too. Something has a grip of you and you are acting madly out of character. Maybe love has you in a spin? But the whirling dervish factor is kicking in. Unravel yourself for a moment and check your dishevelled appearance. Keep your feet on the ground and take a deep breath. Excitement is in the air, but make sure you're not! Don't lose the run of yourself or harsh reality will force an aborted landing.

Magenta assists grounding.

Aries is inspiring.

Lucky Numbers: 3.29.40.16.27.34.

Scorpio: Relish all the attention heading your way, but be aware that it may not last. Stay practical and enjoy what you have for the moment. Trust for the rest. It's all change, but it's for the best! Don't be afraid to let your hair down when it counts. Quality connections matter. Your blessings are many and varied. Appreciate them in the here and now, rather than look back over your shoulder in time to come. The future begins NOW! Fixate on the present. It's healthi-

er than focusing on what you think you need and don't have.
Green for heart and $.
Virgo knows the score.
Lucky Numbers: 13.15.17.19.21.2.

Sagittarius: If your luck is in, you have to win. Strange but
true – or is it? They say you 'have to be in to win', but I'm
not so sure. It's all 'relative' and depends upon your perception of events. Murphy's Law, or Sod's law, works very
actively because we believe it. Someone wins the Lotto and
we look for the plane crash! Why not accept that good
things happen. You are lucky! Ignore the balance of the
Universe for a time and enjoy yourself. We don't want a
self-fulfilling prophecy on our hands.
Reds boost passion.
Scorpio understands.
Lucky Numbers: 3.12.14.16.28.39.

AQUARIUS Time:
January 21st – February 19th

WEEK FOUR
January 22nd - January 28th

Aquarius: Make a New Year statement to all those who
have annoyed you recently! Express the intention not to suffer fools gladly. It's time to make amends and do your own
thing, to the best of your ability. Never mind what loved

ones expect. Lay down the law in the nicest possible way and be true to YOU! Rally your resources and put in a good effort. Things are set to change, but you have to understand certain events and show willing. God helps those who help themselves. So accept responsibility for the obvious and TRUST for the rest. Your circumstances are very much of your own making . . . so UNmake what no longer works. Green for finances.

Leo is guarded.

Lucky Numbers: 13.24.25.17.3.41.

Pisces: Pull your socks up or ship out! Reassess your priorities and make sure you're happy with where you're heading. There's no point casting around for someone to blame. If you were caught in a nasty hook, please God you were thrown back into the deep. Nurse your wounds then swim on to new waters. Learn from your mistakes, and enjoy your newly found freedom. Past difficulty will prove to be a blessing in disguise. And you should be thankful for the huge learning curve you have survived. Be cheerful!

Grey/blues make soft hues.

Cancer is grumpy.

Lucky Numbers: 2.1.7.11.10.34.

Aries: Be careful not to sweep things under the carpet for the sake of appearances. You have risen above adversity, challenges, and affronts to your character. But a particular person is like a bulldog with clenched teeth. They're not going to let sleeping beasts lie! Be prepared for a reality check of the third degree. Honesty and truth will stand you in good stead, when up against it. Remember though, not everyone has the same degree of integrity. Work it all out by doing the right thing – when you know what that is! Red boosts vitality.

Watch Gemini.

Lucky Numbers: 10.20.30.12.33.4.

Taurus: Prepare for a scenario of 'Beauty and the Beast'! You won't understand all the attention you are about to receive, but do be grateful! All offers are extremely welcome, no doubt. Be careful though. And don't add to the confusion that follows you around. Romantically anything can happen and probably will. Mermaids, fairies and magical beings of all kinds light your way into the future. Be 'twinkly' and excited about what will occur – not boring and staid. OK, you're slow but sure, Taurus. But once you get moving you'll be cool!

Regal colours for charisma.

Aries is a nuisance.

Lucky Numbers: 1.7.11.22.33.40.

Gemini: Prepare for a commotion; do the 'locomotion!' Work as part of a team and don't try to stand out from the crowd. It's right to keep your head down at this stage. An independent, stubborn streak won't go down well, but do keep an eye out for opportunities that allow you to express yourself differently. Play ball, but not always in the same court! You can move away from home, if you do so discreetly. Minimum fuss is the key to the freedom you can expect. Don't draw attention to yourself, and people won't notice you're not there . . . charming!

Lemon to support bitterness.

Capricorn is a handful.

Lucky Numbers: 4.7.23.41.35.2.

Cancer: It's all to do with perception. You need to come at IT from a different angle! Whatever bothers you, can be dealt with as long as you adopt a unique approach. Be your own inimitable self when faced with adversity. Your humour keeps you and yours bright and content. Do your worst and stick with the original plan of action. Success is imminent – you just need to access IT. Decide not to be defeated, and you won't be. IT is as simple as that! Choose the best option at all times and don't be afraid to be controversial.

Dark green boosts earth connection.

Virgo is a Trojan!

Lucky Numbers: 22.31.16.6.27.3.

Leo: You may feel so burdened with work and deadlines that you want to curl up and sleep! Actually you could do worse as you need to recharge those batteries in order to work effectively. Don't miss a genuine opportunity to pounce however. Just make sure that the time is right. The road is as rough as you want it to be. So don't pick a treacherous route out of perversity. You love a challenge, but can over-estimate your ability to rise to the occasion. Press on and keep your spirit elevated.

Deep red boosts grounding.

Sagittarius is fun.

Lucky Numbers: 24.33.19.17.35.27.

Virgo: Your courage is legendary. Refuse to give up! On principle Fate owes you a deal or two. But don't expect everything to be that straightforward. Watch your back and don't confide in the wrong people. You attract jealousy without looking or thinking. The agendas of others are dangerous. So you need to be more aware, and less trusting. It's a shame, but it's a harsh reality that not everyone is as nice as you are. Make allowances for this non-negotiable truth, and your way ahead will be safer and more profitable.
Black for protection.
Taurus is a waste of time – for now.
Lucky Numbers: 3.23.15.27.9.30.

Libra:Your balance may be knocked for SIX. Stay as level-headed as you are able and prepare for major adjustments. Things are not as they seem, and there is more to a situation than meets the eye. Look on the bright side. All is not lost. There will be interesting twists and turns in the road up ahead. Be cautious and drive carefully. You may be back behind the steering wheel, but for how long? Ask for timely advice, but don't relinquish control. Do the best possible in a restricted environment.
Yellow to de-stress.
Cancer is leading you on.
Lucky Numbers: 21.34.2.15.17.39.

Scorpio: It's time to see what you're made of! Don't be shy. You may be usually confident, but someone is making you weak at the knees. Be careful not to miss a great chance for all the wrong reasons. Compliance and niceties are all very well. But when the going gets tough, you have to get real. Go for gold! And stop being so clichéd in your thinking. The only restrictions on you are those imposed by your good self. Permit yourself to be bold once in a while. Access your personal freedom, and be all you can be.

White for purity and black for nonsense.

Libra is tough.

Lucky Numbers: 3.11.19.28.42.13.

Sagittarius: Get practical and move carefully through tricky problems. Nifty footwork will guide through a maze of difficulty. But it's not as bad as it seems. Stay philosophical! There's nothing beyond your ability, as long as you remain realistic about what you can achieve! Watch your tendency to be overly optimistic. Use your humour as a secret weapon. It will get you in and out of trouble at the drop of a hat. A fitness and dietary regime will reap dividends, so do persist. Your energy will benefit from an unusual surprise that boosts morale.

Purples for spirituality.

Capricorn gives pertinent advice.

Lucky Numbers: 24.13.26.38.4.2.

Capricorn: There's a good buzz around financial dealings as the New Year progresses. All is not lost with something you ditched or discarded. Give it another go. At second time around it's a different story. The social whirl will get you going and leave you reeling. If your head is in a spin enjoy the feeling! Loss of control won't do you any harm, once in a while. Be open to new opportunities even those you least expect. The element of surprise is good and keeps you on your toes.

Blue for peace.

Virgo is cross.

Lucky Numbers: 15.27.38.41.2.33.

WEEK FIVE
January 29th – February 4th

Aquarius: Alchemy awaits you. Enjoy life's synchronicities at this time, Aquarius. The Universe will provide, and some! You need to keep a sense of humour in a complex situation. Admit you took a wrong turn and make moves to rectify the situation. Don't make premature judgements quite yet, but do follow your instincts, which should be impressively sharp. Pale blue enlivens you.

Virgo is worth it.

Lucky Numbers: 11.24.3.16.37.4.

Pisces: The time is ripe for good decisions. Be the Ninja master (not turtle) of your own destiny. Stop wavering, and read between the lines. You must learn from previous patterns of behaviour that got you nowhere. Avoid the circuitous route and go straight from A to B! It can be done . . . get a map if all else fails. Elaborate plans and grand intentions need to be modified. Be smart and street-wise. Saunter down blind alleys at your own risk – the open road is safer.

Lilac helps transmutation.

Cancer is crabby!
Lucky Numbers: 13.25.37.40.22.1.

Aries: Are you a bit shellshocked or stunned? A strange scenario occurred recently – what can it mean? Life holds many surprises up its loaded sleeve. You have seen your fair share of the goods already, but prepare for more magic, intrigue and mystery. A weird mix of the good, bad and bizarre is winging its way towards you. Enjoy the ghost ride, it is not as scary as you think, and will lighten your load in more ways than one.

Deep blue helps a passing.

Taurus is a pain in the proverbial backside.

Lucky Numbers: 14.29.33.28.19.4.

Taurus: You can fool some of the people some of the time . . . and all that. Are the cracks showing, Taurus? A cover up could backfire big time. Be careful and know who your friends are. The archetypal femme fatale or Casanova waits in the wings. Yeah, right . . . in your dreams! Don't judge a book by its cover. Open it up, savour the contents, and have a good experience before you make a final judgement. Be bold enough to dip your toe in the water, or you will never know what you are missing.

Red boosts passion.

Aquarius knows the score.

Lucky Numbers: 25.14.3.37.40.7.

Gemini: Wish upon a star, as your luck comes through at last! Well, your imagination is second-to-none at least. Stay upbeat and optimistic about the future. Then if all else fails you still have your soul and spirit intact. There is no need to compromise or sell yourself out. Treasure truth and integrity, as they are your most precious commodities. The worst nightmare can turn into the realisation of a dream. If only . . .

Purple for regal prowess.

Libra has insights.

Lucky Numbers: 13.24.35.27.19.5.

Cancer: Stop messing! It is time to get real and desist from merely hoping for the best. A complex emotional situation needs delicate handling. (Kid gloves are available in BT's at discount price!) You may start to wonder what's in a price tag. Do you look at labels, obsessively scrutinise receipts, or simply hone in on what you want before breezing out the shop? Reassess your values sharp or you will lose something very dear through petty haggling. You cannot put a price on your heart's desire.

Green for financial heart and soul.

Time will tell re Virgo.

Lucky Numbers: 13.25.4.37.40.2.

Leo: Creep up on your prey very stealthily or you risk frightening a target. The bush has many thickets and hiding places. So don't expect an easy hunting season. Keep your pride intact whilst on the prowl. Time will reveal where loyalties lie. The Lion will be in cahoots with the lamb before too long. Peace will descend, just not in the way you currently expect. A big roar will get you attention, but will it provide a long-term answer? Act in haste; repent at leisure, as they say. But sure, what do THEY know? Who are THEY anyway? Orange boosts vitality.

Taurus is gallant.

Lucky Numbers: 14.29.38.5.15.17.

Virgo: The Milky Way seems a long way off. But at times you feel as if you herald from another galaxy! Try to lose the feeling of alienation and isolation that 'dogs' your steps. Engage in the here and now with your feet firmly placed on *terra firma*. Close encounters of the delicious kind are highly likely. The consequent attention and questioning should bring you back down to earth with a bang! Never mind the intrigue and mystery, what about the reputation? Something matters, more than words can express. Follow your heart.

Yellow to de-stress.

Gemini brings airy fun.

Lucky Numbers: 15.24.13.15.29.4.

Libra: A potent triangle of events will make your life very interesting. Keep your thoughts sweet and the best scenario will then manifest. Balance and a clear head is crucial for your progress. Take things as they come and be ready for anything. Only Duracell batteries go on forever! Get some rest. Reflect on a significant picture and listen to your dreams. What transpires promptly is unexpected but very necessary. Be philosophical about the things you can't control. And enjoy the things you can!

Turquoise assists creativity.

Gemini makes you laugh.
Lucky Numbers: 3.25.18.39.4.22.

Scorpio: Follow the rainbow and you just may find a pot of GOLD at the end of it. But what if someone got there first? How many pots of gold are there exactly? Is this a symbol for some event in 'cloud-cuckoo-land', or do fairies really boost the coffers in a magical way? Either way you're about to find out! Expect a mysterious and strange boost to your affairs. The twists and turns of fate are going to get very sweaty and intense. Keep a camera close by to plot the evidence. But you will have to believe it to see it!
Silver boosts finances.
Virgo is hot stuff.
Lucky Numbers: 29.3.24.16.18.9.

Sagittarius: Your sense of humour needs a by-pass! Unusually for you, the bright side has done a disappearing act. How then can you look upon it? Trust me, it IS still there. You just have to dig beneath the surface of a complex situation. Use your imagination and find the fun side once again. Don't get bogged down in laborious detail, but do check the small print. Time is of the essence, so take your chance to join the dance. The steps just got trickier, but you are more nimble footed than you appreciate. Press on!
Gold enlivens wisdom.
Aries will share a joke.
Lucky Numbers: 18.24.35.41.29.5.

Capricorn: 'Muggles' need not apply. Life is about to get energetically complex and challenging. You will need a touch of magic to inspire you. Brush down that broomstick, paint the cat black, and find a wand of crystal to make things happen. If only it were that easy. But it IS a case of 'what next?'. Display some trust, focus and imagination and you won't need the props. You will need to kiss goodbye to 'muggledom' however. Miracles, wizardry and magicianship are hot commodities that DO exist! Logic just took a holiday. Wake up and smell potent etheric coffee!

Silver and gold bring magical inspiration.

Pisces knows.

Lucky Numbers: 1.5.7.11.25.19.

WEEK SIX
February 5th - February 11th

Aquarius: Is your head in the clouds, or elevated 'cruising' the heavens? Watch your altitude status– you may need oxygen up there! Aim to find an appropriate landing strip and come back down to earth. Or you just might go supersonic. We are full of admiration. Yes, you're riding high. But you do need to keep a grip on reality. Assess what that may mean in your stratosphere, and act accordingly. Where are you coming from? Even more importantly where are you heading? Look at the flight-deck and chart a flight to somewhere. Please!

Earth colours for grounding.

Fire signs send a rescue flare.

Lucky Numbers: 33.14.25.17.29.6.

Pisces: Make a wish – again! This time your propensity to engage in a spot of fantasy will come good. Your dreams and visions are all set to get you somewhere. Listen to your Byronic poetic heart and don't be afraid to follow through. Have the courage of your convictions, as no one else will. You have to sell a pitch and pitch a sale. That leap of faith is worthwhile. Doubts and fears are unfounded. So reserve judgement for a moment longer. Then plunge into the deep end and swim. The time for treading water is over.

Deep purple is groovy.

Libra is off on one!

Lucky Numbers: 1.14.18.29.40.3.

Aries: What a busy bee you are! Preserve your wild honey by all means, but make sure things don't get too sticky. There's no benefit in acting like the Queen Bee when the droves are no longer obliging. Some of your workers are still on side, but interest is dissipating. Gather your resources for the pending harvest, but be aware that you may have to sting to make an impression. Your honey is not quite so malleable this season. So you may have to squash things into shape for appearances' sake. From the outside the comb looks as juicy as usual. Systematise your activity and things will surely get sweeter . . . maybe!

Yellow for honey and power.

Water signs dampen your enthusiasm.

Lucky Numbers: 2.15.26.38.40.23.

Taurus: Stop playing games! Cat and mouse may be a fun diversionary tactic, but remember there's a rat trap at the end of it. Futile engagements drain you and render you senseless. Avoid over complexity at all costs, for your pocket will suffer if you follow the path of folly. Call a halt to the baiting game. It's a case of least said, soonest mended. Life is like chess at times. And you certainly have a chequered board to manoeuvre. Think tactically. Just don't be overly confident that you will be the one declaring 'Cheque Mate'! It isn't over yet . . . Jeopardy comes to mind

Green for finances.

Scorpio is cute.

Lucky Numbers: 2.4.16.28.39.5.

Gemini: You can sew up a rip or frayed seam, but does it ever look quite the same again? Perhaps appearances no longer count. In which case, start patching things up, I guess, as long as you have something that functions on some level. But is life really about making do? Test the strength of your material. Are you dealing with a wearable, durable, if not classic item? Sometimes it is worth forking out and making an investment. Perhaps stop looking at the price tag and replace all second-hand rags and items past their sell-by date. Don't settle for second-best, it isn't worth it!

Turquoise enhances creativity.

Aries is nifty.

Lucky Numbers: 1.7.11.15.19.21.

Cancer: Do stop ruminating over the impossible. You are not seeing clearly at the moment. Get real and develop your radar for B★★★S★★★! De-fog your specs and if you do have two pairs, lose the rose-tint on both. There may indeed be different ways of looking at something, but the true picture is what you need. If you risk what you already know you may be casting yourself adrift on the high seas. A suitable environment for crabs certainly, but the deep is scary compared to the warmer waters close to shore. Fish in the safety zone to avoid the unforgiving trawler's net.

Deep blue enhances deep peace.

Libra is a head wreck.

Lucky Numbers: 1.10.18.37.40.8.

Leo: Try to find a pitch of activity a bit closer to autopilot. Your routine has got hectic. Re-prioritise your schedule. OK so a quick gear-change always adds to the fun. And there is something to be said for getting behind the wheel and burning up some juice. But joy-riding is dangerous and highly illegal. The quick fix probably is not worth your energetic investment. Avoid the lethal route and calm down. You may feel your engine packs it like a Ferrari, but cast your mind back to the showroom. You invested in a trade-in, didn't you! Be careful and don't over-extend yourself.

Red for vra vra vroom!

Watch for chancing air signs.

Lucky Numbers: 10.20.33.16.19.12.

Virgo: Try to shift that hard-done-by feeling. You have undoubtedly been led a merry dance, but remember aspects of the arrangement you enjoyed. There is no benefit in bearing a grudge forever and a day. Move onto greener, more 'lush' pastures. Air past grievances, then ditch them! Are you sounding like an old record on replay? The scenario has dated now, so don't get stuck in a time warp. Move on with a lighter step, and engage in the next exciting whirl of activity. Show the world what you're made of. You have the wherewithal to turn this whole damned thing around!

Black for protection.

Water signs are supportive.

Lucky Numbers: 1.4.7.11.21.19.

Libra: In for a penny, in for a pound! Do look after your small change, then the bigger, heavy-duty items (gold nuggets) will manifest. Financial responsibility is called for. Download your creativity and make it work. Imagination has a lot to answer for, but it holds the key to your future. Don't be afraid of the unknown, uncertain or unseen. There is a new buzz to connect with. It's not fey, but it is invisible. Substantial returns will land if you follow an illogical but tangible idea. Dig deep and prepare to invest in an unusual but rewarding future. Be brave.

Magenta supports attention to detail.

Cancer didn't mean it.

Lucky Numbers: 15.16.17.18.29.1.

Scorpio: Unravel the mystery that has been bothering you forever. Get your best macintosh, pipe and hat out the closet and go on an investigative spree. Inspector Clouseau, move over! There's an ancient clue hidden somewhere. But you may need to rummage through your karmic drawers to find it! This strangely familiar scenario is bringing on the *déjà vu*. Your intuition and psychic hunches will guide you, but be aware you have met your match, and you may have to surrender to a superior mind (bender). All's fair in love and war! Reach for the nearest power tool to fell the hedges of this emotional maze.

Blue/lemon supports Old Souls!

Virgo is a gas ticket!

Lucky Numbers: 1.5.25.29.19.36.

Sagittarius: All things equine suit your sensibilities. Watch the horses and learn from their ease and grace. A good old gallop down the racecourse will invigorate, but tire you. So pace your step and make things lively but endurable. Don't rush the fences, but do put in the extra effort before the big jumps. Breakneck speed won't assist you in the long run. So ensure that your odds are even, and canter through the hurdles. There's bound to be a photo call once the competition kicks in, but at least you will have made it past the finishing line.

Red Rum disappeared . . . make sure you don't!

Aries keeps up.

Lucky Numbers: 13.17.31.26.6.29.

Capricorn: Your steely determination is about to be galvanised in a grand way. Watch out for empty gestures from the defeated party. Meet someone halfway, as long as you can set the terms for negotiation! A compromise may be dictated, but at least it provides an answer. Pleasure your senses for sanity's sake. Life should not be all hard work. Look for peace and tranquillity in a strange place. Connect with unseen, twinkly fairy folk for maximum entertainment! Yeah, I'm joking, but do give different dimensions some

consideration. What you see is not always what you get!
Pale blue for contemplation.
Cancer emotion riles you– learn something.
Lucky Numbers: 7.11.21.34.29.40.

WEEK 7
February 12th - February 18th

Aquarius: A watershed moment is upon you. Either that or the heavens are opening! As the skies overflow and the rain descends, be grateful that you didn't hang the laundry out to dry. Discretion is really the best policy, though it is tempting to spill the beans on one particular protagonist! Preserve your privacy and that of others and you will be duly reward-ed. Expect a 'crossroads' decision to materialise. Remain calm and the answer will naturally unfold.
Bright blue for inspiration.
Taurus is a challenge.
Lucky Numbers: 1.13.25.36.20.5.

Pisces: This one comes with a health warning (joke!). Check your 'electrics'. Anyone will tell you that water and high voltage energy are not a good mix. Investigate the dan-ger zone and expect a power surge where you splash (play). Water will of course put out fire, but in this instance, the mix is so potent that a more dramatic electrocution could occur. Don't get caught unawares in a compromising clinch. You may indeed look quite fetching with your hair standing on end, but for vanity's sake protect your interests. Take a leap of faith. Just don't hotwire or compromise your circuits before you even get started. A jolt can be stimulating, but charred remains are very unsavoury!

Orange assists shock.

Fire signs inspire excitement.

Lucky Numbers: 23.4.25.18.29.40.

Aries: You may feel justifiably proud of recent achievements. Build on your successes. But don't leave any stone unturned. You are missing a fundamental piece of the current jigsaw. You may feel you have a handle on what's needed to wrap it up. Be warned though – someone 'tricky' has hidden the final shape. The picture may never be completed as you envisage. A gaping hole may not be filled with the wrong part. There is a semblance of artistry about your life, but a more adventurous student has the trump card. An abstract project is underway in the background. Maybe take lessons in cubism to stay ahead of the competition!

Yellow to de-stress.

Gemini is a fun-filled handful.

Lucky Numbers: 1.22.36.35.23.10.

Taurus: Don't just see what you want to in a complex situation. You are an adept reader of people. However, you are not seeing what is right under your nose. Take a cold shower and try to liven up a bit. Inertia is a comfortably 'numb' state to be in, but how long can you keep up this pretence? Plenty of minds have bought into your scheme. So things are fine for the moment. In the long-term though you can expect a controversial shake-up to beat the band! A right old shindig is on the horizon. You will feel invigorated and surprisingly alive, once you let your hair fall into dishevelled place.

Green for an open heart.

Leo is right behind you!

Lucky Numbers: 12.25.37.5.26.17.

Gemini: Oodles of giggly fun will create an interesting diversion. It could be a case of jolly old hockey sticks, or simply a personal private joke between two people. Either way you need to keep, or FIND, a sense of humour! Don't take everything quite so seriously. If your life is bit of a struggle at present, maybe resort to some of the black stuff. By that I mean dark humour not Guinness, though that may hit the spot too! Seriously, there is no need to fret or panic. All will be well. Sit back and do nothing. This alternative approach is not an excuse for laziness. But it will take you to where you want to go!

Gold stimulates wisdom.

Libra is fun.

Lucky Numbers: 1.2.3.14.15.17.

Cancer: Stop scratching around for 'miniscule' fragments of information, evidence, or inspiration! It doesn't have to be this difficult. Give into the flow of life. The tide may carry you in a direction you hadn't thought of, but you will be delighted with the outcome. Surrender to the speed of life-changing events currently kicking in! The best surprise is that things will work out much better than in your wildest dreams. Keep the fantasies revolving around your head, by all means, but prepare for reality to work out just brilliantly. Life's a beach, never mind a ball!

Sea green for flow.

Fellow Crabby is a laugh.

Lucky Numbers: 1.25.37.16.32.12.

Leo: There is no need to be quite so reserved. Be more game for a laugh! As a strong zodiac beast you are proud and resourceful. Do make more time for lesser mortals. Not everyone is worthy of the dismissive attitude you wear too readily. Keep judgements bright and breezy, and let winds of change breathe new life into your existence. There is no need to plod heavily from pillar to post. Leonine paws are weighty and sure, but prepare to lighten your step for an invigorating run across the plains. You are born free, so don't fetter or chain yourself to those who hunt you down. Ignore the threat of danger and you will avoid it.

Orange boosts vibrancy.

Fellow fire signs get you going.

Lucky Numbers: 2.13.15.37.4.28.

Virgo: You are at last truly on to a winner! Expect your magnificent patience to be finally rewarded. Truly you deserve a medal for bravery and persistence. Laugh at your detractors, for you are destined to have the last laugh. There is still no room for complacency however. And you will still have many obligations to fulfil. Don't be afraid to ask for a fairer deal from those who are chancing their arm. Your inherent value is apparent by now. So it is important to guard against abuse and plain ignorance. You have been taken for a ride, even whilst you were running the show. Prepare for victory.

Red/purple protects and grounds finances.

Gemini is lucky.

Lucky Numbers: 2.14.35.26.31.7.

Libra: Perfect your ability to pirouette! You will certainly have to resort to some fancy footwork to keep your head up on the stage (of life). Don't be paranoid about your situation. There will be an interesting outcome that will leave you gasping and laughing! Remain in control and don't lose it with panic. Whatever comes your way is in some measure an important part of your destiny. Even the challenging moments will serve you well if you can maintain your cool. Stay balanced and realistic. A simple approach to a complex scenario will pay off big time!

Purple for dignity.

Scorpio has an idea.

Lucky Numbers: 14.27.38.40.23.2.

Scorpio: Adopt a new way of seeing an old connection. You will be surprised at what you let slip! What a good thing you didn't completely miss out on a golden opportunity. That magical person is still there for you. No, they didn't cast a spell – you did. Yes, they are still hooked. So if you are not going to act throw them back into the deep. A word of warning! You may live to regret not going for what is staring you in the face. Letting go at this point will vastly reshape your destiny and future. It's your call! Don't be duped by those who claim to have your interests at heart.

Events will shortly reveal the true colours of your associates.
Deep magenta helps grounding.
Cancer is wandering off.
Lucky Numbers: 31.27.39.3.17.26.

Sagittarius: A sophisticated (ball) game will get on your
nerves. Let your competitive streak show by all means. But
nothing is worth the compromising of your integrity. Play
to win, but don't cheat. Try some intricate moves and think
on your feet. Intimidation won't work. Your natural ability
and resourcefulness give you the edge anyhow. Relax into
recent events and you will get the result you are looking for.
Don't score an own goal amidst confusion. Take your time
and make sure your back up is in place before you shoot. It's
a goal . . . guaranteed!
Turquoise inspires creativity.
Virgo is interesting.
Lucky Numbers: 19.25.37.15.27.2.

Capricorn: You will find that life is more like chess than
you realise! The cynic within you is afraid of a potentially
destructive domino effect. Fret not! It certainly pays to keep
things black and white, but the difference between the various board games is immense. There is no need to worry
that you are going down along with the best of them. Your
mind is sharper than that. And you always play to win. So it
is unlikely you will get caught in any crossfire. Keep your
head down and work out your next move. It won't be
'checkmate' quite yet. But the final score is as close as you
want it to be. Perhaps you like the suspense of dragging out

the moment! Yes, thought so!

Lilac transmutes negativity.

Taurus is a trooper!

Lucky Numbers: 2.15.26.37.4.19.

PISCES Time:
February 20th – March 20th

WEEK EIGHT
February 19th - February 25th

Pisces: Swimming in a shoal usually brings security and peace of mind. Safety in numbers, as they say. Lately though you are no doubt finding personal independence extremely appealing. The obligation to conform has become a pressure. Access your creativity and work out what a new regime could signify. Freedom of movement means you are not so vulnerable to the nets, pots and hooks that trap fishy creatures. Be a law unto your good self, and see where the tides take you. You may find it unnerving to drift through uncharted waters, but the inherent excitement is a tonic for the soul. Don't be a sheep!

Purple for spirituality.

Aries for oomph!

Lucky Numbers: 21.3.24.15.28.5.

Aries: The cracks are showing – get out the face cream! Nah, I'm just kidding. But you will have to put on your best show biz smile for those watching you. Your body language will tell a juicy story if you are not careful. Transparent expressions are easy to read. You will have to become a thespian during those awkward moments. Use your best acting ability to get you out of a tight spot. Leave a few false trails to put the bloodhounds off the scent, and avoid the spilling of guts and beans! You need to work out whom to trust. May those who scrutinise you have their work cut out! Rummage in your bag of tricks for the best 'fixed' grin you can find!

Deep red protects.

Gemini is a handful.

Lucky Numbers: 1.13.17.26.39.4.

Taurus: You will have no option but to be amused by the antics of someone you love. There are many ways to get attention, but this one beats 'em all! Give a wry smile in honour of originality. And give credit where it's due. Although you will feel vaguely uncomfortable, you will also be stimulated by unusual events. There is no need to stay sitting on that spike! The mischief in the air is entirely under control and you can trust things not to get too scary. Or can you? Expect a perverse thrill as new circumstances unravel. OK, so it takes the biscuit, but it is also becoming really funny!

Berry colours.

Fellow earth is safe.

Lucky Numbers: 23.14.25.36.38.3.

Gemini: Be careful that unpredictable or fragmented behaviour does not trip you up. It's all very well being abstract and artistic, but some logical, sensible decisions would not go amiss! Don't use kooky bohemian vibes to cover up feelings of inadequacy. A 'smidgin' of eccentricity is certainly appealing, but it can also become a form of retreat. Get real and don't be afraid to stare life full in the face! Work out who you are in the midst of transition. At a crossroads you may be, but clear direction will manifest. There are many options, so find the TRUEST path to your destiny. What is the point in trying to be something you're not! Turquoise boosts communication skills.

Scorpio is cool, but complex.

Lucky Numbers: 2.14.26.37.40.23.

Cancer: You have proved yourself to be a master of self-control. Well done! Ignore those who are trying to set you up. And take them at face value. You are wise to their devious antics, but the best way to handle them is to make them squirm. Be as obliging as you know how. That way they will be embarrassed by their misdemeanours. Some people have nothing better to do. They scheme, plot and point the finger, simply because of their own inadequacy. Don't take any nonsense personally. These types want to spark a reaction. So it's dignity at all times and fingers up to their pettiness – OK?

Lilac transmutes negativity.

Virgo is a support.

Lucky Numbers: 2.14.35.27.40.3.

Leo: Let out a rip-roaring growl at the universe! You do need to let off steam. But don't prejudge a situation. At the moment it looks as if you have been madly deceived or misguided, but the beauty of this life is that things turn spookily at the last minute. Panic not; everything will come right. The only way is up. Let yourself go and don't try to control outcomes. You are left hanging, waiting and wondering. Indeed the situation is not fair, but you have the strength and determination to claim victory. Surrender to the flow and trust that you DID receive the correct information. You have no other option.

Orange enhances joy.

Libra is off the rails – but funny!

Lucky Numbers: 23.14.17.19.28.4.

Virgo: You may feel like you're in a pickle, but nothing could be further from the truth! Appearances are deceiving, so believe what your intuition is telling you. Everything is about to be turned inside out and upside down. Major exciting but challenging events will flatten the skyline. The new seeds and shoots that spring up bring the promise of new life. Things will never be the same again. Unsettling as this upheaval may be, in time to come you will realise you would not have it any other way! Remember only you know the truth. Ignore those who get over-excited by your changed demeanour.

Lush green for a fresh start.

Capricorn is resentful?

Lucky Numbers: 24.35.17.29.30.10.

Libra: It is not possible to tie things up before you make a leap of faith. You feel you have lost control in a situation, but do remember it wasn't really yours to control in the first place. Keep a rein on your insecurities and remain professional. You will make a big mistake if you disguise something personal in 'work-speak'. Others won't miss your machinations! Everything will unravel if you get too complacent. Remain modest, kind and tolerant. You are looking at everything too closely – see the bigger picture.

Pale blue for Divine guidance.

An earth sign has rumbled you!

Lucky Numbers: 3.5.11.17.29.31.

Scorpio: You believe that major things are about to happen. You are right in a way, but everything will unfold in a realistic rather than mystical way. It has to in order to ground in reality. Makes sense! So pay attention to your hopes, wishes and dreams, but expect them to arrive in the form of a paler imitation. You will get a measure of what you are looking for. Just not quite the real thing! Maybe stop being so fussy, and you will realise that what you got is thoroughly appropriate. Even better than the real thing, perhaps?

Red assists passion.

Cancer is emotional.

Lucky Numbers: 4.25.16.28.39.26.

Sagittarius: Be careful not to grab or adopt other people's ideas. Don't be afraid to be yourself. There is no need to feed off an established talent. You have plenty of original ideas in your own head. So use YOUR creativity without fear. It is all very well discerning a recipe for success, but be warned. What works for another will NOT work for you.

Everyone's life path is different. There is no point aspiring to be anything but YOU! I guess emulation is the best form of flattery, but you are feeding the energies of the competition by tapping in. You are not doing yourself any favours whatsoever. Respect your POWER, and don't siphon the juices from another.

Green for envy.

Virgo has it sorted.

Lucky Numbers: 23.14.25.16.38.24.

Capricorn: Press on! Persistence is the key to making things happen. All you have to do is steer a steady course to your destination. Be aware that a U-turn up ahead is an important part of the journey. You may have to adapt to an unexpected change of circumstances. Hold steady! Things may not work out as planned, but they will come together just perfectly. At the next stop-off you will be able to assess your position. A massive distance has been covered. So don't be daunted about where you have to go to next.

Blue for peace.

Scorpio is deep.

Lucky Numbers: 3.5.1.7.29.40.

Aquarius: If something or someone has sent you into a spin, panic not. Try to find your feet and settle down! Scan the horizon for a new perspective. A whirlwind of emotion may well descend from the heavens, but there is a harbour in the eye of the storm. Stay centred and focused. The latest string of events does not have to throw you at the mercy of the four winds. Trust the elements and the organic sequence of what's to come.

Green for heart and soul.

Libra has an interesting opinion.

Lucky Numbers: 5.23.17.38.25.30.

WEEK NINE
February 26th – March 4th

Pisces: Different strokes for different folks, Pisces! Be as accepting, tolerant and composed as you have a mind to be. Others will test your limits and boundaries. So rise to the challenge, as only you know how. You CAN perform under pressure – you just have to make the decision to do so. Pull out all the stops and beat the competition at its own game. Magenta boosts practical support and grounding.

Taurus is back for more.

Lucky Numbers: 13.25.42.27.18.5.

Aries: You should be on cloud nine after the events of last week! Did you get enough recognition and adoration? Perhaps the return did not quite reflect your input, but the knock–on effect will be priceless. Watch that the grin on your face does not become too smug. There is an unexpected event that could wipe it off for you, so pay attention. Complacency is the only thing that could trip you up at this stage. So stay cute and look after your interests. Give out plenty of positive vibes, even if you feel like screaming! The stakes just got higher – play to win ...

Bright colours, especially cerise!

Leo has the answer.
Lucky Numbers: 4.16.29.38.40.14

Taurus: Diversionary tactics will work for only so long. Prepare a back-up plan. You will be confronted with some aspect of your behaviour that has annoyed someone dear. You really have to be more careful! Admit the error of your ways. Then appeal for a fresh start. First though, you must accept responsibility for a misdemeanour. Not everything will be merrily brushed under the carpet! Universally admired though you want to be, there are those who see through your 'mindset'! Be honest and clear, with yourself first and foremost. Then get busy to clear up a mess.
Red helps love and passion.
Virgo loves.
Lucky Numbers: 13.24.15.37.29.5.

Gemini: Use your powers of deduction, and don't be hurried into what looks like a new exciting adventure. Be aware that everything is NOT as it seems. Change and challenge are hovering in the ether. Be careful not to be seduced too readily. You are at times blinded by science and love a great diversity of experience. Just make sure that curiosity doesn't get the better of you – it killed the cat, remember? Go over arrangements with a fine-toothed comb and prepare for all eventualities!
Green boosts finances.
Libra is good support.
Lucky Numbers: 22.3.16.27.40.33.

Cancer: Express your deepest emotions as we connect with Pisces time. Do pay special attention to your hunches, visions and dreams. This is a time to generally get spooky! Your intuition is heightened, so do not dismiss anything out-of-hand. Listen carefully to the clues the Universe will present to you. All the magic you need descends to your fingertips. So flex them in anticipation of weird and wonderful events! Shake your crystal wand and prepare for the big time. Or the time of your life, perhaps?

Silver for moon madness.

Scorpio assists intuition.

Lucky Numbers: 4.25.37.26.13.22.

Leo: Speculate to accumulate. You must invest your energy and creativity wisely. Work out what you really want to achieve and go after it no-holds-barred! OK, so there are the humdrum things to be getting on with, but prepare to follow your heart. Open it up to the deepest expression of your soul. Find what lies within and turn the key. You hold all the answers. Prepare for a revelation. And don't be afraid to show the world what you are made of. If in doubt don't speak. The pen is mightier than the sword – remember?

Red assists practical matters.

Aries is a handful!

Lucky Numbers: 3.25.16.38.4.29.

Virgo: A fruit is ripe for the picking. So sense when the juices are flowing and harvest at the right time. The point of salacious fecundity is just around the corner. Wow! Well you will get to sow some wild oats, let's put it like that. Now this could be a creative metaphor for prosperity and general good luck. But something tells me there is more to come. Tap into to the sensuous aspect of your nature. And find your self-confidence in affairs of the heart. Don't wait any longer. A deep connection is RIGHT!

Pink for unconditional love.

Scorpio is a challenge.

Lucky Numbers: 13.24.25.36.17.19.

Libra: Exciting times ahead. The air is full of pregnant possibility. You never know when or IF these opportunities will come around. So make the most of things as and when they arise. Live the dream and build on your 'moment'. Don't fret about the future for it will very much take care of itself. It's now or never, as they say! Play a nifty game of cat-and-mouse with a potential partner. Things look all set to get interesting, but don't be premature in your expectations. Let it unfold . . .

Yellow to de-stress you.

Virgo is competitive.

Lucky Numbers: 22.11.33.19.5.27.

Scorpio: Before too long you will have a lot to celebrate. The bells will be ringing. No, NOT the alarm bells, though you DO have to be careful. Watch out for the agendas of others and be very sure of whom you can trust. This is a warning of good things ahead, but it is 'qualified' by a psychic disclaimer! Don't count your chickens! Take things easy and be assured of your success. Just don't rush anything or you could be looking at infamy rather than notoriety and fortune.

Black protects.
Cancer has you by the short and 'curlies'!
Lucky Numbers: 11.12.13.15.27.2.

Sagittarius: You may want to rehearse an evacuation. Make sure you have covered all the angles of a situation. This is not a dress rehearsal. You will have to think on your feet and have the courage of your convictions. If emergency measures are called for, you will be prepared. This is not a time to take anything for granted. So the excitement and anticipation will suit you. Be keen to show your true colours, but don't bare your soul to all and sundry. Know your own mind and work out who your friends are.
Blue for peace.
Leo knows a thing or two!
Lucky Numbers: 11.22.25.36.4.21.

Capricorn: You may need to get your best undercover operation up and running. There is a riddle to unravel, and possibly a crime that needs to be solved. Be careful how much responsibility to take on your good self. But this is a time to pay attention to detail. Don't wait too long before you make a move. Get to the bottom of something before the mystery defeats you. Find out where you stand, but don't issue ultimatums. Be very sure that you are seeing something clearly before you put your foot in it. You have enough to be going on with.
Purple helps a spiritual perspective.
Gemini is supportive.
Lucky Numbers: 2.13.25.16.38.22.

Aquarius: Adopt a refreshing new approach to an old problem. Things may be festering or mouldy. But there is no need to allow the rot to set in completely. Take pre-emptive action to clear up a mess. Are you in a bind? Cut yourself free. This may be a time to admit a mistake, but you do not need to feel defeated. Things will come right in some shape or form, except the final picture will look quite different to what you had in mind. Get creative and busy with your brushstrokes. Something colourful and abstract is just as good!

Pale blue for Divine inspiration.

Pisces is perceptive.

Lucky Numbers: 3.14.25.37.28.33.

WEEK TEN
March 5th - March 11th

Pisces: This is a time holding great potential for Pisces. Play around with different ideas, styles and approaches. At this point life could move in several directions, and they all look equally exciting. Watch you don't get caught in a self-defeating scenario however. The most obvious choice is not necessarily the best. Trust your intuition. Logic is for amateurs! A natural change will occur before too long. So if in doubt, bide your time a while longer. Answers will manifest in unexpected ways.

Deep blue for peace and healing.

Virgo is witty and truthful.

Lucky Numbers: 13.25.37.24.33.5.

Aries: Sometimes there are things no one can fix. Remember you are not all-powerful but human. Don't expect to be able to save the world, least of all yourself. There are things you cannot change. But do influence what you can. This is not a bleak forecast – honest. Just realise that you have a degree of savvy, but you are not immortal! Respect your talents and skills, and function within reasonable boundaries. Conquer the world in your own sphere of influence. The sky is the limit when you have your feet on the ground.

Deep red assists grounding and protection.

Taurus is leaving, but not forever.

Lucky Numbers: 14.3.21.41.35.17.

Taurus: Be strong, brave and true. Silence in a controversial situation will serve you well. You don't want to ruin all your good work now, do you? Follow your orders and, if you don't have any, create your own. Discipline is important. So monitor your progress and write the report. Find structure and balance in your life. Then you will meet your commitments and make an impression. Be all you can be! Desist from flailing around in the dark. It's time to see the bigger picture CLEARLY. He who dares wins, that's for sure. But do be sensible, practical and realistic too.

Green for a healthy honest heart.

Scorpio is a contender.

Lucky Numbers: 1.10.26.37.42.8.

Gemini: Keep your nose clean! It's not appropriate to be annoyed by another's success. Your time will come. Plenty of adoration and attention is winging your way. Just don't allow your vision to become clouded at this point. Everything is in hand. So don't panic about what you THINK has passed you by. Think again! Negotiate new conditions to inspire you, and look for understanding and sympathy. Loved ones will support you and give you strength. Things come to pass with perfect timing – more haste, less speed!

Yellow to de-stress and inspire you.

Taurus is delaying matters.

Lucky Numbers: 12.32.14.19.27.40.

Cancer: Find your sense of direction. You have no idea where you are going at the moment. In one way this does NOT matter. But in another it DOES! There is no point in aimless drifting. So decide some course of action. Just don't be afraid to modify things as they unfold. Play it by ear. But be decisive and WITH IT. Committing to a person, place or 'thing' will at least bring structure into your life. A routine will ground you. Excitement lurks in the wings. But don't be drumming your fingers waiting for it!

Sea green for tranquillity and homely vibes.

Gemini is a laugh.

Lucky Numbers: 24.10.26.42.8.19.

Leo: Do you feel you are being watched? Well, maybe you ARE! All eyes on you…No, I'm not trying to make you feel paranoid, but you do need to be on your best behaviour. You will inspire plenty of attention as always. Just be sure it is for the right reasons. Certainly you love to be at the centre of things. However, you also need to be discerning. Be smart

about who shares your world. Shape your own reality, but show healthy discrimination even as you do! Ditch negative thinking and toxic people – your load will be lighter.
Orange boosts vitality.
Aquarius is chancing it a bit – nifty mover!
Lucky Numbers: 3.25.39.4.26.30.

Virgo: Confused? Alarmed? Panicked? Don't be! Be very careful not to enter someone's life uninvited. You have enough imagination to create your own party! There is no need to gatecrash. Good riddance to those who DISS you. Let them eat themselves up with resentment and jealousy – you need no part of it. Magnify your own expectations and make things happen. You do not have to be a slave to fear or panic. Let the bells ring! You will be miles away from danger if you follow your intuition. Avoid the challenges you don't need. There is more than enough to be going on with! Gold heals deep fear.
Cancer is a great support.
Lucky Numbers: 34.27.14.19.20.22.

Libra: A surprise is not a surprise if you know it's coming! Don't be so impatient. Life has a cunning and intriguing plan for you. But don't be in such a hurry to get to the bottom of things. Relish the sauce! There is indeed a spicy item on the menu, but choose your flavours carefully. Something will be needed to put out the fire. So have some water on stand-by if things get too hot to handle. An exotic connection is great fun and brings in a different energy. But appreciate the normal things by way of contrast. Don't risk the good stuff – unless you are sure you can get away with it. Purple for spiritual enlightenment.

Gemini inspires you.

Lucky Numbers: 14.8.19.11.26.33.

Scorpio: 'May the force be with you!' Yes – I'm watching *Star Wars* as I write. So, I want to bring you a message from the deep blue yonder – or Yoda? Give out only what you can handle. By the law of energetic return, what you send into the ether will come back to haunt you. So make it good, right. If you remain on your best behaviour, you can expect a nice surprise. Nothing goes unnoticed! Use the magical, mystical powers of Scorpio to turn things around. Healing is at hand – you just need to BELIEVE. Access the truth – it will set you free.

Deep magenta for grounding.

Virgo is a catch.

Lucky Numbers: 31.25.36.42.19.5.

Sagittarius: Potent exciting energies will propel you into the week. Pay attention to finances and the detail of arrangements, or events may trip you up. You will need to think on your feet. So rehearse your nifty footwork! Prepare to move quickly. But don't overlook important priorities. There is no reason why you can't achieve everything. This is not the time to buy into a limitation theory! Don't restrict yourself in any shape or form. See the big picture and play the reel that guarantees endless possibilities. Think 'HUGE' and expand your horizons!

The forty shades of green boost finances.

Capricorn is insightful – sometimes.
Lucky Numbers: 13.25.19.40.5.6.

Capricorn: Reassess and re-juggle your priorities. There is no time like the present to make amends. Remember you ARE allowed to change your mind if things are not working out. Mistakes are a learning curve, and you may have experienced some big ones lately! All is not lost. Pick up the pieces and start again. Some things have to be written off as an experience, but it is possible to transmute the negativity of a disappointing scenario. Invest positive vibes in a tricky situation and turn it all around. It will be as if it never happened. Calm your thinking – then proceed.

Lilac assists transmutation of negativity.

Virgo is competitive.

Lucky Numbers: 1.11.6.31.16.37.

Aquarius: If you feel you have come unstuck, find the glue! Encapsulate a bright energetic moment. Imprint the thought in your brain and lose the stuff that is dragging you down. It's all about perspective. A new way of seeing the world brings the freshness back. Don't become all 'old' and jaded! Use your imagination and by the end of the week you will be a winner. Hold onto the ball that lands in your lap. A whirlwind of change is all set to spin into your reality. Rest in the eye of the storm 'til it passes. Peace will descend thereafter.

Pale blue to connect with Divine will.

Pisces has your number!

Lucky Numbers: 24.19.38.25.17.28.

WEEK ELEVEN
March 12th – March 18th

Pisces: There is a great event just around the corner. OK, so there are no corners in your heart and mind, but that's a point to consider. Are you too free with your thoughts? Preserve your boundaries and privacy a little more carefully. Have you been 'cruising' the air miles of outer space lately? Come back down to earth, please, Pisces! Use the power of the Moon to claim a release from past difficult emotions once and for all. Lunar energy will inspire and elevate you if you allow for the transformation. Connect to nature. Never return to what hurt you so much. What's the point? A fresh start is the way to go…no limits.

Green for nature links.

Fellow Pisces will boost your confidence.

Lucky Numbers: 22.34.42.17.11.19.

Aries: Don't lose heart! OK, Valentine's day bit the dust in style, but it's all about perspective, right? Stay dignified amidst defeat and be assured that what goes around comes around. So if someone has done you a wrong, bide your time and let the Universe deliver. All you have to do is watch. Just don't gloat too much, OK? Keep your wits about you and don't repeat a past mistake. The future is as bright as you want it to be – beam away!

Yellow to lift your spirits.

Virgo has some inside information for you.

Lucky Numbers: 40.14.33.25.36.4.

Taurus: Have things got a bit grubby, Taurus? Pay attention to your demeanour, behaviour and general outlook. Time for a spring-clean perhaps? You can pretend certain things are not really happening if you like, but before too long you will have to address the real thing. Never one to let go, you hold onto the bitter end. Commendable tactics! However, I detect a change of heart. Once this happens you will be inspired to bite the bullet. A sudden whirlwind is set to turn you upside down. Hold onto your hat!

Browns and greens assist grounding.

Aries is clever and persistent.

Lucky Numbers: 14.25.38.30.11.7.

Gemini: Persevere and pursue your goals as if there is no tomorrow. Who knows what the wind will bring? Or what will happen when the tide turns? Make the most of the here and now. And give something your best shot, for you won't know unless you try. Lose the monsters in your head and don't hold yourself back with negative thinking. Your circumstances will change between this and then. So be prepared for anything! Literally, your life is unpredictable at this point. Remain grounded and focused.

Deep magenta and turquoise will help you to go with the flow.

Virgo has the answer you want to hear.

Lucky Numbers: 2.13.15.17.19.42.

Cancer: There's a lot reaching boiling point in your life. Fasten your safety belt as the ride could get a bit bumpy. Let's just call it turbulence. As with a choppy flight, you know that technically you are safe. This is very much the case. But it won't help the rather hairy possibilities that threaten to 'land'. Remember the disaster scenario is a potential ONLY. Stay positive and in command of the cockpit. Chart your route carefully. All will be well, just expect it to be!

Bubbly electric blues for vibrancy.

Libra is compelling.

Lucky Numbers: 34.35.36.27.12.4.

Leo: It's your time, Leo. So seize the opportunities winging your way. Don't hold back or be afraid to commit yourself. There's a wonderful energy supporting you at the moment. Make the most of it, ye Zodiac Lions! Let go of anything that no longer hits the spot. Assimilate your experience to date. And think carefully about the future. A lot rests on your shoulders, as your responsibilities to your good self and others are set to increase. Integrate your emotional experiences and work out what you REALLY want. Wait a while to shape your on-going tactics. Think smart and be proud of what you have achieved. Protect your heart and please YOU!

Green and turquoise boost deep heart connections.

Aries will fire you up.

Lucky Numbers: 8.16.18.29.34.6.

Virgo: My! The complex web you weave is getting very interesting. Without intending to, you have wound several important people up to the point of no return. If only the rest of the world were so trusting and open hearted! But the reality is there are complex agendas at play. You need to exercise discernment and discretion. Don't be quite so free with your words, thoughts and feelings. It's a sad reflection, I know, but the world is a place that bites on occasion. You need to protect yourself. Not everyone is as nice as you are! Black for protection.

Taurus is very skilful at backtracking.

Lucky Numbers: 13.25.36.27.30.10.

Libra: Take advantage of the beautiful banishing moon, Libra – check your charts for the next full moon. Let go of past hurt, disappointment and regret. Be as nostalgic as you like, but use this time to put mistakes and negativity behind you. Have you been asleep at the wheel? Not paying attention? Fret not, you can't change your circumstances quite yet, but you CAN sort out your INTENTION and perspective. Look on the bright side. Once you have made the decision to be more in control of your life and destiny, the blessings will descend. A completely natural process!

Lime green is fresh and inspires a new start, from the heart! Aquarius had information you may want to hear.

Lucky Numbers: 3.13.30.33.41.29.

Scorpio: Keep your pecker up! Pardon the expression. But you DO need to cheer up a bit, Scorpio! Events may well be stirring up your emotions. This challenging energy heightens the heart issues you need to address. Express yourself freely and don't be afraid to tell it as it is. Let go of anything that doesn't do it for you any longer. It's time for honesty, plain talking and action. Get hot and sweaty if you need to. Whatever floats your boat, as they say. The important thing is that you STOP PRETENDING! Find some authentic behaviour, and be true to what you know. Black and white will help you to see and think clearly. Capricorn may be able to help.

Lucky Numbers: 16.26.35.21.19.40.

Sagittarius: The fiery energy flying around at the moment will serve you well. Expect to be revved up BIG TIME! Well after you have had a good rest that is! Seriously, look after yourself a bit better. Don't get up to that nonsense that sometimes tempts you. Yes . . . you know what I'm talking about. Life is not something to be messed with. Take things more seriously, and place more value on the special things. Treasure your time. Send past angst and distress into the ether to be transmuted. Claim your luck and salvation. It's free, but comes at a price.

Reds will give you added energy.

Virgo is matter-of-fact.

Lucky Numbers: 31.6.27.38.4.26.

Capricorn: Steer a safe passage through heavy choppy waters. I'm not quite sure what you are doing out on the ocean deep, Capricorn. Your terrain is the mountainous tracks of the intrepid Billy Goat Gruff! But I detect a sea change. A refreshing attempt to try different scenery at least. Pay attention to your emotions and feelings. And work out why you are going off the beaten paths you know so well. You are right to look for a new perspective, but remain in touch with YOU. Don't try to be something you're not. Find a way back to dry land.

Deep purple will inspire you spiritually and philosophically. Gemini is hilarious!
Lucky Numbers: 26.37.41.19.17.36.

Aquarius: Dream harder! The light of the silvery moon will inspire you! Let go of heartfelt 'niggles' and move away from a negative situation. This is a potent time for you, Aquarius. Make the most of it. There's a BUZZ in the air, and things will happen if you REALLY want them to. Prepare for dynamic action re location, finances, and the time of your life. Don't miss the moment. There is a window of opportunity that comes around once in a blue moon! Grab it with both hands. Be not afraid.
Silver for femininity and finances.
Virgo is right more often than not!
Lucky Numbers: 10.20.30.1.7.11.

ARIES Time:
March 21st – April 20th

WEEK TWELVE
March 19th - March 25th

Aries: Pay attention to your own agenda. You need to assess your '*raison d'être*'. No, this is not some strange reference to dried currants! But it does mean that you must give your approach to life the 'once over'. Don't monitor the activities of others too closely. It's time to do your own thing. Do as you would be done by, and most scenarios will be sorted. This Biblical sentiment covers a multitude of sins. There is no point in following through a revenge plan. The consequences won't suit you, and I don't want to be wiping egg off your face next week! Learn the art of putting yourself first in an unselfish way…

Gold attracts riches.

Virgo is onto something.

Lucky Numbers: 33.31.24.25.16.7.

Taurus: Falsity is never a good idea. Take that mask off and show your true colours. You can aspire to nobility, but the genuine touch has to come from deep within. Find the route to authentic behaviour, and get real about what is going down. Don't act out a part any longer. You may have to be gracious amidst defeat. Be assured, however, that a fresh start will blow your mind away. I know you can't stand the thought of anyone upsetting your apple cart. So perhaps if you do it first, the opposition won't have that satisfaction. One way or another, a change is gonna come!

Pale green and turquoise link to the deepest part of your heart.

Libra is funny.

Lucky Numbers: 23.14.25.36.27.3.

Gemini: Feel the wind in your sails. Use key days to make pertinent points. Act when it counts, listen when challenged, and generally busy yourself. Communicate clearly and speak the truth AT ALL TIMES. Be sure anything less will creep up behind you and bite when you least expect it.

You may love to claim ownership of ideas, people or items, but loosen your grip. Sharing is fun too! No one is out to get you. So stop expecting the worst. Project good vibes into the ether. Then things will turn around in your favour. Resentment is an unhealthy mindset – stop wallowing!

Green for heart and finances.

Fellow Gemini may need your support.

Lucky Numbers: 23.4.41.15.36.17.

Cancer: Never mind the ocean deep. You should be riding on the crest of a wave at this stage. Stay steady on that surfboard. Balance is the energy that will ensure a safe landing. Expect to come to shore triumphant. So hold your own amongst the beach bums. OK, so you may not have the rippling muscles, wind tan, or athleticism of the pros, but no one does it quite like you do! And there will be plenty of compliments winging your way before too long to prove it. There's no need to fake it – you ARE unique! Play that ace up your sleeve, and those smug smiles will be wiped before too long.

Yellow for cheery brightness.

Leo is big-hearted.

Lucky Numbers: 1.13.24.35.17.39.

Leo: A bit of harmless 'slap and tickle' will put a smile on your face. Shock tactics are needed. We have to smooth out that furrowed brow somehow! No, there's no need to resort to the Botox jabs. Poisoning your system is certainly NOT the way to detox or 'rejuvenate' your existence. Lighten up and smile a bit. Laughter lines are more attractive and will bring you what you want. That frown is preventing things. The happy approach will reel in the good stuff. The best anti-ageing treatment is an inner resolve to remain youthful from the inside out. And it's FREE! Take some things seriously, but don't go too far.

Pale blue for Divine Will.

Sagittarius is nervous.

Lucky Numbers: 13.26.37.18.9.22.

Virgo: You can't quite figure out whether things are going well for you. Maybe disaster is lurking around the next bend? But somehow the moment of impact keeps getting averted. The delays are starting to do your head in! If you knew one way or another, you could live with it and adjust to the circumstances. Life seems to be having a merry giggle at your expense. Start to laugh back, and see what happens! You may feel like you are tottering on a tightrope traversing a precipice. Don't look down so . . . and you will come back from the brink just fine. Trust me! Re-educate your perception of what's going down, as it isn't you!

Purple for finesse.

Aquarius is tolerant.

Lucky Numbers: 1.17.11.22.33.41.

Libra: Is it my imagination, or are you a different person? Something has changed in the last while. I hope you are feeling better. The spring in your step 'suits you, sir'! It is only a matter of time before the big turnaround. So prepare for what you have been focusing on. If you are determined enough, it will come about. Persistence holds the key to your success. There is no point giving up now. Don't lose heart, and carry on with that positive vibe. You're emanating the good stuff. Keep it right and stay within the remit of your dreams. Hold onto good luck- it's in the air and fast approaching!

Black for protection.

Gemini is a challenge.

Lucky Numbers: 28.19.30.31.2.11.

Scorpio: Wipe that sweet, innocent look off your face. You know it doesn't paint the real picture. Stop misleading the rest of the world. You're making an impression all right – Just be sure it's the right one. Impressionistic masterpieces are very colourful, but get up close and the detail of what you thought you saw disappears. If you are going to give a sketchy appearance of where you're coming from, please keep your distance! Pay attention to detail, or your artistry may trick you out of what you want to clinch! Anyone would be seduced by the magic you are weaving. Use your powers wisely, or the critics will rumble you!

Deep blue for peace.

Cancer is beguiling.

Lucky Numbers: 3.31.25.37.22.9.

Sagittarius: Tap into your own creativity and originality. There is no point siphoning from the success of others. OK, so, emulation is the finest form of flattery. But it does have a way of making the person who plagiarises look a bit stupid! You are a fountain of information, but is it all useful – and is it your own perception? Are you spouting in an attempt to impress the right people? Silence is golden if you don't have an original thought in your head. You WILL get noticed, but on your OWN merit. All in good time, right? Don't put your foot in it, and your patience will be rewarded. Stepping on toes is an uncomfortable experience best left to the nibble footed!

Sunny vibrant colours will cheer you up.

Leo is stiff competition.

Lucky Numbers: 23.14.16.37.28.19.

Capricorn: You can spin a tall tale for it will serve you well, but do remember the details of your fabrication, or you could end up embarrassing yourself BIG TIME! Those who are adept at seeing around corners will see through your best attempts. So I would NOT recommend pulling the wool over the eyes of those older, wiser or smarter than you – now, there IS a challenge! Avoid elaboration unless you know what you are dealing with. You would regret a misdemeanour at this stage. So play straight, even as you play to win. Cheating will likely trip you up. There is more than one way to skin a rabbit, as THEY say!

Purple for regal grandeur.

Virgo is intelligent – listen carefully.

Lucky Numbers: 23.15.26.17.28.19.

Aquarius: A dose of Triple XXX should sort you out. Enjoy the trip and buzz of an exciting ride! High-octane energy will get you revved up. There's no need for RED BULL, or other sickly stimulants. Get your kicks from a natural source. Love will find a way to send you into orbit. Use the traditional route to fulfilment and leave dubious substances out of the frame. Let your fingers do the talking. You have all you need. So there is no need to ramble around looking for what you THINK you are looking for! You already have the recipe for success…YOU! Believe in yourself, and don't expect external factors to lift you out of the doldrums.

Silver for financial fizz.

Gemini should keep you amused.

Lucky Numbers: 2.3.15.27.38.19.

Pisces: Dangle a hook and see who takes the bait. You never know what or whom you will entice. But things are all set to get interesting. If the morsel is juicy enough, pick it up quick. Assess what is on offer – you deserve the best. Choose wisely and line 'em all up if necessary! Perhaps a trial run is in the offing. If all else fails, choose randomly. The lucky dip is a lot of fun, or the test drive may serve you well. You could end up with something pricey and temperamental. So follow your instincts and make an intelligent trade-in. The deal is worth negotiating. An older model may be more reliable than the sporty one with the fancy 'paintwork'! What are you looking for?

Lilac enables transmutation.

Scorpio is intense.

Lucky Numbers: 36.17.28.19.32.2.

WEEK THIRTEEN
March 26th - April 1st

Aries: This is a good week for Aries financially. It's time to get moving on all those financial deals you have been neglecting. There may be some hassles to sort out at work but if you avoid getting entangled in work politics all will be well – stand back and let the troublemakers hang themselves. Dampen down your frustrations with a swim or walk by the sea. You need to cool off emotionally. Leave the object of your affections to their devices and you will be pleased later when they volunteer their attention. Watch your need to be in control. You cannot control all of the people all of the time. In the long term any manipulation will backfire, however subtle. So be true to YOU and, if the rest of the world doesn't like it, good riddance!
Be careful with your diet and digestion. Do you need to take more exercise?
Wear green to attract luck and money.
Taurus is a law unto itself.
Lucky Numbers: 22.14.32.26.36.29.

Taurus: Taurus should be careful of any financial deals. Make sure that the legalities and paperwork are correct. You will regret it if you rush through any business transaction. There will be travel soon that you will feel mixed about. Go ahead with confidence. You will achieve everything you are setting out to do and more. Be gentle with yourself emotionally. It is time to put your own needs above those of others for once. If you do not, you will get sick. You will be no good to anyone least of all yourself if you ignore what your heart is telling you. Taurus hates change, it makes them insecure, but sometimes when things don't go to plan it is better to cut your losses. Take a risk for once. You will not regret it. Take time out and reflect on your next steps. Eat plenty of protein for energy.

Blue for peace of mind and tranquillity.

Virgo is out to get you – in the nicest possible way.

Lucky numbers: 4.10.31.25.6.21.

Gemini: There are big changes in the air for Gemini so focus on your goals and do not waver. This is a time of profound change and transition. Family members will be a great support. Also do not be afraid to take advice from someone older or wiser. Gemini does not always grow up. This is a mixed blessing: on the one hand you can look youthful at fifty; on the other you can flit around like a child when you need to make important choices. An important message will arrive soon regarding money. Be patient. The stress you are feeling will pass, and by the summer you will look back at this time and wonder what all the fuss was about. Things may be a bit quiet romantically, so get out there- flirt away and stop looking for the big one! Love will arrive dramatically out of the blue when you have stopped waiting.

Watch that you are not eating too many dairy products, and go kick a ball around.

Yellow will make you feel less stressed and depressed.

Pisces has a romantic answer – or several.

Lucky Numbers: 12.32.41.5.26.2.

Cancer: All Crabbies, sorry, Cancerians should wrap themselves up in home life over Easter. Enjoy the company of family and friends, and switch off from work for the moment. Relaxation is really important and so is taking time for yourself. Hide away a little to recuperate and if you feel so inclined meditation or yoga would not go amiss. You need to stop running away from important emotional decisions. Home is important but so is peace of mind. Communication is the key to sorting out any conflict or difference of opinion. Come out of your shell on this one or you will regret it later. There is an important new contract to clinch. Follow your sharp instincts and trust your gut reaction to people and places. You need to make a decision about personal finances. Do not panic. All judgements will go in your favour.

Eat fish for extra brainpower and get swimming or bathe in warm water.

Turquoise is a good colour for creativity and inspiration

Fellow water signs, Scorpio and Pisces, understand.

Lucky Numbers: 2.13.15.18.21.40.

Leo: Leos should make the most of family gatherings and celebrations. There will be many parties and opportunities for social intercourse! A warm glow will descend on the Leonine community, so remain open. It is a good time to propose, make wedding plans or move house. Also begin making plans for that hot holiday in the sun. You will need it sooner than you think to help keep your regal dignity intact. Watch carefully with any legal matters. It is probably better to delay any court cases or decisions for the moment. You are being watched by an admirer – be kind to them even though you may not be interested. A bunch of flowers would not go amiss for a female friend or lover you have neglected lately. It is a potentially lucky week for Leo. Plenty of energy and determination will bring in extra money.

Red and orange boost your pulling power, but really you never have to try too hard, so black will do!

Lucky Numbers: 42.21.32.26.4.33.

Virgo: You are about to be swept off your feet, Virgo. Life is moving at such a pace you can hardly cope. Your mutability is proving more difficult at the moment, as you are confused emotionally. It is best to go with the flow and not expect any overnight answers. There is major change afoot so keep your head and fasten your seat belt. By the end of the summer there is plenty of money around for you to put any business or investment plans into action. There may be an unexpected romance and whirlwind engagement on the cards. Follow your heart, for logic does not touch what is about to happen. It is difficult for Virgo to let their mind rest but for once this is what you must do. There is a higher plan afoot so you must surrender and trust the process of life.

Make sure your nervous energy has an outlet: power walking or step classes will do the trick. Eat carefully and do not be too fussy about your food.

Use red for extra energy.

Taurus will keep you waiting

Lucky Numbers: 23.17.19.21.11.40

Libra: Love is in the air for many of the Zodiac signs – well, it is the spring. Take your time with romance, Libra, you need to be sure a certain someone is genuine. Proceed with caution. It will take a few weeks for the situation to clarify. You may feel in a bit of a rut in your working life. Extra training would boost your career, and it would be fortuitous to consider a slight change of direction. Use your initiatives and your contacts to make your wishes come true. Do not stand on ceremony. There may be some conflict over a trip abroad but it is your destiny to take that trip. The health of a loved one will improve but do be prepared for major adjustments in time. The family will be a great support and peace will descend. Sit back and take your time with any legal or financial issues. Haste at this point would spell disaster.

Eat plenty of salads for a gentle detox.

Pink will make people well disposed towards you.

Gemini will keep you amused.

Lucky Numbers: 23.25.40.39.16.5.

Scorpio: Wow, Scorpio, you are hot at the moment! But be careful. You are being watched at work. Everything will be cool if you keep your secrets and hold the energy of your secret love. It can wait, but enjoy thinking about it in the meantime. You have commitments that you have to fulfil, so get stuck in and make a success of yourself. There is marriage or fulfilment in love sooner than you think. And this goes hand in hand with a passionate sex life. You really can have everything. Just let a bit of time pass, then follow your heart. It will not mess up your work or your social life. You will have the freedom to be both independent and committed. Besides the object of your affections needs exactly the same space as you do! This is a meeting of soul mates so don't blow it. These connections only happen once in a life, if at all. Do not deny what is happening or you risk losing everything. You are blessed that you have these opportunities. Eat plenty of carbohydrates but avoid salt.

Wear white for purity!

Lucky Numbers: 31.14.32.40.29.18

Sagittarius: Sagittarians should aim to enjoy themselves socially. It is important to distract yourself from any emotional hurt you may be feeling. Do not worry. You have been through a lot of difficulty and have had to make adjustments. Your determination to be happy will succeed. You may want to propose to your long-term partner, or take a second honeymoon. It is important to take positive steps and action rather than to wallow in past failures. If you are disillusioned about work, just stay put. The energy will change dramatically of its own accord. It is better to bide your time than to make premature changes. You will have legal choices to make. Go ahead with legal papers or documents, as the process will free you up in ways you could not imagine. It is important for you to drink more water.

Magenta will keep you grounded.

Aries is a great laugh and support.

Lucky Numbers: 13.25.26.28.7.11.

Capricorn: It is important for Capricorn to preserve energy. Take a bit of time before rushing into a work contract or financial deal. You run the risk of embarrassing yourself if you let pride be the arbiter of your behaviour. Sometimes it does not pay to be ambitious if you are deliberately treading on toes. Your overconfidence is your potential downfall, so make sure you step back and take stock. At times you spread your many talents too thinly. It is better to master one trade than to attempt to excel at everything. Romantically things look promising. You will have to let the past go so that new relationships can flourish. There is a financial offer imminent which it is your destiny to accept. Avoid bitter foods, and try to rest your stomach.

Wear black for protection.

Taurus is a head case-but funny with it!

Lucky Numbers: 1.11.17.19.30.14.

Aquarius: It is a good time for Aquarius to take time out and rest. There has been a lot pulling at your resources recently and you have faced some disappointments since Christmas. Pay attention to your health and listen to your body. Keeping fit is very important at the moment, so strenuous exercise should be top of your list. Wait a little while before you change a car. The situation will be better financially by the summer. Surgery for a family member will be very successful, so proceed with confidence. Hang in there! Things will work out in your favour if you keep cool. Focus and determination on a family matter will pay off. If a child needs discipline do not be afraid to be firm-handed. Eat chocolate!

Wear sky blue for Divine support.

Virgo is spot-on, most of the time!

Lucky Numbers: 26.14.34.31.15.35.

Pisces: There are many blessings coming into the lives of Pisces. Great peace of mind is on the way after a lot of adjustments and difficulty. An earth sign will play a supportive role in your future working life. There is a move on the horizon that is work-related. You may be uneasy about the future but there is no panic. Everything will work out perfectly. A harmonious relationship is about to take off. The connection with your soul mate will take an unexpected turn and peace will reign. Any money concerns will balance out in the long run, and you will have the means soon to follow many lifelong dreams. There may be a slight delay with a planned pregnancy, but everything will work out perfectly. Eat a lot of fruit.

All shades of blue will bring peace and tranquillity.

Scorpio is deep and meaningful.

Lucky numbers: 23.41.32.40.19.33.

WEEK FOURTEEN
April 2nd – April 8th

Aries: Be a bit careful with money matters this week, Aries. It is not always right to push ahead against the odds. Financial deals may be wrecking your head but you WILL look back at this time and laugh – honest! A Virgo person is all set to become very supportive to you. Do not try to dominate them but listen to their sensible and grounded wisdom. There is victory for you in family relationships this week, but do not try to win arguments at all costs. It is good to let a feisty female have her way at the moment. Anything for a quiet life! Do not be overly concerned about a troublesome child – maybe check their diet for too many additives. Marriage is well starred and any wedding plans look straightforward. A worry about pregnancy will soon be allayed. Take proper precautions with birth control. Brighten your environment with flowers and air fresheners. Eat colourful foods.

Vibrant colours are good for confidence

Pisces is kindly and empathetic.

Lucky Numbers: 2.14.33.26.37.12.

Taurus: Your family and romantic life look brilliant at the moment, Taurus, so if you are feeling down do not despair. There are many surprises for you this year, and the big changes set in around the time of your birthday. Money matters are well starred and you will reap the rewards of past investments. You may have to support a female with a sum of money. It is better to settle the issues between you quietly. A relationship that you had given up on will resurface – surprise! This person could very well be your soul mate. However complex your situation, do make careful decisions. Work victory overseas is yours – proceed with confidence. Material abundance abounds in your chart but is money everything? Be sure you follow the prompting of your heart. It is your emotional guide and will never let you down.

Wear green for financial reward.

Virgo is nicer than you think!

Lucky Numbers: 3.10.26.24.14.30.

Gemini: After a lot of wrangling and debate you should be able to close a deal. Keep your head in business matters. Someone is watching you at work. Hold your head high and smile sweetly. You have nothing to hide; it's just that those who do are projecting their issues merrily onto you. In a long-term partnership do everything you can to reassure the other person – any conflict between you will naturally pass so do not force things! Is it the right time to trade in that car? A new deal is well starred and you should be able to negotiate an upgrade. The lover of your dreams could be just around the corner, so keep your eyes open! Do not put that special person too much on a pedestal – they are flesh and blood and need you to warm up a bit. Finances and investments you have been worried about will break even. Eat plenty of pasta for slow-burn energy.

Wear browns for grounding.

Cancer is emotionally supportive.

Lucky Numbers: 5.8.16.34.32.40.

Cancer: Financial and security issues are probably doing your head in at the moment, Cancer. Try not to worry. You should have more faith and confidence in your abilities. Part of you wants to zoom off into the sunset while the other part is fighting to hold onto the stability that you know. Remember the grass is not always greener. In fact it is usually the same colour when you look closely. Try to curb that tendency to feel sorry for yourself. Be thankful for the good things in your life. The situation is really not as bad as you think. It is a perfect time to commit fully to a relationship you have left up in the air. Leave the past behind and crack on with life. Passionate relationships leading to marriage or re-commitments are well starred, so don't be nervous. Money difficulties will ease if you exercise discipline. A move of house that you have been putting off will actually go well if you take the plunge. Eat simple foods and whole grains.

Wear red for passion if you can handle it!

Virgo is better connected than you realise.

Lucky Numbers: 23.32.42.31.16.7.

Leo: Be open to new relationships, Leo. Romance in general is well starred. Take your time to cosy down with your loved one. If single you may meet an ex and it could make sense to reconnect for old times' sake. Be sensitive of others' moods this week. You are not always good at noticing the subtleties in people's behaviour. If only everyone were as straightforward and up front as you. If a family member has a choice concerning surgery or a medical procedure, it is beneficial to go ahead. Do not pay out for shoddy workmanship. Make sure the job is well done before you pay that vastly inflated rate. Sorting out a marriage contract will end years of uncertainty.

Wear blue to cool down and eat lots of ice cream for the same reason!

Virgo's analytical skills will help you.

Lucky Numbers: 9.24.30.19.23.4.

Virgo: You are in two minds whether that special someone will phone. Do not fear they have other commitments at the moment but you are on their mind – more than you would care to realise! There is a huge celebration soon with a finan-

cial resolution to a very tricky situation. You have been sadly misled. You placed your trust in someone who has deceived you. Your simple faith will not be ignored and the Universe will make sure that you are compensated. All your dreams are about to come true in many unexpected ways. Sit back and enjoy the ride. Your detractors will pay a heavy price without you having to do a thing. Reserve judgement about a work offer; a small delay to negotiate your terms would be sensible. You are spiritually protected, so leave all lies behind. Eat yellow foods to boost your personal power. Wear colours that give you courage. Scorpio is a hot little package!
Lucky Numbers: 6.31.19.21.30.16.

Libra: There will be a greatly unexpected turn-around with a legal issue. Do not panic if at first it goes against you as in the long run you will be victorious and justice will be served. Perhaps it is time to upgrade your computer? Your working life is set to change after a stretch of time where you have felt thwarted. You are about to step out of a rut in many respects. That new contract is promising. Take opportunities to extend your field of training. If you have an important date make sure you are on your best form. If this means delaying the meeting by a day or two you will be glad you did. Fighting over a legacy will eventually end. It is better not to get involved. Keep your dignity in one piece. It is important that the wishes of the deceased are respected. Financial security in the long term is assured. Get a bit more rest and relaxation. Eat fruits with high water content. Wear greens and beige for camouflage!

Cancer is cheeky and a bit inclined to interfere.
Lucky Numbers: 7.11.39.24.1.30.

Scorpio: Is it all work, work, work for you at the moment, Scorpio! Keep dreaming of your loved one. It is important, if you are apart, to hold your feelings steady in your heart. Absence makes the heart fonder even in the fragile stage of new love. This relationship is worth fighting for. Do not listen to those who are trying to interfere. They are jealous for their own reasons and do not have your best interests at heart. The stress of your situation may be getting on top of you. You do not miss much but unfortunately you are not free to express your opinion. Keep smiling to yourself and everything will work out brilliantly. There is no need to force issues. Just trust that the Universe is steering you towards something brilliant. You should eat a more balanced diet.
Wear black to seduce.
Aquarius is an eye opener!
Lucky Numbers: 26.6.31.40.22.11.

Sagittarius: If you are feeling insecure about a trip abroad, do not worry as it is well worth the effort. Part of you will be homesick, but the long-term benefits of the journey far outweigh any negative aspects. Your family life may be hectic at the moment and there seems to be no peace or time for your own thoughts. This is frustrating for Sagittarius. You need to spread your wings and fly! Ignore anyone who is being deliberately obnoxious in your working life. They will soon tire if you walk away. Romantically you may be tempted to make a judgement. Do not be too quick off the mark – you would regret hasty behaviour at this point. Just insist on more time to yourself rather than upset the apple cart completely. If a parent has been giving you cause for concern the trouble will soon pass. Leave family members to find their own way forward. You cannot live somebody's life for them – right? Eat curry!

Wear purple for spirituality and healing.

Leo is hot and wants to get involved.

Lucky Numbers: 32.14.22.11.33.1.

Capricorn: Money matters look great for Capricorn at the moment. There is money to be made with the sale of property, and the energies are good for a lottery win. Use the birth-dates of family members who are deceased for extra luck. Romantically things will take off after a rather fallow period. There may be love waiting at a wedding or family reunion. A relationship that went wrong near Hallowe'en will be back on track very soon. If you have plans to extend or build a property, go right ahead. Your wishes will be granted on a medical matter and any illness will be short lived. A very expensive car is of significance and a business deal will be the outcome. In the next three months your earning capacity will increase and money will flow towards you.

Eat plenty of seafood as you may be short of iodine.

Wear light green for a good laugh!

Pisces has is sorted – exercise more trust.

Lucky Numbers: 16.24.19.20 21.3.

Aquarius: Marital harmony is well starred and a move of house looks very positive after a time of delay. Go right ahead with any contracts connected to property. There may be some frustrations on closing a deal, but all will be well. Be strong where finances are concerned. Focus on what you want to achieve and it will come about. Aquarians are masters of their own minds, so make use of your brainpower to weave some magic. Be careful not to be too complacent about your life and do not use your natural authority to railroad others. You have coped with a lot of shock and disappointment in your life so there is reason to be proud. However, not everyone has the same perceptions as you so take time to listen and understand. A family pet may need treatment. Eat porridge if you can stomach it!

Wear turquoise for creativity.

Virgo may get annoyed – watch your step!

Lucky Numbers: 27.14.32.13.3.22.

Pisces: Despite any insecurity you may have about work and finances your life is on track. There is a new car, travel and work victory within a short space of time this year. Any business undertaking is well starred provided you make the most of the earth signs in your life. Stand firm on a matter close to your heart. The determination you have displayed will reap its own rewards. You must resist any temptation to fall back into old patterns. These are destructive to you, and it is not a good idea to undo all your brave decisions. Go with the flow in love relationships. There is romance on the horizon, but maybe stop gazing at the horizon too intently! It may feel like you are on a rollercoaster, but enjoy the ride

and life will get very exciting shortly. Eat more protein.
Wear yellow or paint a room in this colour to lift your spir-
its.
Gemini is mildly amusing.
Lucky Numbers: 21.41.3.11.7.2.

WEEK FIFTEEN
April 9th – April 15th

Aries: You may feel reflective this week, Aries, if not a little
subdued. Things are not as bad as they look, so keep your
head. Changes afoot at work will turn out in your favour.
Do consider going for a contract and it is a fortuitous time
to clinch a property deal. It may be time to move on from a
relationship that is not bringing you the happiness you
deserve. If you take a courageous leap of faith it will all look
very different down the road and you will be glad you took
the plunge. Get plenty of fresh air and do breathing exercises when you feel stressed. It is worth fighting for your rights
with a legal issue but it will take time to resolve – definitely persist.
Wear red for confidence this week, and eat properly.
Libra brings a different perspective.
Lucky Numbers: 24.32.11.40.39.5.

Taurus: The raging bull causing havoc in a china shop is
not a pretty sight. Do curb your temper this week. There
may be frustrations in your working life and a delay with
money matters. Do not chase rainbows with a particular

business deal. It may not be all it's cracked up to be – exercise caution. You are better waiting until the time of Taurus before clinching important transactions. Romantically you may be going through a lot of uncertainty. Look within at what your heart is telling you. Sometimes it is more honest to follow the illogical route. All will be well if you trust in the process of life. A chapter has to close but there is an exciting new book on the horizon! Take things easy and do a lot of thinking. Your logical mind will catch up with your heart eventually. Eat raw foods and red meat. You need to be fitter to cope with what's coming.

Stand your ground in greens, browns and reds this week. Capricorn helps financially – take advice.

Lucky Numbers: 36.5.41.33.11.24.

Gemini: Use your intuition this week. You are unusually creative at the moment, but do use tact to get your ideas across to superiors. A business plan will work out but do be careful of extra stress. It is not a good idea to be stubborn this week. Some situations cannot be salvaged and in this case it is probably better to walk away with your head held high. There is victory over a marriage issue so remain diplomatic and your feelings will register. The big news you are waiting for has been delayed until the time of Taurus. Panic not. Plan that summer holiday, as there will be a great deal waiting for you. Spend time by water as its sound will soothe you – turn on the tap if necessary! Use any spare time to sort out your abode. It is important to de-clutter and tidy your environment. Avoid fizzy drinks and sweets.

Wear sky blue for creativity and freedom.

Taurus is wise and all-knowing.
Lucky numbers: 12.2.13.5.27.41.

Cancer: Cancer should be on a bit of a roll at the moment despite hidden insecurities. It is important to have more confidence and to trust yourself more than you usually do. There are many good things on the way that will manifest if you just relax and accept your situation. You do not have to try too hard as the Universe has big plans for you. Be brave with any health issue in the family, there is great potential to fight off any difficulty. Do not hesitate to accept a job offer or promotion at work as it will go swimmingly for you. A family celebration will go according to plan if you do not get stressed about the details. Wait a while for a decision on a car, and travel is well starred. Eat plenty of vegetables.
Wear yellow and orange for vibrancy.
Virgo knows a thing or two.
Lucky Numbers: 22.7.26.17.39.40.

Leo: There is a very definite love choice in the air for Leo. Put family considerations first and stay cool. It is not often that someone manages to ruffle your mane, but forewarned is forearmed. Rise above any personal insecurity and speak your mind. Your instincts are on top form, so rely on your gut reactions rather than any doubts that surface. Take stock of a relationship. Does that person really love you? Or are they along for the ride? It is a good time to invest and save money. Make what you have work for you; it may be multiplied with careful planning. Leave a difficult relative to their own devices and they will soon stop the drama. Stand your ground in all matters this week and you will be well pleased with the results.

Wear warm clothes, and eat warm food this week. Your system needs TLC.

Reds and oranges will heat you up nicely.

Sagittarius gets intense. Unusual!

Lucky Numbers: 33.8.14.36.29.3.

Virgo: Stop worrying, Virgo! Everything is going to be fine. You are looked after and you are luckier than you realise. Financial difficulties will soon be a thing of the past, and a lottery ticket looks as if it will come up trumps. Be patient for a while longer. You are all set to be whisked away for a romantic break. Go for it despite any nervous reservations you may have. Your soul mate and spiritual partner is on the horizon. You will be able to leave the years of heartache and missed opportunities behind. It is a good time to purchase property but check the fine print of any contracts you are about to sign. An older member of the family may need extra attention and support this week. Do not get stressed unduly, everything will make sense by the summer. It is OK to indulge your sweet tooth this week!

Wear pink to attract unconditional love.

Taurus is full of love and admiration.

Lucky Numbers: 18.25.14.16.37.40.

Libra: Well, Libra, it may not look like the sun is shining on you, but it is! A court case that has been dragged out painfully will finally resolve. Be careful of any out-of-court settlements; it would actually benefit you to go the whole way with this. Property issues may be causing you a headache. Take your time to find the house you really want. A person close to you who is separated or divorced will find love again and true happiness. Be careful to keep up any loan repayments. Spend fearlessly and pay the bills. All monies will come back to you in kind. A family reunion that you are dreading will go better than expected. By the summer practical problems around the house will be sorted and any DIY or decorating will be complete. Red wine is a tonic for the system

Yellow is good for well-being this week.

Gemini is respectful but good fun too!

Lucky Numbers: 14.37.31.6.27.18.

Scorpio: Your heart may be all over the place, Scorpio. Don't panic. Everything will work out just fine if you keep your head. The object of your affections will wait for you. Focus on the work that you have to do, and ignore any frustrations you are feeling creatively. Unfortunately you have signed up for something that does not give you the free rein you would like. You have to ride with it at the moment. Stay centred and the pressure will relax by the early summer. Be careful with pregnancy in any new romantic 'liaisons' as the fertility between you is strong. If you are planning a family, this month should get you a result! Weigh up a possible training programme or college course; it may not be the right thing at this point. Avoid eating too much wheat if you are bloated.

Wear red. It's as hot as you are!

Aquarius is a challenge.
Lucky Numbers: 12.8.14.15.17.29.

Sagittarius: You may be feeling restricted within a relationship. If your emotions are turbulent do not despair, there is love, passion and balance not far away. The energies are great for marriage and pregnancy, so if you want to propose go right ahead. It will work out better for you to leave the past behind and take a risk. You can connect with the person of your dreams, and if they are already in your arms build on the relationship with confidence. If you are hurt, keep quiet. People have no right to interfere with your privacy. Keep your secret and those who are trying to control you will kick themselves in time. A move of house should go according to plan. The next home has a lucky vibrant energy. Your career is flying and you are destined for the big time in your chosen field. Avoid refined foods.

Use orange for personal vitality and zest.

Pisces drops you in it – but don't panic. It's a good thing!
Lucky Numbers: 15.26.14.33.2.25.

Capricorn: Although it will antagonise proud and determined Capricorn, it may be time to admit defeat with a particular investment. You went ahead for the wrong reasons with a project because your ambitious nature got the better of you. Sometimes even Capricorn has to cut losses! You are set to win out in more subtle ways if you give up the need to be top of the class. Put your stubborn nature to one side and sit back. This will work in your favour with relationships also. A brilliant offer is on the horizon that will make

any sense of failure evaporate. Your focus is better channelled into your own ideas so do not be on the look-out to
poach the inspiration of others. Harness your own creativity. Victory is yours by the summer. Eat plenty of leafy green
vegetables and salads.
Wear white to reflect attention.
Leo is lively company- a tonic, so!
Lucky Numbers: 16.9.4.30.26.5.

Aquarius: This is a good time for any surgical procedure,
Aquarius, so proceed with confidence with any medical
matters. Peace of mind will be the outcome. If a marriage or
long-term relationship is stressing you out, do not despair.
Focus upon your day-to-day work and the problems will
eventually disperse. You could make things worse by insist-
ing on answers within your social and emotional life.
Sometimes it is better to go with the flow and ignore the
hitches. Follow your instincts with finances and be a bit
braver: speculate to accumulate. Any depression or feelings
of melancholy will lift by the end of the spring. May is a
good time to buy a new car, and book the church pronto if
marriage is on the cards. Eat fewer high fat foods and stop
smoking – certainly do not even THINK about starting!
Silver and gold are good for luck this week.
Capricorn identifies with you.
Lucky Numbers: 19.32.14.25.36.40.

Pisces: If someone is keeping you waiting at the moment,
you will have to get on with the next thing. You may be in
two minds about a marriage and feel not a little sour. Do not

worry. Any emotional difficulty you have experienced over the last two years will pass. It would be good for you to take that trip. All things linking you to America are well starred. Romantically, change is afoot which will work out for the best in the long run. Be determined to succeed, and focus on what you want to achieve. You can make things happen as long as you do not undermine yourself with doubt. The sea air is good for you at the moment, so clear your head with plenty of walks. Country lanes will do the trick if you live in Meath! Press on with a new job. The recent decisions you have made are going to work out in your favour. Avoid stodgy foods at the moment.

Wear turquoise for inspiration.

Aquarius is insightful- a true visionary.

Lucky Numbers: 33.11.21.34.28.4.

WEEK SIXTEEN
April 16th - April 22nd

Aries: Any work or project that you attempt this week is destined to succeed, Aries. Applications for future college courses also look good. There may be difficulty concerning an earth sign in your life, and watch that Taurus, as all is not as it seems with him/her. Romantic uncertainty will eventually clear by June, and there may be a dramatic end to a relationship. Do not be floored by the shock as everything will work out for the best. Great peace of mind is on its way after a time of exciting turbulence! Please do not try to control those in your charge, as the constraints you place upon people will come back to haunt you. Move forward with courage and hold your head high. By the end of the year you will have reason to be proud. If you find that you are frustrated, try some sublimation in the form of charity work or altruistic gestures. Make sure that you do not eat on the hoof! Blue will keep you cool.

Taurus excites for all the wrong reasons!

Lucky Numbers: 23.27.21.3.40.1.

Taurus: Money matters are well starred, but it is important not to be complacent about a particular contract. There is an emotional entanglement with an earth sign that you must sort out. You have been unfair to a person and they are waiting patiently for you to speak. Travel to a poor country will be an eye-opener and you will be able to co-ordinate a relief project. Watch out for an unwanted pregnancy but if it can not be prevented accept it as a fateful intervention. A new relationship will transform you in ways that you don't expect. Marriage that takes place abroad will herald a new era in your life this year. Be careful with the purchase of land or property as it may be worthwhile to wait until you are absolutely sure. You may take out a loan to extend your abode. Go right ahead - you will be delighted with the result. If an older family member needs medical intervention do not worry as any treatment is timely. Links with America for business expansion look like a good idea. Eat venison and rabbit if you like fair game!

Wear red and black in combination for extra energy.

Virgo is clever and won't give up.

Lucky Numbers: 26.10.33.11.24.16.

Gemini: Love and money are destined to make a dramatic entrance into your life soon, Gemini. This will end a time of work-related stress. If you are waiting for love – be prepared. You are about to be blown away! You may not believe in love at first sight, but something extraordinary is about to hit you right between the eyes. Trust this and follow your instincts. For a newly married couple or first-time buyer now is the opportune moment. If you are a gambler, it is likely that an outsider will romp home. So make sure you put your money where your mouth is. A legal matter will be settled in your favour so relax and leave the procedure to run its course. Spiritually there is a rebirth on the cards. You may find you are full of the joys of spring, and your innate trust in life will blossom. Lobster, crayfish and mussels are good for you.

Wear serene colours for their calming effect.

Cancer has a lot of patience.

Lucky Numbers: 22.33.1.7.11.30.

Cancer: There are changes on the horizon in your working life, Cancer. This may leave you feeling hard done by. Try to accept the upheaval as a challenge that will steer you ever onwards and upwards. 'Crabby' Cancer resists anything that threatens personal security, especially if it involves finances. Do not worry unduly, as there is a high possibility that someone close to you will come into money soon. A trip abroad that has been on your mind since Christmas is worth following through. Working overseas is a good idea at this point and if you don't go for it now, when will you! The purchase of land or property near water is important in the future. Go for the house by the sea rather than the one inland if a move is on the cards. Be careful that you do not blow a business venture by being overly confident in your management skills. Sometimes it is better not to tamper with something that has a life of its own and works. If it's not broke don't fix it! Eat rich foods this week; it's allowed! Wear or use yellow for personal power.

Virgo is smart – keep watching!

Lucky Numbers: 6.16.31.27.14.5.

Leo: Reserve judgement at the moment about a possible work venture abroad. It is not quite the right time, so do not make plans prematurely. You may be disillusioned about a relationship that has an overseas connection. The person concerned is a live wire so please handle with care! At times you tend to accept your situation for the sake of a quiet life. This year will change the status quo. It is highly likely that you will raise both your standards and your expectations regarding romance. This is not a bad idea as in the past you have sometimes settled for less than you deserve. A work offer is on the way that looks very positive and perhaps involves a slight change of direction. Proceed with confidence, as this career move is timely. If you are trying to extend your family, now is the prime time to get busy! Eat mushrooms and foods such as venison and Stilton.

Wear and use pink for fertility.

Libra is amusing and worthy of your time

Lucky Numbers: 19.8.14.31.6.22.

Virgo: It looks as if you are doing battles in your head about your working life, Virgo. Take heart and review what you have achieved in the past year. Are things really that desperate? You are certainly working hard and at the moment there will be no relief with deadlines or commitments. Pace yourself and persist with what is required, and more exciting work offers will manifest by the summer. If you are waiting for someone to get in touch it will happen if you get on with the next thing and forget it. There is a relationship that has broken your heart in recent years. Healing is on the way, and reconciliation is highly likely if you can both resolve your differences. Communication is the key word in both your career and private life. Remain open and roll with the changes and you will come out a winner by the autumn. Eat high protein beans and pulses.

Wear something trendy to impress.

Turquoise inspires creativity.

Lucky Numbers: 24.34.16.33.2.17.

Libra: If you are feeling turned upside down by a family bereavement, please hang in there. A peace will soon descend upon you as you learn to let the loved one go. Be assured that they are in a better place and will be watching over you into the future. Your independent spirit is triumphant by Christmas and you will understand that life follows its own pattern. There are many things that we cannot control so remain balanced and philosophical during testing times. Work victory is on the horizon and a romantic offer with a link to the past will surprise you. In many ways you are being pushed to the limit. It is worth staying upbeat and do preserve your energy rather than expend it on negative thinking. You can tip those Libran scales in your favour with positive attitudes. Keep your boundaries defined in a relationship and do not allow yourself to be pushed into things that are not for you. Eat complex carbohydrates at the moment.

Wear lilac or purple for healing.

Gemini will help you along.

Lucky Numbers: 11.42.10.30.1.2.

Scorpio: Be careful not to let politics in your working life upset your personal relationships. You may be quite overloaded with stress and work commitments. A project that looked as if it would open up the world to you may not be all it is cracked up to be. There are people behind the scenes who have unspoken agendas and in some ways you are a mere puppet performing at their beck and call. It is time to demand some privacy for your love life, which has been sadly neglected of late. Make an effort to connect with your loved one, and take time out for family and friends as well. Those in authority must not be allowed to totally commandeer your life. You should make contact with an exciting newcomer as they will turn your life around in more ways than one. Keep your sense of humour and things will work out just fine. Eat Greek salad and olive oil!

Wear red for passion.

Aquarius is watching.

Lucky Numbers: 6.11.31.14.25.33.

Sagittarius: Playing happy families was never your strong point, Sagittarius, so you are wondering how a particular situation crept up on you. It is important to take responsibility for your actions and get on with the task in hand. Uncertainty over a property issue will soon be resolved so you can rest easy. You may not get as much profit as you would like for a particular transaction but it is worth taking the settlement because it will make sense in other ways. Twins are destined to make an entrance into your extended family and parental responsibilities will in general be challenged. A firm word and the appropriate discipline will make for an easier life in the long run. Do not try to buy peace of mind with a manipulative bargain. Financial problems will clear over time if you take the practical approach at this point. Your bank should be supportive of any investment you may wish to make. Eat plenty of red meat or fibre. Wear black for protection.

Taurus has a great sense of humour.

Lucky Numbers: 2.23.14.36.27.30.

Capricorn: Love is in the air this week for Capricorn, and earthy Taurus looks set to arrange encounters of the intimate kind. Be careful if you are in a long-term and committed relationship, as the temptation to stray may be strong at the moment. If you are single what may begin as a casual affair is destined to get serious quite quickly. Trust your instincts with the passion that is flying around and do not falter in the heat of the moment. Sometimes strong connections are made at such times that defy logic and turn your life around. A professional work offer is destined to change the pattern of your future career. Take decisive action and within six months you will know that you made the right move. If emotions are running high be careful not to lose your head. When you have made up your mind on an issue you are usually immovable but just this once be prepared to compromise. If you do not, your stubbornness will cost you dearly. A close friend or family member will get the all-clear from the medical profession. Eat whole foods and plenty of grains.

Wear turquoise for creativity.

Capricorn brings a smile to your face.

Lucky Numbers: 9.16.32.11.14.25.

Aquarius: You have a dream in mind, Aquarius, but finances are blocking its potential to become a reality. At least this is what you are telling yourself. Sometimes dreams do come true but they often need a commitment from us to manifest their full potential. Aquarius is ruled by the mind so will often get caught up in flights of fancy. But what this Zodiac sign sometimes misses is that it possesses the focus to make things happen. Grounding is difficult for the air signs but of course it is fundamental to reality. Assess any projects carefully and do not commit yourself to contracts unless you are sure. Aim for the stars by all means but do not get caught up in silly ideas that will remain up in the air. Focus upon a plan of action and you can achieve everything you wish for. There may be battles with a loved one about finances, but any disharmony will fall away by July when a windfall is due. Eat three square meals a day.

Wear green for luck with blue for peace of mind.

Virgo knows best.

Lucky Numbers: 40.32.3.12.14.16.

Pisces: If you have been going through a difficult time emotionally, Pisces, victory is just around the corner. Any grief for a missed opportunity or failed relationship will soon turn on its head. An important liaison will develop within two months and this will bring harmony back into your life. Do not be tempted to give someone another chance. There would be no long-term change to the situation, never mind the promises they might make. Actions really do speak louder than words in this instance so monitor the relationship accordingly. Your instincts are razor sharp at the moment so follow those hunches! A 'Dear John' letter may be a necessary evil that will clear up a lot of uncertainty. Do not let a jealous person destroy your life. Links to America are well starred in the near future and it will be important to make quick decisions regarding work. Eat plenty this week; you need the extra energy.

Go for gold!

Taurus is sensual and exciting.

Lucky Numbers: 19.24.23.14.16.5.

TAURUS Time:
April 21st – May 21st

WEEK SEVENTEEN
April 23rd – April 29th

Taurus: Family life may be a battleground for Taurus at the moment and important life choices are on the horizon. It is crucial to keep your perspective and give personal space a priority. Do not make hasty decisions but bide your time until the perfect scenario reveals itself. Love is but a breath away so do not miss out or tie yourself up in knots of guilt. Exciting life-changes are at hand so fasten your seat belt and enjoy the ride. A rest from a hectic work schedule would be ideal but if this is impossible pace yourself until the summer. Finances look stable but you need to invest for the future and get practical with business transactions.

Red and black will help your energy levels.

Aries may get nasty- tread carefully!

Lucky Numbers: 24.32.2.12.33.4.

Gemini: Do not lose heart if a work project is causing you frustration. It is possible you are feeling hard done by but do not despair, as before the summer your hard work will pay off. Please remember that you cannot please all of the people all of the time and it is definitely time to give yourself more priority. Use the full force of your intellect in a legal matter and trust the system to serve justice in this case. A family move is indicated after a time of delay and you may proceed with confidence. Wait for the ideal property and do not be impetuous, as things will download at the perfect moment.

Yellow will restore your confidence and bring good vibes.

Taurus is stubborn but probably right too!

Lucky Numbers: 39.42.27.14.23.3.

Cancer: Any uncertainty and conflict in your working life is part of your destiny at the moment, but disillusionment will dissolve by the summer and you will realise that the turn of events makes sense. In fact by this time next year you will appreciate that you could not have planned your life better if you had tried! An independent spirit will serve you well. Make sure that you go with the flow if a particular relationship is causing you grief. Do not fret about outcomes as the Universe will as always keep your shell upright. Swooping seagulls need not torment you and there is more faith in the process of life at your disposal. Be careful not to manipulate those in your care as the more freedom you give, the more reward you will reap.

Pink will help you to give and receive unconditional love.

Virgo is a great friend – always.

Lucky Numbers: 5.26.9.2.41.22.

Leo: Guard your financial and legal concerns carefully, and do not be too free with confidential matters. By all means take colleagues at face value, but do be aware of their agendas at the same time. Your instincts are on good form so capitalise on the inside information that seems to be dropping from the skies. Spend quality time with family and friends to help keep your feet on the ground amidst exciting developments. There is a charming child close to you who will bring joy to many throughout their life. Perhaps it is time to look at your fitness regime and take on physical activity to counteract couch potato syndrome! A medical problem for a parent will be correctly diagnosed and efficiently treated.

Green will support you with matters of the heart.

Scorpio is very unusual.

Lucky Numbers: 19.5.25.11.31.4.

Virgo: An exciting romantic offer is on its way for Virgo. Follow your heart and do not make a hasty negative judgement. Many people will be affected by your decisions in the future so be both responsible and true to yourself. A time of stress and worry is drawing to a close and finances are assured in the years ahead. The purchase of a property will happen sooner than you expect, so be careful of what you commit to in the meantime. Be wary of jealous people as your career moves up to another level of success. Do not be so free with your time and be cautious of whom you trust. Violet will support you psychically.

Pisces is different but enchanting.

Lucky Numbers: 37.22.12.4.33.21.

Libra: If you are hurt and disappointed by the end of a relationship, do not lose heart. This change in your life is profound and will lead to greater things. Destiny has exciting plans for you if you can just sit back and relax. There is no need to panic even though people around you are tense and paranoid. Keep your famous balance and serenity intact and all will be well. Take the leap of faith with a financial offer and commit yourself fully to your career. Make sure that you do not get sidetracked by a romantic liaison that is doomed before it begins. If you hold onto your emotional and professional integrity, everything will work out in your favour. Turquoise will enhance creativity and communication.

Taurus offers something different.

Lucky Numbers: 11.34.8.9.32.41.

Scorpio: You will have to exercise some patience, Scorpio, and be prepared to give up control to a superior. Difficult as it is to surrender your perspective, this person does claim to know the ropes. Your instincts never let you down, so continue to trust them even though you might have to act against your better judgement. Do not neglect your love life. Contracts may rob you of your freedom but they can not buy your soul. So make your move and never mind the consequences – you will be glad you did! Travel plans may look uncertain but it is worth persisting with the commitments you have made. Personal finances or business interests will turn around as long as you keep focused.

Dark blue will add mystery and brings protection to your life.

Cancer is emotional and links to you down the ages.

Lucky Numbers: 4.31.6.16.37.20.

Sagittarius: If you are thinking of following up a work opportunity abroad, question it no longer. Foreign connections are very important for the next few months. Emotionally you may feel torn but the changes on the horizon are, in fact, good for everybody. Life brings major events soon which reflect the inevitable cycle of decline and rebirth. A financial surprise is a distinct possibility and the sale of property finally resolves. Concentrate your energies upon your hopes and dreams. Why shouldn't they come true? Do stop undermining yourself and begin to trust that your future looks as good as you intend it to be.

Pale blue puts you in touch with Divine Will.

Leo and Aries are soul mates.

Lucky Numbers: 23.4.5.8.7.21.

Capricorn: It looks like it's time to make that relationship decision you have been putting on hold, Capricorn. If you are feeling sorry for yourself, please be reassured love is in the air. Give someone that you are in two minds about a second chance. A work situation needs to turn a corner before you can be sure, so reserve judgement. The summer is full of promise for life, love and romance. Therefore steer a steady course through disillusionment at this point. Make careful financial assessments and get a clear picture of a proposed business venture.

Black and white will help you see clearly.

Gemini will keep you amused.

Lucky Numbers: 32.9.24.33.10.1.

Aquarius: By the end of May great peace will descend for you, Aquarius. So hang in there. Out of the blue a work offer will manifest and you may proceed with confidence. Opportunities abound to leave negative situations behind. Refuse to allow unhealthy relationships to drain your energy, and take the chance on a fresh start. The conditions are right to leave a major rut or sticking point behind. You may skip into the future with a lighter step and a joyful heart, but you have to honour your integrity and independent spirit.

Orange will add zest to your life.

Leo is very different but has something worth writing home about.

Lucky Numbers: 12.20.33.23.15.3.

Pisces: You may be feeling insecure about your intuitive ability. Pisceans are the visionary dreamers of the zodiac and many possibilities float through their heads in any given moment. Learn to discern and trust the pictures you see, but be aware that not every insight will ground itself in reality. Your imagination is powerful and you can manifest events if you remain focused. There is plenty of money for Pisceans and future security, but you have to trust what is being offered to you. A move of location is a strong probability and you can be confident that if you take a major leap of faith it will pay off.

Reds will focus your mind in a practical way.

Virgo is insightful.

Lucky Numbers: 21.24.4.3.30.40.

Aries: Things look quite challenging for Aries at the moment. There are major shifts and changes afoot and at times you may feel as if you are jumping across quicksand. At least you are not sinking, so do remain confident and in control of your reactions to complicated events. There will be celebrations for you at the end of this journey and you will appreciate that life delivered what was needed. Destiny is at the helm of the next few months so you will have to brace yourself and honour the bigger picture. Uncertainty in relationships will clarify by the end of the summer if not sooner. Work hard and keep your head down so a lot of the potential angst floats over your head.

Black will bring you protection.

Libra is light and fair.

Lucky Numbers: 23.16.2.31.41.5.

WEEK EIGHTEEN
April 30th – May 6th

Taurus: It is important to get your house in order financially, so review commitments and make intelligent decisions. A block in your working life may be removed if you display determination and tenacity. Get moving with those travel plans, as a break is long overdue. Family support is guaranteed if you keep communication honest and true. Don't give up with a long-term goal, for your tenacity and persistence will be duly rewarded. Make the most of your opportunities as and when they arise. A love from the deep distant past will not give up – have you really let go?
Blue brings peace.
Virgo offers a fresh start.
Lucky Numbers: 22.10.12.4.33.2.

Gemini: Romantic issues may be getting you down, so look at the reasons for disillusionment or uncertainty and the answer will become clear. Expect a magical summer with plenty of social interaction. It is important to make headway at work so that you can find the time to enjoy the celebrations. Retraining or a college course will lead to favourable career options. A wedding plan looks set to roll and is a very lucky choice for those concerned. Keep a control of financial investments and pay attention to detail or you will regret your carelessness.
Yellow will lift your spirits.
Libra is funny but a little wired!
Lucky Numbers: 26.24.6.32.16.7.

Cancer: It may be time to leave the past behind in a work situation. Do not worry. Any financial uncertainty will naturally sort itself out. A move of location is a strong possibility and will go very well for you if you take the plunge. Romance looks set to pick up and you can move out of the rut you are resting in. To honour the status quo is not necessarily your most intelligent choice at this point. It is a good time to buy a car or take up those driving lessons. New confidence and peace of mind is on the way.

Green brings financial luck.

Virgo has the answer.

Lucky Numbers: 4.23.28.14.25.1.

Leo: Stop lagging behind and quit looking over your shoulder. The future begins now and because plenty of water has gone under the bridge it is time to move on. Legal documents that initially gave you cause for concern will finalise in your favour. Show determination and ambition in your working life and fight off low self-esteem or security issues. You need more physical activity, so do not succumb to laziness, enjoyable as it may be. Check the running condition of a vehicle and make sure all papers are in order. There is encouraging news with a medical condition.

Purple brings healing.

Scorpio is enticing.

Lucky Numbers: 28.7.2.33.24.16.

Virgo: Keep your counsel with work projects, as there are many people who wish to emulate you by stealing your ideas. There is victory for you with a relationship that has stood the test of time. Trust your finer feelings as dreams really may come true if you dream them for long enough! You might grieve the end of an important connection, but be assured it is for the best. This time next year you will not recognise your life with all the changes that are afoot. Destiny has many exciting twists and turns in store.

Orange will bring joy.

Scorpio holds the key.

Lucky Numbers: 7.32.39.13.4.25.

Libra: You may be in two minds about the future of a relationship, but what's new? Happiness is yours in the future but you need to leave the past behind and enjoy life's mystery. Do not overstress yourself about finances, as the long hours you have to put in will be rewarded eventually. Reach for the stars and in time you may grab one! A sudden change of plan feels like destiny and will work out in a perfect way. The sun is shining on you despite all evidence to the contrary. Be careful not to interfere in big decisions that are out of your hands. Some things are best given over to the professionals.

Black will protect you.

Capricorn has legal or financial clout.

Lucky Numbers: 19.11.42.33.2.14.

Scorpio: You really must trust your instincts where love is concerned, never mind convention. Do not allow other people to dictate the details of your life. Hold onto the control and objectivity that is naturally yours for the taking. Dreams may come true, but you have to make a few intelligent moves to help them along. If your nose is out of joint, straighten it! Major passion is dangling under that nose, so dust yourself down and enjoy. In a complicated work situation victory is yours if you steer a steady course. Finances look promising in the long term.

Red will liven you up!

Taurus is your opposite, but provides balance.

Lucky Numbers: 11.19.22.31.14.6.

Sagittarius: Follow your instincts in complicated business dealings and make sure financial agreements are secure before you broadcast them. If you are under a cloud or drowning emotionally, take positive action. Do not wallow in your melancholic mood, as it is in part self-contrived. You have more power at your disposal than you realise, so smile upon the world and it should return the favour. Check the brakes on a vehicle or put your car in for an overdue service. Tenacity and ambitious drive are needed to put the spark back into your working life. Do not get too entangled in emotive family matters. Stand back and let any problems right themselves.

Dark blue brings serenity and mystery.

Pisces is understanding and empathetic.

Lucky Numbers: 2.34.21.3.4.13.

Capricorn: Put aside any jealousy relating to work, as there is no point in resenting someone else's success. Focus upon your own future and channel your ambitious nature into independent projects. There is a lot of creativity at your disposal, so paint, write or sing your way through this week! Relationships look wonderfully supportive if you keep them equal and show respect. Do not allow control issues to spoil partnerships, and keep that ego locked in a drawer marked private. Your future is blessed if you can be all things to all people in a straightforward way. Do not attempt to manipulate situations or bend things to your strong will.

Turquoise inspires you.

Aries is feisty and stimulating.

Lucky Numbers: 16.32.27.14.5.3.

Aquarius: Try to put stress that relates to the past behind you. Wipe the emotional slate clean and press on as one relationship needs a fresh start and positive input. A win of money looks highly likely in the near future - keep tickets in something yellow for optimum luck. That legal matter is not all it seems, so do tread carefully through the small print. Work choices are inevitable by June and wise moves reduce tension and financial commitments. Be prepared for a surprise offer relating to property.

Lemon yellow will reduce bitterness.

Taurus doesn't want to know quite yet.

Lucky Numbers: 4.17.40.5.31.25.

Pisces: It is important to walk away from relationships that have brought you difficulty and disappointment. Passion is lurking around the corner and will pounce when the time is right. Be prepared to be surprised when after interminable waiting, what you have given up on comes to pass. Finances in the long term look positive and a new work contract is to be trusted. Healing is at hand for family grief, and peace will descend shortly. Make a decision to embrace your future wholeheartedly and do not wobble about demands made by others – they will make sense. Trust your judgement about a move of house.

White brings clarity and purity.

Gemini will keep you happy – well, amused anyway!

Lucky Numbers: 21.4.14.5.6.11.

Aries: It may be swings and roundabouts where a particular relationship is concerned. Take personal space and come up with an emotionally intelligent solution. Your integrity and freedom are more important than holding onto something for the sake of appearances. A work situation may not be going according to plan and you may have to sacrifice your dream when reality sets in. Unexpected news about a contract or papers will leave you reeling but there is a bigger picture at stake. Be assured that you will be looked after and that sanity will prevail. Go with the flow and keep focused upon your goal. Things may not go quite as you plan so be prepared to enjoy life's little jokes.

Pale blue will freshen you up!

Sagittarius shares your sense of fun.

Lucky Numbers: 6.13.42.26.34.7.

WEEK NINETEEN
May 7th – May 13th

Taurus: Love choices are looming for Taurus, so be careful if you are about to put a long-term partnership at risk. Follow your heart in all things and be assured of your success with an important project. Do not get tripped up by dodgy politics at work – step aside and leave troublemakers to hang themselves! Take a leap of faith with a contract and turn your back on paranoia and frustration. Finances and family matters look promising. Have the courage to put yourself first for a change. The right people will adjust to your changed circumstances.

Violet will clear your head.

Leo is all heart – like you.

Lucky Numbers: 3.14.6.27.4.30.

Gemini: Double-check all documents linking to travel abroad, and make sure that the practical details pertaining to a wedding are in order. If you are being challenged at work, be grateful for the opportunity to clarify a situation. Speak plainly this week and follow the logical route to success. Retraining or further study is a very good idea in the long term so proceed with confidence. Walk away from arguments with a loved one. You will only aggravate the situation if you engage in a fight. Single Geminis may look forward to a romantic encounter.

Sky blue will elevate you.

Scorpio is intense and challenging.

Lucky Numbers: 22.33.11.24.40.5.

Cancer: Things are not all they seem in a work situation. You can expect a surprise judgement that will knock you off your feet. The wheel is turning very much in your favour, so trust the process of life. There is every reason to be optimistic about your future happiness, especially if changes in relationships are afoot. Do not give into the blues – take a trip abroad if things are getting on top of you. Be gracious and kind to those in your charge as this will benefit you more than watching everything in paranoid detail. Balance your books, and finances in the long-term will accumulate. Silver equals money.

Aquarius is all-knowing, or likes to think so!

Lucky Numbers: 24.31.25.36.7.2.

Leo: There will soon be a big celebration over the settlement of a money matter. After a time of uncertainty, wishes will be granted. Leave the past behind and ignore sticky situations. If you remain clear-headed and hold onto your integrity, all will be well. You may be in two minds about a particular person so reserve judgement for a few more weeks. All will be revealed in more ways than just one! A work offer looks timely. Even though coming events are unexpected, you can trust that fate is looking after you – hold onto your hat!

Orange brings zest and vibrancy.

Gemini is a great communicator.

Lucky Numbers: 4.2.33.11.25.7.

Virgo: You may feel hoodwinked by a person who claims to have all the answers. Give them the benefit of the doubt at the moment as despite their smugness they do have innate wisdom. Things are not as they seem in a long-term relationship. An issue close to your heart will be settled eventually. Even though you are completely fed up, you can expect a good outcome to your ongoing concerns. Stress with

233 *Taurus Time*

finances will level off but you have to make a commitment to keep your head down and work hard. Love will win the day. Never mind all the nonsense and interference from other people.

Pink supports you unconditionally.

Capricorn is useful, but be cautious too.

Lucky Numbers: 33.22.11.24.5.16.

Libra: You may be missing a loved one from the past or need to connect with someone who has gone abroad. Everything will balance out for you so do be patient and trust the hand of fate for the rest. There are no missed opportunities so do not hold onto regrets. Stand by your decisions and raise a glass to the future. A dramatic legal issue will be settled financially but do not feel hard done by. The loss of your freedom is a heavy price to pay so embrace your circumstances, and you will have the last laugh. Work requires determination and persistence.

Red will attract passionate encounters.

Pisces is interesting.

Lucky Numbers: 12.4.26.37.4.11.

Scorpio: Embrace work offers from overseas wholeheartedly. If you throw yourself into team project, despite difficult conditions, success will be your reward. Major financial deals will be dangled in front of you so use discrimination and do not count your chickens! Try not to be duped by superiors and keep your wits about you. Stop being quite so sure of yourself as regards the opposite sex or you may be in for a rude awakening! Conditions are ripe for a successful pregnancy and family matters will naturally resolve. Follow your instincts in love and do not allow others to interfere, as you know best on this one.

White shines the light on confusion.

Cancer is a fellow partner in crime.

Lucky Numbers: 6.31.24.35.27.3.

Sagittarius: Stress relating to family issues will resolve but you need to be practical. A time of transition where your life moves to a different level is about to begin. You may be in two minds about leaving the past behind but it is best not to look over your shoulder. Things are set to become more challenging and you will need to draw upon your best qualities to succeed. Patience is needed and you must keep your cool rather than fly off the handle. A financial loss will be compensated for with new investments and shrewd property deals. By the summer, work contracts are worth accepting. Do not idealise a loved one but be prepared for wonderful romance.

Purple brings regal serenity.

Aquarius may hold a secret.

Lucky Numbers: 2.5.3.4.15.6.

Capricorn: You really do not need to be quite so competitive. Have more confidence in your abilities and leave others to express their talents without interference. You have natural authority and your need to be in control is admirable but worrying. Do not be afraid to bend a little and give others credit where it is due. This summer financial peace of mind lands on your doorstep so please remain humble.

Travel abroad and a move of house are blessed by the gods, but please remember complacency is not a pretty quality. Love can be blissful – perhaps money really does buy happiness!

Green brings healing for the heart.

Leo is entertaining, but not your cup of tea!

Lucky Numbers: 24.33.26.37.9.10.

Aquarius: A moment of spiritual epiphany may occur like a bolt of lightning out of the blue. Expect to be shaken in an exciting but profound way. Keep a philosophical perspective with financial matters and do not question your path of destiny. A wake-up call is on the cards, which will lead to humanitarian gestures of goodwill. An open heart and mind manifests a better life experience than paranoia or suspicion. Trust the Universe to provide for you at every level and do not get hooked into issues of survival. Expect the best and it will surely arrive, expect the worst and you bring trouble to your door. Victory in love and romance are yours.

Gold releases hidden fears.

Taurus is stubborn and needs some convincing.

Lucky Numbers: 22.14.26.37.4.25.

Pisces: Do not lose heart if you wish to expand your family, as success with pregnancy is likely soon. Leave a negative work situation behind and make sure you find study or employment that utilises your creativity. Peace of mind is a breath away if you can ditch that sense of feeling hard done by. It is important to move on and let those who have hurt you be judged by life itself. Clear your head of thoughts that weigh you down, and rid your environment of clutter. It is time to detox yourself on all levels. A legal settlement may enable you to fully leave the past behind.

Pale lilac brings transmutation of negativity.

Aries is vibrant and brings good energy.

Lucky Numbers: 7.33.35.26.37.1.

Aries: Be wise to the shifts and changes of a partner's moods – all is not as it seems. Trust your instincts and the sense of unease that may be creeping up on you. Keep your counsel but observe everything. There are many clues surrounding you which herald the positive changes on the way. Independence of mind and spirit are called for. You can cope if you steer a steady course and do not expect people to act as normal. New contracts relating to property are trustworthy, but an unexpected upheaval may occur in the family home. Prospects for a complete turnaround in fortune are good. Destiny has many twists and turns in store so do not settle into complacency.

Fiery red will help you win.

Libra is hilarious.

Lucky Numbers: 40.11.13.25.4.37.

WEEK TWENTY
May 14th - May 20th

Taurus: Be very careful to protect your interests, Taurus, as you are not as infallible as you believe. Follow your heart by all means but do not get caught out in the process. It is important to make definite decisions and follow them through. Keep your focus and people will modify their behaviour accordingly. Do not be tempted off the beaten track or a merry mess will ensue. But if you like living dangerously, opportunities for a great time abound. Watch your back especially if you have hurt someone recently.

Red and black will rescue low energy levels.

Fellow Taurus may not be persuaded.

Lucky Numbers: 10.5.4.24.16.42.

Gemini: Work stress should ease if you keep all lines of communication clear. That delayed message you are waiting for will arrive if you get on with the next thing. Love may hit you between the eyes like a bolt out of the blue – be prepared for delicious complications! Family life looks settled and content so spend quality time with children and keep your better half sweet. Stop all that fretting and relax.

Yellow boosts personal power.

Cancer will mellow things nicely.

Lucky Numbers: 22.14.26.42.8.4.

Cancer: If you are in two minds about your current job, a change certainly looks positive. Leave the past behind and accept an offer or promotion based upon your gut reaction. Disillusionment could cause disruption if others are depending on your consistent commitment. Follow your emotions and trust your deeper feelings as people will adjust and be happy in time. It's a great time to get engaged or make a deeper connection with someone who interests you. Go with the flow and you will reach your destination unscathed.

Bright blue lifts your spirits.

Leo is on the ball.

Lucky Numbers: 24.8.36.2.6.31.

Leo: I suggest you accept that unexpected offer, as surprises both romantically and at work form part of this week's planetary design. Do not be lazy about either aspect of your life. You can lift yourself out of a rut by focusing upon that new contract. Life is not about scraping by with second-best, so draw on your Leonine pride and stroll towards what's staring you in the face. If you have the blues, do not sit around playing them! Get out and about, and life will soon take on a different complexion – as will you if you take that holiday abroad.

Lemon dissolves bitterness.

Capricorn can be relied upon.

Lucky Numbers: 8.4.7.32.42.25.

Virgo: You may be disillusioned about your destiny: have you been told one thing but something else is happening? Do not lose sight of your dreams and expectations as, if anyone can turn things around, it's you! After a time of conflict, confusion and delay in your love life, clarity is on the way. A large sum of money will manifest if you forget about it. Do not fixate on what might have been or you will miss opportunities in the present and create more turmoil for your future. Go for gold and you just might wander into a goldmine - your career is about to fly.

Black will protect you.

Libra has an independent idea.

Lucky Numbers: 1.2.3.4.5.21.

Libra: The world is turning in your favour so there is every reason to be optimistic about the future. Take a fresh start as a healthy way forward and do not turn to salt by glancing too frequently over your shoulder. You can expect a sudden improvement in your financial dealings so make pertinent choices regarding contracts. You have reason to be proud of an improved appearance – looking good! Get practical in your love life. If you have to timetable a rendezvous, bear with the situation, as any upheaval is only temporary. Expect a lucky winning streak in the near future.

Pink will attract lasting love.

Gemini will keep you on your toes.

Lucky Numbers: 19.24.32.36.2.21.

Scorpio: There is more to life than work, stress and money. You do not need to work so hard, as what you are striving for will arrive more easily if you give up trying. Do what is required, of course, but make more time for your personal life and do not take your work home with you. There are many ways to the top so be more open and you may be able to hitch a ride! Give up control issues – someone may buy that car for you. Do you really have to do everything on your own terms? Give love a chance, and display more trust in the Universe as life is not out to get you. A person you have misjudged misses you madly.

Red should get you going!

Aquarius is bright and breezy but quite kooky too!
Lucky Numbers: 6.26.31.4.3.22.

Sagittarius: It is a good time to propose, Sagittarius, or renew your commitments. Do not worry. Making a romantic promise does not have to rob you of your treasured freedom. In fact you will feel strangely relieved if you take the leap of faith. Follow your heart in all things and do not let logic mess up your natural instincts. A decision to travel is fortuitous – buy a lottery ticket in the country you visit. Sale of a property is guaranteed if you make a decision and follow it through. An impressive work offer can be trusted. Your destiny has some surprises in store!
Green for financial luck.
Taurus is patiently waiting in the wings.
Lucky Numbers: 26.2.8.12.17.27.

Capricorn: Disappointment with a business venture can be turned around if you cut your losses. Consider going back into employment rather than put yourself on the line financially. If unemployed, work offers are forthcoming – take a job offering in-house training. Make positive judgements within relationships, and communication may move up a notch. It is time to forgive and forget so stop tying yourself up in knots. Work abroad looks good and is worth making the relevant sacrifices for. Base lottery numbers around the birthdates of distant or absent relatives.
Use dark blue for deep peace.
Pisces knows more than you – for once.
Lucky Numbers: 16.8.21.11.22.33.

Aquarius: Try not to feel hard done by, as your circumstances are better than you appreciate. Everything is in hand and will work out not necessarily as you expect, but perfectly none the less. A new vehicle is a good investment for a business venture, and watch out for the mechanical failure of an old family car. Approach contracts with caution. Be careful of hidden agendas at work. Make sure that you get justice this week and do not tolerate fools. Personal space will breathe new life into a relationship. Romance is on the way if you want it.

Silver enhances femininity and finances.

Cancer is moving and eloquent.

Lucky Numbers: 23.21.9.6.3.40.

Pisces: A planned pregnancy will work out very well for everyone concerned. Do not grieve family losses forever or you will rob yourself of life's joy. Smile and the world will smile back! Cynicism and bitterness do not become you, so do not get stuck in sticky emotions. Life is set to turn around in your favour but it is important to remain focused in each moment. Fresh air, sunshine, and flowers are important natural remedies that you should get more of. Appreciate the beauty of simplicity and detox yourself of any residue negativity. Mischief and the joys of spring are nearer than you think!

Reds and pinks attract a mate and passionate encounters.

Sagittarius is spicy fun.

Lucky Numbers: 33.6.42.12.4.22.

Aries: Wake up Aries. You are being taken for a fool by

someone close to your heart! Proud and determined as you may be, sometimes admitting defeat is the lesser of two evils. Peace of mind will be a deserved reward if you can find the courage to stand up for yourself, despite the complications. Stand in your own power and remember it is not in your nature to be floored by anything. New status symbols are on the way and material benefits are guaranteed. Persist with a work plan even though it is not practical, as it will win you favours and admiration.

Magenta brings Divine love into everyday life.

Libra is balance – sometimes!

Lucky Numbers: 4.25.32.41.5.2.

GEMINI Time:
May 22nd – June 22nd

WEEK TWENTY-ONE
May 21st - May 27th

Gemini: Do stop battling against the inevitable especially as it is staring you in the face this week. Take time to rise above personal insecurities and make sure you think before you speak or you will alienate a loved one. Finances will be corrected if you trust normal procedure and suspend judgement until the autumn. Exercise patience in matters dear to your heart. You will come good at the right time. So don't force anything along. Await opportunities, for they are hovering and imminent. But you must NOT upset the balance of things by being too hasty.

Green to support finances.

Libra will be magnanimous at just the right time.

Lucky Numbers: 2.34.37.42.33.21.

Cancer: An unexpected injection of cash could see you heading for the hills, but make sure that you tie up the loose ends before you go! Work uncertainty should be sorted by the end of the month so you can take time out to relax. Check documents relating to a vehicle, and legal matters will be settled in your favour. Do not allow your stubborn streak to jeopardise a special relationship. Go and cool off rather than risk confrontation that will backfire on you.

Blue to calm you down.

Capricorn could prove difficult.

Lucky Numbers: 14.27.32.39.23.16

Leo: I've told you this before, Leo. You need to work on your fitness and get into shape for the summer! Do not laze around feeling sorry for yourself but get busy and life will automatically turn around. It certainly will not oblige unless you exercise that leap of faith. Work contracts abroad and a romantic union are part of destiny's plan. But things are not going to fall into your lap. Stop feeling hard done by and expect the best.

Red will fire you up.

Gemini is a breeze.

Lucky Numbers: 26.4.33.41.22.1.

Virgo: Quite unusually someone has succeeded in pulling

the wool over your eyes. If you gave your heart away to the wrong person, do not waste any more energy on them. No one should be allowed to damage your self-esteem in that way so make sure it doesn't happen again. Pregnancy and romance are on the horizon possibly in that order, so do be careful out there! Finances linked to a Taurean look promising and investment in property is fortuitous. Stop going to other people for advice when you know the answers already!

Yellow for the sunny times ahead.

Aries has some insights – listen carefully.

Lucky Numbers: 3.12.30.29.14.24.

Libra: Draw upon family support if you are feeling emotionally challenged. You can rise above grief and stress, so keep your head held high and be determined. A work offer that looked promising may fall through unexpectedly. Please remember that time-worn phrase 'what's for you won't go by you'! Try to remain objective and neutral in emotive situations, as victory is yours if you keep a cool head. New love interest is worth waiting for.

Pink for unconditional self-acceptance.

Aquarius may have good advice, but make up your own mind.

Lucky Numbers: 19.24.29.32.33.14.

Scorpio: It might be timely to review your priorities. Are you focusing upon finances, work and success at the expense of loved ones? Security is important but so are love, sex and romance. How true to yourself are you being when you neglect these! Follow your instincts and give someone special a listening ear. A lot of carrots have been dangled in front of you and you have been forced to make a judgement prematurely. Make sure you do not lose one of the most important contacts you are likely to make.

Black to attract a mate.

Pisces is all over the place in the nicest possible way!

Lucky Numbers: 24.26.31.6.22.11.

Sagittarius: Imminent work or travel abroad may put a relationship under stress but the contract is important. Loved ones will benefit from some independence and what seems like a pain will turn into something positive for everyone. Passionate encounters are likely and your powers of attraction strong, so take your pick! Purchase of a property is worthwhile and recognition with added status is winging your way. Take time out to help someone who needs your help.

Orange brings in joy.

Virgo is mysterious – surprisingly.

Lucky Numbers: 21.15.35.41.23.14.

Capricorn: An unavoidable transition is underway that will bring you to a better place, and more self-confidence will be yours as a result. Leave personal difficulties to one side whilst you focus upon an important work project. A summer wedding may not go quite to plan so prepare for the unexpected. Honeymoons and holidays to exotic locations are a great idea. Watch out for someone manipulative and sneaky as they have an unspoken agenda, which could scupper your plans.

Purple for spiritual dignity.
Aries will fire you up, if you allow it.
Lucky Numbers: 4.34.27.43.26.11.

Aquarius: Do not allow insecurities that have their roots in the distant past to mess up the present. Make sure that you are direct and honest to those who are dependent on you. Expect things to move very quickly as this is not a time to sit back complacently on your laurels! Be on the alert for atypical behaviour in loved ones and use your antennae to work out what's wrong. A medical check-up is timely for a niggling health complaint. Love is in the air but do not take anything for granted.
Pale blue for tranquillity.
Gemini needs patient handling.
Lucky Numbers: 3.27.33.16.23.41.

Pisces: Try to put hurt and disappointment behind you, as you need to be ready to take a chance in love. Do not expect the past to repeat its patterns, as negative expectations will not help. Victory is yours if you can lose the storm cloud brewing overhead. It is your own creation so let the rain fall and shed tears if necessary so that you can move forward refreshed. An important career decision will be made soon but a few things have to happen first. A romantic encounter beckons which you should embrace, never mind all the questions!
Use magenta for deep protection and grounding.
Taurus is special.
Lucky Numbers: 22.23.34.42.1.11.

Aries: It is OK to admit defeat sometimes and you cannot always be expected to soldier on regardless. Move forward at this point to preserve your dignity and reputation or you will be made to look rather foolish by someone you trusted. Pregnancy and creativity are heightened possibilities and sensational news will knock you for six! You need the protection of the heavens at the moment so ask and you shall receive. An offer to travel should be accepted. Give yourself more priority and stop trying to accommodate everybody. Gold will attract heaven's riches.

Cancer is really connected.

Lucky Numbers: 23.27.42.10.3.21.

Taurus: You may need to extricate yourself legally from a sticky situation. Leave behind frustration and anger, as it is not doing you any favours. Everything is not as it seems in your life and don't you know it! Perhaps it is time to reveal yourself and let the truth be told. Honesty in relationships is essential to future happiness. Work may jog along while you reassess priorities. Go with the flow but not to the point where you risk losing everything. Pre-emptive measures will retrieve precarious situations. Money is the least of your worries.

Browns keep your feet on the ground.

Fellow earth signs can help you.

Lucky Numbers: 11.17.19.24.32.4.

WEEK TWENTY-TWO
May 28th - June 3rd

Gemini: This week should heal emotional wounds so plaster up those love rifts and kiss everything better! Single Geminis can expect a major romantic connection to materialise soon. Keep communication clear on all fronts this week. Do not allow misunderstandings to sabotage plans. Investments and finances will turn in your favour. Bide your time with important issues. Don't be too hasty, for this won't do you any favours. Life has a destiny plan for you. Look forward to how things will manifest and enjoy the journey. Green for money.

Capricorn is very wise, but may have an agenda.

Lucky Numbers: 24.33.12.6.17.18.

Cancer: Be careful that an earth sign does not seduce your partner right under your nose! Play it cool and you will win out against the odds. Certain work projects may struggle to make headway, but stay committed to them nonetheless. Documents that set you free are worth signing. Finances will balance satisfactorily if you accept that new job offer. Destiny has an interesting sense of irony this week, so wear a smile at all times.

Blue for calm.

Virgo is holding you suspended in mid-air – interesting!

Lucky Numbers: 32.14.2.34.27.3.

Leo: Give romance priority over work this week or you could end up regretting your stupidity. Offers and contracts look very positive, so trust your instincts and go right ahead. The sun is shining upon major financial transactions. A trip abroad is really important for your equilibrium and sanity, so book those tickets. Do not remain stuck in the past. It is necessary to leave something behind – you know what I mean!

Orange boosts vitality.

Gemini is very funny, but you must take them seriously too.

Lucky Numbers: 42.13.23.41.5.27.

Virgo: Not everything is as it appears in the lives of Virgoans at the moment. There is intrigue, gossip and potential scandal on the horizon, so be careful out there! A love wish will be granted and the connection is controversial but unavoidable. Do remember that love is not necessarily sensible! Put travel plans on hold for the moment and it is good to de-stress and de-clutter your life in preparation for what lies ahead.

Red attracts passion.

Taurus is just not interested – move on.

Lucky Numbers: 33.14.35.27.38.2.

Libra: Independence is a good thing, but make sure the baby is not thrown out with the bathwater when it comes to romance. Regardless of work commitments love will catch you out and leave you gasping for more! A move of house will be very positive, never mind the annoying delays. Finances look a bit 'ropy' but stop being anxious about long term security as that is guaranteed. Do not allow worries that have their roots in the past to sabotage the present. It is time to move on.

Yellow for clarity.

Aries is a feisty handful.

Lucky Numbers: 22.31.41.21.13.4.

Scorpio: If things are not developing as quickly as you would like, show determination, for your efforts will bring their own reward. Romantically you may be at sixes and sevens! Perhaps it is time to make a move you have put off for the wrong reasons. Stop messing with your own heart never mind everyone else's. Keep your eye on a work offer with an American link, as it may not be what it seems. Try not to be overly fussy this week. You will have to accept that there are some things you cannot control and love is one of them!

Black for mystery.

Taurus is practical.

Lucky Numbers: 31.6.16.27.34.4.

Sagittarius: Perhaps it is time to review a relationship. Have you delayed a run down the aisle? If so, do some serious thinking about your commitments and priorities. Be honest and follow your heart and do not create a bigger mess for all concerned. A contract should come good, and financial dealings are blessed. Build upon your current success and your career will benefit. Keep a close watch over someone you do not trust. Relax in the sun if possible.

Lilac for psychic ability

Gemini is to be considered.

Lucky Numbers: 29.33.35.26.17.31.

Capricorn: Watch your integrity, as it is quite possible that indiscretions will come back to haunt you. Honesty is the best policy in all matters this week. Leave the past behind and move forward towards greater clarity and peace of mind. A move to a new location may be the best way to claim a fresh start. Be prepared for a jolt re finances and work but be confident that change is good. Love will warm your heart and the support of friends is comforting.

Turquoise assists creativity.

Virgo is a hot contender.

Lucky Numbers: 16.14.35.22.33.1.

Aquarius: There may be some disillusionment over finances. But do not despair, as there is money to be made through property and intelligent investment. A marriage is blessed and there is a pregnancy on the way. For negative relationships this is a wake-up call. It is time to leave stress and trauma behind. Single Aquarians should take a chance on love and make that phone call. Past patterns will not repeat. Be brave and open that heart!

Deep blue brings peace.

Taurus will check you out.

Lucky Numbers: 21.4.25.33.17.29.

Pisces: It may be time to get practical and leave certain dreams to one side. Think of your long-term happiness and security above all things. Do not go back to something you have decided to leave behind for good reasons. Stress regarding money and work will clear up if you focus on the task in front of you. Acceptance of the way things are is a realistic way to approach the future. A new relationship will bring love, excitement and happy memories.

Brilliant blue boosts inspiration.

Aries will solve a mystery.

Lucky Numbers: 14.35.26.37.18.39.

Aries: You may be laughing all the way to the bank in the very near future. Sure take the relevant party to the cleaners if it makes you feel better, but do also accept this opportunity to move forward in a positive way. Lose any resentment and frustration and reserve judgement with certain issues until you know the truth. A property matter will be settled and a change of scene looks like a good idea. If a relationship is at an end, be assured that it is for the best. Love is in the air in a new unexpected way.

Pink for unconditional support.

Leo is a good companion.

Lucky Numbers: 40.21.22.23.11.7.

Taurus: If your heart is broken, Taurus, it is your responsibility to mend it. You know where the truth lies and sometimes love requires us to be brave and controversial. Make a statement and live up to it. A trip abroad will go really well and work-related matters sort themselves out. Victory is yours on all fronts if you give someone the benefit of the doubt. There may be news shortly that rocks your world. Brace yourself for the rest of your life, as major change is afoot.

Browns to earth you.

Libra provides an interesting insight.

Lucky Numbers: 6.14.23.35.26.1.

WEEK TWENTY-THREE
June 4th - June 10th

Gemini: You are looking good and the gift of the blarney is in full flow. Expect to see an old face from the past unexpectedly. Your energies are flying at the moment so make the most of extra oomph. Don't be afraid to ask for professional help with an important matter. Use witty banter to champion a cause. You can get most people on side without much bother. Kiss the Blarney Stone and don't be afraid to come on strong. Guard against deviant behaviour, but draw on alternative techniques to lay people open to your charms. Be careful not to over-stress your system. A detox programme is in order on many levels. Monitor your integrity – may the best man/woman win! It is inadvisable to hover because of someone else's success. Leeches fall off once they have gorged themselves. So avoid vampire behaviour and make your own splash!

Violet brings spiritual inspiration.

Scorpio is deep and intense.

Lucky Numbers: 2.32.4.23.16.8.

Cancer: Breathe a sigh of relief. Your most recent challenges will soon disperse. Take this opportunity to get on with paperwork and important communication. Travel will no longer phase you, so book that holiday. There is a new fresh start in the air but you must keep your secrets closely guarded. People are receptive to you. Make the most of this but avoid confrontation over controversial issues. Rise above a sense of feeling hard done by as everything will work out

just fine in the long term.
Blue brings peace of mind.
Sagittarius is fun.
Lucky Numbers: 24.33.30.15.16.3.

Leo: This is the optimum week for travel linked to work or romance. Your vitality is high so play this to your advantage in career matters. If you are signing important documents, make sure that you understand future commitments that arise from your decision. Virgos and Geminis should be willing to extend favours without strings attached! Move forward at last and rectify stuck financial situations. A great time to plan weddings and all things romantic. Be inspired by the good vibes floating in the ether, and steer clear of toxic people.
Red for grounding and survival issues.
Scorpio has it all.
Lucky Numbers: 18.4.35.27.38.11.

Virgo: You will be attracting admiring glances at the moment. Just smile and lap up the attention rather than put your foot in it by opening your mouth! Avoid awkward people and watch for clumsiness in particular this week. Reaching a compromise in emotive situations is possible, so do not lose heart. Use your powers of communication to the full at the beginning of the week, and bingo! Your patience will be rewarded. Be patient with love complications.
Pink for unconditional love.
Fellow Virgo may be competitive.
Lucky Numbers: 8.14.23.16.27.39.

Libra: Bite your tongue this week rather than be too hasty to point out injustice. Those concerned will address the difficulties in their own way. You need variety and stimulation so take to the road or enjoy the company of people who interest you. Romance looks favourable, but keep expectations realistic. Be a good friend rather than ruin something positive with demands. Finances will come good but you need to make an effort to achieve your ambitions.

Green for an open heart.

Gemini will see the humour in most things.

Lucky Numbers: 40.2.33.21.4.5.

Scorpio: Pace yourself this week and take everything slowly and steadily, especially if your energies are at low ebb. It is necessary to leave the past behind to find peace of mind. A romantic choice is imminent so prepare to be swept off your feet and into a haystack or down the aisle! Stop doing battle in your head over the things you cannot control. Lighten up and have more fun. You can reach a compromise with someone important if you negotiate carefully.

Black for protection.

Capricorn is special, but controlling.

Lucky Numbers: 31.4.35.6.16.27.

Sagittarius: Relax and enjoy the sun, especially if you are sluggish like the moon at the moment – by the end of the week things look more hectic. You are able to influence loved ones, and those in authority will want your perspective amidst controversy. Expansive horizons beckon so if you can't fly to the moon at least aim for the skies! Property issues settle and a move of house will go well. News of a pregnancy will bring a smile or a scowl to your face depending on your disposition!

Lilac transmutes negative energy.

Taurus is a performer.

Lucky Numbers: 23.14.33.25.16.7.

Capricorn: The blocked energy has turned about, so you may relax and sign important documents or sort contracts with ease. You have definite work choices to make. Follow your instincts and aim to manifest long-held ambitions. Focus and believe that dreams come true because for Capricorn they surely will! Be philosophical about financial delays and trust fellow earth signs with business decisions. Try not to be too perfectionist if hosting an event. Detach yourself and enjoy life's twists of fate – all will be well.

Turquoise assists creativity.

Virgo is loyal.

Lucky Numbers: 27.14.35.26.37.2.

Aquarius: Please do consider the facts of a situation before you make a premature judgement! It may be time to admit defeat in one situation. You are not always right so eat humble pie if necessary and move onto the next thing. Family life brings contentment and support. If there is a legal matter to clarify go right ahead now retrograde Mercury is no longer sabotaging settlements. Personal disillusionment will evaporate if you get practical and focus upon the present moment.

Yellow to de-stress you.

Fellow Aquarius will see through you.
Lucky Numbers: 29.14.35.26.7.9.

Pisces: What was once an interest or hobby may now become a way to earn your bread and butter! Be careful whom you trust this week and with the new moon in Gemini make sure communication is constructive and clear. An Aquarian is backwards about coming forwards because of depression. Be patient, and romantic answers will bring natural harmony into your life. Pregnancy is a strong possibility this summer. Integrate the past into the present for the best results.

Aqua for invigorating freshness.

Breathe deep with fellow Pisces.
Lucky Numbers: 21.14.35.26.1.5.

Aries: Do not neglect a long-term relationship or you will pay the price. Be careful you are not being altruistic for personal reasons. Honesty and manipulation sometimes go hand in hand so keep your eyes peeled. Leave the past behind and focus on the future. It is too late to control the momentum of events, so ride the rollercoaster with glee. Your energies should be high but a different and surprising insight will shake you up. Expect change on all fronts. Gold for wisdom and to support fear.

Gemini may need looking after.
Lucky Numbers: 41.32.14.15.28.40.

Taurus: Fresh fields and pastures new beckon the old Bull throughout the summer, so graze away and decide where you want to settle. Colleagues and associates are very supportive and you can make great strides towards a personal goal. Socially you are on form but be careful amidst family dissension.You are in demand and romantically things are set to get passionate and intense. A shock is in the air but you will realise it is meant to put you on a track you have avoided. Exciting times!

Green for an open heart.

Virgo holds deep feelings – so do you!

Lucky Numbers: 6.27.38.33.14.2.

WEEK TWENTY-FOUR
June 11th - June 17th

Gemini: This should be a positive time for Gemini. Avoid confrontation and make the most of good vibes. Financial circumstances will improve but delay signing a contract until you have tied up loose ends. Move forward and leave the past behind, as the road ahead looks clear. Be independent and strong in all things. Do stop worrying! Inner tension will naturally disperse if you adopt a positive attitude. That is about all it will take to provide the release of energy needed to turn things around in your favour!

Wear blue to enhance your desirability.

Leo is a challenge, but nice with it.

Lucky Numbers: 23.4.15.17.38.20.

Cancer: Make intelligent love moves and give peace a chance. A major about-turn will bring peace into your life so be careful to forgive and forget. Do not bear a grudge or allow resentments to fester. Social events will be lively and it is important to accept invitations. Not all work projects will lead to the success you wish for. If others are dependent on you, be honest and do not give false hope. Get medical niggles checked by your doctor.

Wear green to attract good fortune.

Fellow Cancer understands.

Lucky Numbers: 10.20.30.40.16.27.

Leo: Avoid personal stress based on low self-esteem and insecurity, and you must not beat yourself up about the past. You are a generous spirit so be careful that 'chancers' do not pull the wool over your eyes! Follow your instincts if in doubt. Good luck links you with America this week and travel plans run smoothly. Keep a lottery ticket in something silver, and base numbers upon your most valued relationships. Leave complicated behaviour and immaturity to one side.

Silver for finances.

Virgo is very canny.

Lucky Numbers: 29.24.15.36.27.4.

Virgo: Be aware that you inspire professional jealousy and watch out for agendas at work. Someone important does not believe in you but don't despair as you will have the last laugh. By the end of the summer you will leave many people gawping in wonder! Trust yourself and confide only in the people who have your best interests at heart. Be meticulous with finances and pay attention to the detail of forms and contracts. Everything will work out better than you expect.

Red attracts passion to spice up your life!

Gemini will keep you on your toes.

Lucky Numbers: 14.17.19.24.32.36.

Libra: A long deserved rest is in order, so kick back and switch off the phone.

Passion, proposals and property make for an interesting summer. Take time to look good and give yourself centre stage for a change. Be confident about recent decisions and do not dither any longer in matters of the heart. Lose the sense of feeling hard done by. Really, don't you know which side your bread is buttered! Relax and enjoy life. Wear pink for self-esteem.

Yellow will help you de-stress.

Aquarius passes judgement.

Lucky Numbers: 11.13.14.25.36.17.

Scorpio: Does an age difference in a love affair matter as much as you think it does? Stop being so cautious and follow your heart. Life is not always logical, nor can you control the chemistry between two people. The best things have no rhyme or reason attached to them, so let go and enjoy! Leave restrictive behaviour to one side and do not allow yourself to be dictated to. Work stress should pass and a time of leisure is well deserved.

Wear black to attract – and keep.

Pisces gets interesting.

Lucky Numbers: 1.7.11.23.35.26.

Sagittarius: Stop all those arguments in your head about things that are really inconsequential. Put issues in perspective and make a list of priorities. You do have a lot to get done and several people have high expectations. Learn to be a bit more selfish and say 'no' once in a while. Be cautious regarding contracts until you are satisfied all angles are covered. Make time for love and enjoy romantic attention. White for purity of mind and heart.

Green will open your heart.

Leo is insightful.

Lucky Numbers: 23.14.35.26.37.4.

Capricorn: Make a decision to leave stress and upset well and truly in the past. Equilibrium and balance are key words this week, so do not let anyone knock you off-centre. Finances and contracts look good and there is the possibility of a win if you play your cards right! A loved one is missing you and needs renewed contact. Don't be too proud in affairs of the heart – be willing to forgive. A medical procedure is destined to go well and give the patient a new lease of life.

Violet for healing.

Taurus hits the nail on the head.

Lucky Numbers: 31.24.35.26.3.4.

Aquarius: You won't know whether to laugh or cry at life's irony this week, so maybe try both! A ferry journey or trip abroad will go swimmingly. A financial shock on the home front is destined to work out for the best. Do not wallow in disillusionment or feel defeated, as your determination will pay off eventually. Victory is yours but it is important not to be complacent or act ahead of time. Family life looks settled and harmonious.

Sky blue for vision.

Libra is impartial and wise.

Lucky Numbers: 25.19.21.3.26.1.

Pisces: It is a great time to feather your nest and wield a paintbrush to good effect. Finances and DIY go hand in hand this week. A breathing space in affairs of the heart will work to your advantage. Do not be phased by stress, as making definite decisions is certain to ease any complex situation. Peace of mind is yours if you leave the past behind and allow yourself to prosper. Gentle exercise will benefit you and a business plan has potential.

Yellow to lift your spirits.

Virgo is all you need.

Lucky Numbers: 24.16.37.4.8.18.

Aries: Move on and party is my advice for this week! You have not had an easy time lately and a loved one is running rings around you. Clarity is needed and an honest heart-to-heart. Your life is in transition and there is major change in the air. Destiny has plenty up its sleeve for you and you should enjoy the challenges winging your way. There is no way events can defeat you, so chin up and smile. Finances are secure but a personal project may need a different approach.

Gold will inspire riches.

Taurus wants to move on.

Lucky Numbers: 14.23.5.16.27.3.

Taurus: When you have stopped saving the world, perhaps you will find time to save yourself! Seriously, do stop running around and call a halt to altruism for just a minute. If you can manage this, the noise in your own head may deafen you. Do stop being an ostrich and tackle your personal problems effectively this week. Rumours abound but just ignore them – no one knows the truth anyway. Discretion and silence are the best policy, as you are not obliged to explain yourself.

Gold assists wisdom.

Virgo is unnerving.

Lucky Numbers: 3.33.30.4.6.31.

WEEK TWENTY-FIVE
June 18th - June 24th

Cancer: Try not to be over-anxious or disillusioned about a personal situation. Learn to recognise when something is not happening and detach from it emotionally. Weigh up your options and make sensible decisions. Time and energy is one thing: peace and wisdom another - do not commit to something that won't work. Use all the resources you have at your disposal to make intelligent moves. Sideways motion is second nature to you, so try some lateral thinking!

Use magenta for discernment.

Aries is not great in the mix.

Lucky Numbers: 16.27.38.9.2.33.

Leo: If you are in a rut it is time to get things moving. It is important to take action rather than let a situation fester. Only if you leave the past behind can you walk towards permanent peace of mind. Promotion and recognition at work are highly likely. Spend quality moments with loved ones and speak up in the name of love. Frustrated communications should ease, but you need to make a move rather than wait politely.

Turquoise boosts creativity.

Taurus are kidding themselves.

Lucky Numbers: 32.14.35.4.22.11.

Virgo: You are stronger than you know and can rise above emotional hurt and disappointment. More than one person has deceived you and out of the goodness of your heart you gave them the benefit of the doubt. Take control of your own life, as you do not need the advice of other people to make progress. Things go wrong if you stop trusting yourself and hand your personal power over to other people. Victory is yours, so channel your own creativity into the future and things will come about.

Pink for unconditional self-respect.

Pisces is inspirational.

Lucky Numbers: 12.34.25.38.1.2.

Libra: Expect a delay financially as work takes a while to reap its rewards. Be independent and ignore insecurities within complicated relationships. Guard against pregnancy at the moment if it is not part of your game plan. Family links overseas look positive and the return of someone unexpected forms part of your destiny. A delayed message will reach you and do give a partner the benefit of the doubt. Keep a marriage ceremony straightforward. Red assists passionate energy.

Gemini will bring a different perspective.

Lucky Numbers: 34.24.13.25.3.4.

Scorpio: If you have had to put your love life on hold, don't worry! What transpires this summer will more than compensate. Persist with work and try to leave stress behind. Be careful with money and think long-term regarding investments and cash return. Free up your energies and leave the past behind. Do not give any time to people who drain you or who leave you uninspired. Move onwards and upwards. Blue for peace and calm.

Cancer is a calming influence.

Lucky Numbers: 42.14.25.36.37.28.

Sagittarius: There is fire in your belly - hopefully for passionate reasons rather than because of acidity! Seriously, check out both your love life and your diet this week. You will not regret a new approach to life so be positive and sort things out. Exercise ambition and determination to succeed in your career. Transition time is upon you so expect change on the home front and amongst your circle of friends. Purple for serenity.

Fellow Sagittarius is a philosopher.

Lucky Numbers: 33.4.30.31.16.41.

Capricorn: Consider a change of direction and assess where you are headed at this point. Be assured that you would not be disappointed with pastures new. Life can be magical so do not place restrictions upon yourself. Trust the flow and expect miracles. But there is a catch – you need to relinquish control and surrender everything to Higher will. Pale blue to connect with Divine Love.

Virgo is streets ahead of the game.

Lucky Numbers: 4.14.40.41.25.33.

Aquarius: You might need to pull a few tricks out of the bag this week! Think on your feet to good effect or you may find yourself being hauled over the coals for something. Take a well-deserved rest but make sure you have a clear conscience first. Do not be impatient with finances. It is important to remember that there is a rhyme and a reason for everything. Life is serving you up with a riddle – solve it! Green for space.

Taurus connects from the heart.

Lucky Numbers: 41.21.33.24.15.25.

Pisces: Be content with what you have. If things are moving slowly, you can be sure that there is good reason. Never mind the planets! Go after what you want for a change and expect the best outcome. Do not undermine something before it has even begun. Fish don't have feet, but keep them on the ground anyway! Pucker up those lips, as you will be smooching to good effect before too long. Let the sun shine on your life.

Yellow for bright spirits.

Taurus may never forget.

Lucky Numbers: 2.19.30.20.40.16.

Aries: Wear a smile only if you mean it and do be very honest this week with your emotions. Family life is blessed so appreciate the good things however they pan out. Build upon a firm foundation but do not try to hold onto what is no longer yours. Extensions to property may be a hassle but worth it nonetheless. Cut a big slice of cake and eat it too, but forget the second helping. Your waist may be swelling for other reasons before too long!

Orange boosts vibrancy.

Gemini engages you.

Lucky Numbers: 23.14.33.2.16.21.

Taurus: Marriage and commitment are in the air for single Taureans, but there is legal hassle for those who are spoken for. Life-changing events are imminent. Give yourself a pat on the back for a job well done. Recognition is on the way so stop undermining your achievements to date. Be watchful of your feelings and be aware that emotional infidelity is just as damaging as a physical fling. What you are looking for lies within you.

Red to rouse you.

Scorpio can match you every step of the way.

Lucky Numbers: 34.22.31.24.25.8.

Gemini: A time of ambiguity and financial uncertainty will soon end. Keep up the good work and be vigilant. Victory is yours if you make clever connections. Remember that there are no mistakes, and stop beating yourself up over apparent failures. Get a grip of the good things in your life and clear out the debris. De-clutter your environment and

do not waste time on time–wasters!
Silver will bring financial luck.
Cancer inspires the light of the moon to get busy.
Lucky Numbers: 35.34.21.6.31.7.

WEEK TWENTY-SIX
June 25th – July 1st

Cancer: Expect your entrepreneurial skills to be challenged
this week. You may feel out of your depth or pushed to the
limit in a work situation. Hang in there! If you weather the
storm brewing overhead, a fresh breeze will liven your step
in the weeks to come. Leave the past behind and change a
situation that no longer works. Plum the depths of your
imagination. All the answers you need lie within your
unconscious. Learn to access the intuitions you need from a
deeper level.
Blue for calm.
Capricorn is not really good for you.
Lucky Numbers: 26.27.28.31.2.4.

Leo: There may be high jinks over a legal or financial matter. Stay balanced and keep your feet on the ground. Follow
your instincts in all things this week and honour your generous heart. Be careful over a change of job and check the
small print on all contracts. Surrender control issues. Trust in
the bigger picture as events have a special momentum. Love
will warm the cockles of your heart!
Red boosts.

Sagittarius gets you going.
Lucky Numbers: 32.14.33.25.11.2.

Virgo: Keep an eye on the clock this week. You need to run punctually and efficiently to make the best of good opportunities. Do not be afraid to be powerful! The rest of the world can watch and wonder as the magic unfolds. The Universe reflects back to you what you expect, so make sure you do not undermine your own progress. Get down to business with a loved one and transcend emotional hurt.
Pink for unconditional acceptance.
Taurus hits the spot – finally!
Lucky Numbers: 24.25.34.6.16.37

Libra: Stop walking around with your nose in the air as you might miss something important! Uncertainty and disillusionment in your working life will lift in the long-term. You need to exercise trust at this point and invest your time in good things. Do not tolerate fools gladly, and walk away from negativity. If you use creative energy to boost your ego, you can expect it to backfire. So stay calm and cool and the Universe will provide.
Orange boosts joyful activity.
Leo has it in spades.
Lucky Numbers: 23.4.26.27.18.9.

Scorpio: Things look great, Scorpio, but don't get too big for them boots! You are on track for major success and happiness. Give love a chance and fit romance into your schedule, or you will regret a lost chance. Destiny has more in store than you bargained for and it will knock the socks off you! Be patient re finances as you will be rich in every way before too long. Sex is good – remember?

Black to seduce and smile a lot for luck!

Pisces may be pushing for answers too.

Lucky Numbers: 23.14.15.26.17.18.

Sagittarius: If you are deceiving a loved one – stop! And if you are deceiving yourself about something, stop even quicker. Peace of mind is yours if you reach out and grab it, but you have to have integrity. Romance and contentment are a breath away so trust the opportunity and trust life. Lose the cynicism and all will be well. Make a clever financial judgement and prosperity is guaranteed.

Violet for head stuff.

Cancer gets under your skin.

Lucky Numbers: 40.16.27.28.9.19.

Capricorn: Expect love to zap you between the eyes very shortly! But remember love is all around us in many guises so do not judge situations prematurely. Draw on your tenacity and resilience this week to fend off competitors. No need to get nasty but be alert to the agendas of others. Express your creativity and foster generosity of spirit as life will reflect back to you what you put out.

Green for personal space.

Aries may be helpful, finally!

Lucky Numbers: 44.11.23.15.16.27.

Aquarius: Try to live and let live a little this week. That does not mean you have to accept any nonsense but it does mean you need to show kindness and empathy where it is needed. Finances look very positive and your strength will bring things about. Focus upon where you want to be and do not allow doubt to undermine your resolve. Spice things up a bit and hit the town for a curry!

White for clarity.

Gemini gets lively and inspires you.

Lucky Numbers: 42.13.16.17.38.5.

Pisces: Another sign that can expect love to manifest very soon. Keep your eyes peeled and never say never! That feeling of disappointment will pass and you do not have to feel hard done by for much longer. Pisceans are very challenged at the moment so batten down the hatches as the storm will pass. The skies will lift and a healing warm sun will melt your mind and heart. Sounds ominous? Not a bit of it: lie down and bask awhile!

Yellow to lift spirits.

Fellow water signs will see you through.

Lucky Numbers: 39.25.28.19.4.2.

Aries: Can money buy you love and happiness? Well maybe, but you know deep down that you need more than that. Draw upon your own resources in the future and be careful you are not being used. Protect your interests and think ahead. This is a time when you need to be smart and with it to hold onto what you have. Change and a new direction are part of your destiny so enjoy the status quo while you can.

Gold inspires wise decisions.

Fellow fire signs keep your energy levels up.

Lucky Numbers: 3.33.30.31.16.27.

Taurus: Do not feel a failure or believe that you have to prove yourself all the time. Emotional wounds will heal but be prepared to bear a few scars. These will add to your depth and interest, and enhance your ability to help people. A legal settlement is important so that you can make a fresh start. Expect a new relationship to enhance your life and to bring along more than you have at the moment. Do not be afraid of the future.

Dark red brings energy and protection.

Aries is best avoided for now.

Lucky Numbers: 10.11.21.31.4.25.

Gemini: Do you still believe in true love? Try not to get too cynical as the world still contains the magic that cynics would love to dismiss. Hang on in there, as your dreams will come around. It is important not to lose faith or be despondent. Your mind is powerful so be careful what reality you create as you just might have to experience it! Work and creativity are at your disposal so don't throw it all away.

Magenta assists grounding.

Libra is full of hot air.

Lucky Numbers: 22.11.33.16.41.20.

WEEK TWENTY-SEVEN
July 2nd - July 8th

Cancer: Take your time this week to do the right thing. If work stress is getting to you, organise a break or you run the risk of making bad decisions. Extra preparation is needed in a work project before the investment pays off. Spend quality time with family and friends and try not to get so wound up by unimportant things. Not everyone has your depth of perception and sensitivity, but please remember life does not have to be as difficult as you make it.
Violet for head stuff.
Virgo will sort out a problem.
Lucky Numbers: 32.41.35.26.27.18.

Leo: A tricky situation will at last come to an end. Do not allow yourself to be thrown off track by heartache or personal doubts. Keep centred and focused and you will successfully move through any difficulty. Be careful not to get caught out by a tempting affair, unless you want to face the music! Extra training and intelligent decisions boost your career. A legal matter may cause hassle so try to be philosophical.
Blue for peace and authority issues.
Gemini throws interesting shapes!
Lucky Numbers: 40.25.17.19.11.5.

Virgo: Try not to let a sense of feeling hard done by weigh you down. Everything will work out perfectly and much better than you expect. Take delays in your stride, as there is a very good reason why you have to wait. A big contract is in the offing and great celebration before too long. Be patient with love and do not run ahead of the natural course of events. Victory will belong to you.

Pink for compassion.

Capricorn is a great pretender.

Lucky Numbers: 36.14.27.16.25.3.

Libra: It is time to spread your wings and fly a little. Do not allow someone to dominate you. Keep your independence in all things. If you need personal space make sure of it and stop being so obliging. Learn to say no especially when energies are low. A romantic proposal is set to end disillusionment and disappointment. Trust your instincts and go for it.

Turquoise boosts creativity.

Aquarius is a visionary that sometimes mixes things up.

Lucky Numbers: 42.31.4.25.36.2.

Scorpio: If you are stuck on the horns of a dilemma, break free and claim your freedom. For some reason you are buying into manipulation. Is it worth it when you are being controlled to the point where you no longer recognise yourself? Do not sell your soul in the hope of getting somewhere. Life's riches are accessible to all not just to those who scale the heights. Make sure you do not miss the precious things. Love is more desirable than a hefty bank balance – isn't it?

Yellow for stress.

Taurus will rescue you if you are open to help.

Lucky Numbers: 24.32.33.16.15.7.

Sagittarius: A riot of colour and intense emotion should surround you this week – if not, get thee to Rio! Samba your way through difficulty in the knowledge that you are a winner. Romance is in the air and a trip up the aisle will be in order before too long. Take stock if you are already committed and count your blessings before taking action you may regret. Do not lose the run of yourself and dampen down any misplaced ardour! Work hard to boost finances.

Aqua inspires coolness.

Pisces brings romance to town.

Lucky Numbers: 4.33.34.21.15.41.

Capricorn: Control your stubborn streak! The time has come to get real. Do stop pretending things are as they should be. Tackle stress by relaxing. There is no need to get so wound up or uptight. Use your intelligence and savvy to get ahead but do not resort to devious manoeuvres. Leather and lace might spice things up a bit. Do take precautions and try not to let someone mess with your head. Be cautious in love and appreciate the good things in life. Simplicity enhances beauty so don't try too hard.

Magenta enables grounding.

Fellow earth signs offer insights.

Lucky Numbers: 34.25.26.33.6.7.

Aquarius: The planets are in alignment for a spectacular win of money. Well, maybe not, but you may at least expect the unexpected! Property matters will get the green light shortly. If you do gamble, choose numbers that have unusual significance. The obvious route is not always the correct one. Extend the hand of friendship even though you do not feel like it. You will benefit if you adopt a magnanimous attitude with a difficult person. Love is in the air though spring has sprung!

Sea green for serenity.

Gemini is wittier. Is that possible?

Lucky Numbers: 28.16.33.21.24.2.

Pisces: You might be feeling a bit of a flatfish at the moment. Connect with water to re-energise your fins. You are being challenged in many ways, so swim fast and true and you won't get caught. Life will liven up if you adopt a lighter attitude. Do not focus on the difficult things as you have every reason to be optimistic. A new business contract is sound, so trust the wheel of good fortune to spin in your favour.

Wear emerald green for a dose of Irish luck.

Cancer is comforting.

Lucky Numbers: 24.32.35.36.27.8.

Aries: Watch your fiery nature and don't jump your guns! You may believe you have sniffed out foul play, but actually the truth is even more interesting. Reserve judgement and hold that tongue. Be balanced about a legal matter and overlook personal frustration as much as possible. A whirlwind tour is on the horizon, so be prepared. You are about to be swept off your feet in more ways than one. Reputation and prosperity fall into your lap but do not be complacent.

Gold enhances wisdom and complexion.

Scorpio gets all romantic – run?

Lucky Numbers: 24.33.25.26.18.19.

Taurus: Do not delay emotional decisions for financial reasons. Your peace of mind is far more important than your bank balance. Love will win the day so there is no point in hiding your true feelings for much longer. Foster independence and healthy interaction with loved ones. Plod along for a while but recognise the boundaries of your field and ignore them at your peril. The bull should stand firm and let the storm rage around his head. Honour the glint in your eye or alternatively fall asleep for a very long time!

Browns for grounding.

Aries has an agenda.

Lucky Numbers: 41.31.26.7.18.29.

Gemini: Please do not fry your brain too much with your mobile phone! Seriously, look at the time you spend on needless communication! Sure it's the Gemini prerogative to be fiddling endlessly with keyboards of all kinds, but do reassess priorities this week. For once you may be lost for words and have to pull a few tricks out of the bag. A new approach to old problems is needed. Be patient with loved ones and please ask that person out for a drink. Politics be hanged! Follow your heart!

Red makes a change.

Capricorn is stubborn but right, no doubt.

Lucky Numbers: 4.11.33.21.40.19.

WEEK TWENTY-NINE
July 16th – July 22nd

Cancer: Cancerians should review all contracts and commitments and make deeply emotive decisions this week. Uncertainty needs to be confronted head-on. To be effective into the future you need to trust your own judgement and not waver once you have made a decision. Be careful that you do not make a premature mistake with your heart. Destiny will grant a wish. Think about what you wish for first. Be wise and circumspect. It will not benefit you to rush things through.

Sea green for homely vibes.

Libra is helpful and supportive.

Lucky Numbers: 43.16.27.34.25.18.

Leo: Finances look very promising for Leo, so invest with confidence and even expect a lucky win. Enjoy the peace that should descend and leave past difficulties behind. Weigh up all of your options and plump for the extravagant gesture, as it will pay off. A leap of faith in a work matter will come good. Be confident about travel plans and expect a property issue to settle amicably.

Yellow to connect with the sun.

Fellow Leo will warm your heart.

Lucky Numbers: 26.14.35.4.27.18.

Virgo: Stress over finances could be shifted with a move of house and change of career. However you are not one to follow the straightforward route. A challenge is more up your street and you will tackle the trickiest option with aplomb! Look after yourself more and listen to gut feelings. If you are churned up emotionally do not fret, as the end result will make sense. Be courageous and exercise trust. Magenta boosts support.

Aquarius is eccentric but wise.

Lucky Numbers: 32.14.34.25.16.7.

Libra: Is your heart light as a feather or heavy as a piece of meat? You have a choice, and a change of perception can turn everything on its head. A spring in your step and a smile on your face will make all the difference this week. Do not miss opportunities by sulking. Keep your equilibrium and do not panic over a long-term goal. Things will creep up on you if you just get on with the job in hand – so maybe watch out for the office jerk!

Turquoise boosts creativity.

Fellow air signs will elevate your soul.

Lucky Numbers: 17.14.16.19.33.23.

Scorpio: Stop dithering! There is the possibility of disappointment if you do not have the courage of your own convictions. Desist crawling to further your career, as a cooler attitude with a superior will work in your favour. Do not be afraid of a new romantic connection – the most logical route is not always the right one. Try not to be snooty or prudish in love. Where is the Scorpio dynamo this week? Go for gold and give passion a chance.

Red to rev you up.

Virgo is all that you want and need.
Lucky Numbers: 21.14.23.24.35.26.

Sagittarius: Step away from the monsters in your own head, and do not allow them to get a grip of you. It is important to lay all demons to rest this week and adopt an optimistic approach to the future. Lose the negativity and turn things around. Your destiny is in your own hands so make it a good one. Study contracts relating to a move of work or property. Sorrow will be replaced with joy over a pregnancy. The urge to get away is strong, so why not?
Lilac enables transmutation.
Virgo is out to get you!
Lucky Numbers: 24.32.4.12.13.16

Capricorn: Someone could be less than straight emotionally. They are confused so give them the benefit of the doubt for now. Distress from grief will lift, and healing is at hand. Clear the air over any deceit and be as forgiving as you possibly can. Life is good and peace is yours if you reach out and accept the things that you cannot change. Be independent and keep your own counsel with a controversial issue. Hold your head up high and be proud of your achievements to date.
Royal blue boosts peace.
Libra inspires you.
Lucky Numbers: 2.12.21.33.24.25.

Aquarius: Be careful not to place your perfectionist expectations above the needs of loved ones. Detach yourself from attachments that threaten your equilibrium and do not be drawn into a game of cat and mouse. Your fortunes are about to turn upside down in an unexpected but positive way. Calm down in the face of adversity. Acceptance of things as they are is the key. Then life can dish out the prizes.

Aqua boosts serenity.

Aries will hold things together.

Lucky Numbers: 42.29.24.15.17.28.

Pisces: You deserve a pat on the back for your composure. Many a storm has been weathered recently and you have held it together. A loving embrace to warm the heart is around the corner. Fortify your energy with strong foods and exercise. You will need added oomph to get through the next chapter. Be firm and direct with people and make sure you defend your rights. A joker will play a game and give you a laugh. You must stay flexible, as life will keep you on your toes.

Pink for softness, and unconditional love.

Taurus is grounded.

Lucky Numbers: 3.14.32.33.16.27.

Aries: Are you the cat that got the cream at the moment? Just be sure not to take anything for granted and remember that cream turns sour very readily. Leave tears and emotional distress in the past. You are a survivor who knows how to win by trying not to! Mixed feelings about travel plans will fade as soon as you make the effort. Stir the pot to keep your pet project bubbling nicely. Is a loved one acting out a role to keep you sweet?

Green for space.

Cancer is growing more independent.

Lucky Numbers: 33.30.14.25.6.2.

Taurus: Go on, Taurus! Grab the bull by the horns and take the plunge. Do not resort to the demon drink to drown out a problem. This won't go away even if you run forever in the opposite direction. Surely it is better to avoid that haunted feeling and face the truth? Finances are not important: a sense of personal completion and arrival is. Reach out and accept the inevitable or your torment is set to continue. The power is in your hands.

Violet for head stuff.

Gemini has held you in place.

Lucky Numbers: 41.14.35.26.27.1.

Gemini: Do not let work commitments scupper your chance of romance. Certain things can wait so make sure you prioritise your existence. Be aware that you do not need to win approval. Just be your good self and everything will land perfectly into your lap. Use intelligence and communication to shift the energy of controversy. Try to make peace with the past. A soul mate is shining like a beacon – open your eyes!

Lime green for tang.

Cancer will enhance your security.

Lucky Numbers: 22.19.10.30.4.23.

LEO Time:
July 24th – August 23rd

WEEK THIRTY
July 23rd - July 29th

Leo: Don't waste your time this week with time-wasters. You are on a roll creatively so do not let outside interference scupper your progress. Drive carefully around all the corners in your life and if you cannot see further than the next bend panic not! Take it easy, sit back and enjoy the ride. Make the most of your opportunities and talents. Things are not necessarily going to drop into your lap. You can improve your chances though by being receptive and willing. Prepare for a spot of jealousy as your well-earned reward lands in your lap. Red assists survival issues and grounding.

Taurus is at last ready to get on board.

Lucky Numbers: 11.9.23.34.25.16.

Virgo: An immanent decision is looming, so make sure you see the bigger picture and take everything into account. You have unusually been led astray against your better judgement. Perfectionist that you are, this is not an easy reality to accept. Self-forgiveness is vital if you are to avoid dissolving in a heap. Get down to the job of picking up the pieces, and fight to survive despite those who wish to undermine you. Silver boosts financial opportunity.

Gemini will assist you if you ask.

Lucky Numbers: 33.11.22.40.14.7.

Libra: Aren't you looking gorgeous? All power to you! A romance is looming with someone that you perceive only as a workmate. Enjoy the intrigue and merrily wind people up as they try to work out what's going on. Watch your diet. Happiness is in the air and all will be well. Do not worry about things that are past their sell-by date. Ever onwards and upwards should be your motto as you skip into the sunset with a beaming smile.

Yellow for sunny vibes.

Pisces may be a bit lost.

Lucky Numbers: 33.1.24.26.37.12.

Scorpio: For richer and poorer! Was that really in the work contract you signed? Do make sure you are not married to your work, and know when you are beginning to look ridiculous. Nothing is worth the sale of your most precious commodity. So ask Old Nick for your soul back and you can retrieve the situation before it is too late. Never live and breathe your vocation at the expense of loved ones. Temptation is on the horizon.

Black for protection.

Virgo holds you dear.

Lucky Numbers: 23.14.35.6.27.38.

Sagittarius: Your hunger for the big wide yonder may be heightened this week, as claustrophobia sets in. Take little steps towards your goals as this is more effective than jumping in with two big feet. Mellow out a bit and try to be philosophical about the changing landscape. Life has its own map to follow and we get lost if we try to find the short cuts.

Cruise on 'autopilot' for a while and see what happens.
Pale blue enhances your connection with Divine will.
Aquarius may have the advice you need.
Lucky Numbers: 33.12.14.25.16.7

Capricorn: Are you devastated by the recent turn of events or secretly smiling on the inside? Try not to gloat at other people's misfortunes, even if it is a case of 'told you so'. As the Billy Goat of the Zodiac you can be gruff at times. Gargle and clear your throat, as only plain-tempered speaking will save the day. No, that does not mean horns down and charge! Fix them with your stare by all means, but keep that voice under control. Reassess a financial venture and get your house in order.
Purple enhances a spiritual link.
Virgo is elevated.
Lucky Numbers: 36.27.18.19.10.4.

Aquarius: Try not to be complacent about a subtle victory. Be aware that you cannot impose your perceptions upon other people. Well, actually you can and very effectively, but whether you ought to or not is another question. If it is time to retire from a performance, do so gracefully. Throw caution to the wind and let the breeze catch your hair. It is time to relax and let others find their own way. Let your cares vanish on the wind and listen to the voice within.
Lilac boosts transmutation.
Libra keeps you laughing – all the way to the bank?
Lucky Numbers: 33.12.4.5.17.29.

Pisces: Give up trying so hard. You can barely please your self at the moment, never mind anyone else. Enjoy the bare bones of life and things will soon flesh up to your satisfaction. Do not chase a dream around the sky, as it is more likely to creep up on you surreptitiously if you are otherwise engaged. Take what is on offer in its entirety and stop chasing your food all over the plate! A hearty bite of something wholesome is better than the dregs of a banquet.

Hearty reds assist passion and survival.

Cancer will see you through.

Lucky Numbers: 12.24.35.26.33.7.

Aries: Socially desirable you may be but are you hurting yourself in the attempt to keep up appearances? Take stock of where you have got to and make sure your determination does not spread you too thinly. Being all things to all people is a tiring game. You need to mellow out and make measured decisions. It is a lonely view up there and you wouldn't want to fall off your perch now, would you! A few smart moves and your feet will be firmly back on *terra firma*.

Tranquil blues will help you unwind.

Libra is a good friend.

Lucky Numbers: 3.15.16.27.38.9.

Taurus: What's eating you, Taurus? Looks like you are feeling a bit hard done by and misunderstood at the moment. Bless! Seriously, do not worry and certainly do not sulk. It is not possible to control the Universe or bend it to your will – not all the time anyway! Be proud of where you have got to and be assured that you are destined to make an impact.

Things won't pan out in quite the way you expect so you are going to need a lively sense of humour to cope. Laugh at the ironic twists of fate and you will stay sane!

Berry colours for succulence.

Virgo has it covered.

Lucky Numbers: 2.15.16.33.8.40.

Gemini: Lines of communication are in full flow, so make the most of this time of creativity. Your senses are heightened and reading minds could become an amusing pastime! Have full confidence in your instincts and do not be afraid to follow apparently obscure hunches. You may get a rap on the knuckles from life but in an amusing way. If your head is in the clouds, you might as well read them while you are up there! Hints and messages abound so enjoy the heavenly view.

Light olive green for inspired feminine leadership.

Cancer is right in front of you.

Lucky Numbers: 14.3.25.17.11.18.

Cancer: Why are you scuttling sideways through life? I know you are a crab but this is getting ridiculous! Try looking at issues head-on and do not be afraid to expose yourself when you have to. Some of us like vulnerability and respect it. Your fear of predators that threaten personal security is becoming a bit extreme, *non*? Being 'crabby' your stability is vital to you but do avoid being overly complicated about it. Relaxation is the key to success – if it ain't broke, don't fix it.

Green for an open heart.

Leo loves you unconditionally.
Lucky Numbers: 1.2.3.4.16.40.

WEEK THIRTY-ONE
July 30th – August 5th

Leo: You need to be ambitious and determined to succeed. If you remain modest, philosophical and true, the rest of the world will catch up and acknowledge your talents. Emotional turmoil can be turned upside down if you lighten up and take that leap of faith. Follow through all contracts and obligations. Peace of mind is imminent – just accept it. Shine on in your own sweet way. May criticism and jealousy be water off the duck's back! Be a law unto yourself.

Yellow for sunshine.

Taurus will help – just ask!

Lucky Numbers: 18.29.14.25.35.2.

Virgo: Lose those Virgo worries and insecurities, as the wheel is about to turn in your favour. Sit back and allow fate to take a hand. At the moment you are hampering your own progress with doubt. Be careful whom you trust and protect your interests. Love is dragging its heels but good things are worth waiting for. Be self-sufficient and you will be delighted in your personal strength. Laughter lines look nicer than a furrowed brow!

Black to protect.

Capricorn may have an interesting insight. But do you

really want to hear it!
Lucky Numbers: 32.36.27.38.29.3.

Libra: Try to lose the scourge of being Libran this week –
make definite decisions. You can only sit on the fence for so
long. De-clutter your mind and living environment, to help
stop the rot. It is time for a much-needed break. Go with the
flow with matters of the heart and certainly don't force
issues. Get a medical check if you are under par. Running
on empty only works as an emergency measure. Insist on
your human rights this week, and do not allow yourself to
be used and abused.
Blue enhances peace.
Cancer is peaceful company.
Lucky Numbers: 14.31.24.15.36.7.

Scorpio: Stop acting out the role of 'loser in love', as it is
not a true reflection of your sexy spirit! You are sounding a
bit like a puppet on autopilot. Who is pulling your strings?
Dare to be defiant if someone or something has taken you
over. The current state of play doesn't suit you. Great rewards
are around the corner but you do not have to compromise
to win recognition. Love is set to wake you up and catch
you out! Don't leave things up in the air this time around.
Red enhances passion.
Pisces may be a bit wishy-washy.
Lucky Numbers: 42.16.23.17.28.9.

Sagittarius: Read Scorpio above as the same can be said for
you this week! Do get your act together and do not be taken

for a fool. Enjoy the ride you have signed up for but keep it in mind that you can jump off and abort your present destination. Take the initiative and make contact with someone special. This is not the time to be too proud. Drink more water to energise your system and avoid spicy food. Laugh at life's irony and you will live to fight another day.
Purple for dignity.
Leo has it about right.
Lucky Numbers: 40.23.12.21.5.2.

Capricorn: Peace will descend closing a matter dear to your heart. Never mind finances. You deserve that trip of a lifetime. Your plans are feasible so proceed with confidence. Put emotional upset or disturbance to one side and do not get drawn into conflict. Rising to the bait is not a great idea at this point, so keep calm and hold onto your equilibrium. Cheer someone up with an important message and surprise them with your thoughtfulness. Magnanimity brings benefits!
Royal blue enhances healing power.
Gemini is funny, but too much for you!
Lucky Numbers: 43.32.21.5.27.19.

Aquarius: Try to display more trust in friendships and your good nature will be rewarded. There are only certain things you can control. Other human beings may not be relied on to indulge your every whim. But love and emotional support are available to you. Do not allow your independent streak to isolate you. A delayed celebration is joyful and a pleasant financial surprise is imminent. Try not to worry unduly

about loved ones and let people make their own mistakes.
Lemon to counteract bitterness.
Taurus is open-hearted – don't abuse this trust.
Lucky Numbers: 7.24.33.14.15.27.

Pisces: Streamline your life, Pisces, so that you can swim freely and make headway. Give loved ones a bit more personal space and enjoy your own company. It is time now to relax after a testing episode, or several! The old is making way for the new so do not repeat past mistakes. Open your eyes and marvel at life's beauty and rhythm. Nature will remind you of her strong influence shortly, so be adaptable. Patient waiting must give way to specific action.
Pale blue for Divine intervention.
Libra is a bit mad, but funny with it.
Lucky Numbers: 5.14.33.21.6.27.

Aries: We can all tamper with the external look of our image and lives. Look within and be honest from the inside out. A sense of feeling a bit hard done by will give way to a genuinely sunny disposition. 'Survivor' is your middle name so take a bow and review what you have held together. Remember you can sew up a tear but it may be still visible on close scrutiny. But you are an excellent tailor or seamstress so perhaps only you can identify the flaw. If not for that twitching magnifying glass, I would tell you to relax permanently.
Orange boosts vibrancy.
Gemini is a live wire.
Lucky Numbers: 2.6.3.20.30.16.

Taurus: You can fool some of the people some of the time but you can't fool all of us – not even for a minute! At the moment the only person you are deceiving is you. How long will you play out the farce? Bucket-loads of forgiveness and understanding are needed. So do not hand around the peace pipe unless you mean it. A playful sense of humour and old fashioned charm will help matters, but your timing has to be good. Expect everything you touch to turn to gold as the Midas factor is in full flow.

Gold boosts riches and wisdom.

Fellow Taurus is a challenge – stay cool.

Lucky Numbers: 2.4.6.8.10.12.

Gemini: Call a halt to the conflicting voices in your head and enjoy a bit of silence. Reserve judgement on a situation and leave certain things to the hand of fate. Love finds a way through the direst trials, so have faith in that at least. Trust your sensitive antennae to steer you out of a maze of difficulty. Be practical and there is no need to lose your nerve. Prioritise your working life and shelve the things that can wait. Money delays will work out well in the long run.

Green for finances.

Cancer may be difficult.

Lucky Numbers: 4.11.31.22.34.33.

Cancer: If life is all work and no play at the moment try to redress the balance. Have a bit of fun and enjoy the mischief in the air. Romantically you will be the focus of attention so do not let it go to your head. Be realistic with a work project and do not push people too far. You will pay in the long run if you overstretch your limits. Be respectful of boundaries and scuttle under cover for protection if you need to. Try not to get too greedy and remember that short-term gain does not necessarily guarantee long-term prosperity.

Blue enables peace.

Gemini is witty and wise.

Lucky Numbers: 24.33.13.15.17.8.

WEEK THIRTY-TWO
August 6th - August 12th

Leo: Leo can expect rich pickings shortly. They are set to defy convention and win against all the odds. Your degree of success will directly reflect the degree of risk you have taken. New contracts and opportunities increase your chances of self-expression. Your creativity is in full flow, so capitalise on this.

Be proud of who you are, and what you are about to become. Some people will look for ways to trip you up. Hold onto your integrity and your hat. The rest should be a breeze!

Orange boosts vitality.

Fellow fire signs could overwhelm you.

Lucky Numbers: 1.7.4.11.23.14.

Virgo: Do not lose heart, Virgo. Your circumstances at present indicate the amount of blind trust you have put in a person. Pull yourself together and take back the reins of your life. In the long run this difficult stretch will prove to be a blessing in disguise. Try not to give into temptation, anger or resentment. Forgiveness is required so that the stress you are under does not defeat you. Smile and laugh as you have repaid your karmic debt. Grace is free and easily accessible – reach out and accept Divine help.

Pink for unconditional love.

Taurus has been very bold.

Lucky Numbers: 24.41.35.16.27.8.

Libra: Balance the scales, Libra, and maintain your equilibrium. You have made good choices recently so do not undermine them with doubt. Streamline your life and refine your existence. Be careful of the company you are keeping and stay away from negative influences. It is a time to prune, chop and clear away the debris. Give your heart some attention. Enjoy flirtations and flattery – you never know where they will lead! Sure, I do, but I will keep that secret for now . . .

Red boosts attraction.

Gemini may get you places.

Lucky Numbers: 3.6.9.20.16.7.

Scorpio: Scrub that tan off. Is it real or fake? Remember appearances can be deceiving. You might want to assess your honesty levels at the moment. Love is a seriously important part of your life so do not chase it away with silly behaviour. You are looking hot, never mind the tan. Take advantage of your good fortune, and build a worthwhile future. Do not squander opportunities or lose the run of yourself. If success goes to your head sober up with a cold shower – but remember the tan might run!

Blue enhances peaceful vibes.

Virgo will assist your equilibrium in a healing way.

Lucky Numbers: 4.35.26.17.19.40.

Sagittarius: A sense of feeling hard done by will diminish if you go with the flow. Do not battle uphill or deliberately go against popular opinion. You will have the last laugh and victory is sweeter if you don't try too hard. Take the plunge in love and make contact. Keep your secrets watertight and be careful whom you trust. No need to be paranoid though. So relax when it counts and pull a winner! You have a mischievous streak that puts the little green men to shame.

Gold for 'the pot of' and rainbow colours for luck.

Taurus may know a thing or two.

Lucky Numbers: 11.29.30.4.33.12.

Capricorn: Determination will reap you rewards in abundance, but your stubbornness may undermine things. Be careful to distinguish the difference, or mistakes will prove costly. Keep those cloven hoofs firmly on the ground and do not be tempted to gallop ahead. The natural course of events has an excellent outcome organised. So do not blow your opportunities with impatience. Love needs attention and quality time.

Purple for regal composure.

Gemini is a mentor.

Lucky Numbers: 4.28.39.41.22.11.

Aquarius: Your humanitarian nature will be in demand this week. Make sure that you offer your services in good faith. The road to hell is paved with good intentions, so assess your ability and integrity at all times. Keep things in perspective and remember that arrogance and false humility are not pretty qualities. Do not be afraid to shine, but be gracious with it. Finances pick up, so take your pick!

Green to boost love and luck.

Libra is cool but challenging.

Lucky Numbers: 21.28.39.33.1.25.

Pisces: Wriggle free of a situation that curtails your freedom is my advice to all fish! Do not get caught or tempted by attractive bait. Keep your distance until you have evidence of someone's good will. Independent action needs careful assessment – sometimes it is safer to swim with the shoal. If you are stuck in deep water, keep your head down until the tides subside. Kisses may be secret, but they are plentiful!

Turquoise boosts creativity.

Scorpio may help you get to the bottom of something.

Lucky Numbers: 40.28.19.30.42.11.

Aries: Smart action is second nature to all Aries heads, but even you may be up against it this week. Life presents a challenge that tests you to the limit. Express your passionate side rather than frustration or anger to win hearts and minds. Love is set to get hot as temper flares. Is that blind eye you are turning starting to look a bit 'squiffy'? Either get glasses with strong magnification or correct your vision. Oh, and gazing into the middle distance is not a viable alternative!

Yellow to de-stress.

Virgo will not give up.

Lucky Numbers: 14.33.26.17.19.20.

Taurus: Actor or actress you may be, but you can keep up an act only for so long. Eventually you have to step off the stage. Personal control is important to you and anything that threatens your security will get short shrift. However be aware that you may be undermining yourself by not listening to your heart. Which better protects your long-term options – honest expression of emotion or the denial of recent events? Why not actually be as brave as you have led people to believe?

Cobalt blue for protection.

Sagittarius may leave you feeling restless.

Lucky Numbers: 26.32.14.15.27.39.

Gemini: You may need to jump-start your heart this week or at least hot-wire your energy system. Try to identify the cause of tiredness or lack of vitality, then act to improve your performance. Your emotions may flip with unexpected feelings of love. Enjoy all the pleasant surprises and shocks winging your way. If your nerves are frayed by the end of the summer, at least you will have a smile on your face! Persist with creative projects and display trust re finances.

Sky blue for Divine inspiration.

Aquarius may be able to help.

Lucky Numbers: 22.33.11.4.5.6.

Cancer: If you are scuttling around in a panic, do stand still and take a deep breath! Slow down your pace a while as you do not want to burn out or get smashed. Protect your space from predators and scan the horizon for anything that may threaten your progress. However do not work against yourself by spreading your activities too thin – quality is better than quantity at this stage. Love will flock to you in many guises so be prepared.

Sea green for calm.

Libra can lift your spirits.

Lucky Numbers: 6.24.33.25.37.39.

WEEK THIRTY-THREE
August 13th - August 19th

Leo: Try not to be too demanding this week, or loved ones will rebel. Take your time over an important choice. It is best not to be in too much of a hurry. Everything will work perfectly if you relax and trust. Don't walk into a financial trap and make sure all paperwork is in order. Wear a broad grin to attract a mate – that is all you need to get lucky! A positive attitude will bring you guaranteed success in all things. Stay with it and be all you can be.

Bright colours to lift your spirits.

Sagittarius may inspire you.

Lucky Numbers: 42.13.24.25.17.8.

Virgo: Leave your workaholic tendencies to one side this week and attempt to relax. Anything could happen with affairs of the heart and probably will. You are not reading a loved one correctly because of those rose-tinted spectacles. Sure, they suit you, but I'm a bit concerned they are ruining your vision. Be understanding, forgiving and pragmatic in that order and you will get what you want. A romantic trip should take place despite your reservations. Trust me, if you give them another chance you will be happy.

Pink for unconditional love

Taurus is worth another go!

Lucky Numbers: 32.33.11.25.16.27.

Libra: Look after yourself as you are spreading everything too thinly. Life is Chocolate Spread not Bovril! Spare us all the pernickety behaviour, and enjoy. A little indulgence goes a long way. Lose all guilt. Never mind what you should be doing, it's time to live a little. Show mercy to someone who has annoyed you and let bygones be bygones. Make sure you are not burning yourself out with internal stress. If you can't think clearly, don't think at all! Have courage in matters of the heart.

Blue assists peace.

Fellow Libra will help keep you balanced.

Lucky Numbers: 12.34.25.16.27.4.

Scorpio: Why are you leaving us all dangling? The suspense is killing me! I know- it's your only option . . . You sure about that now? Seriously do review your behaviour and be more up-front about your intentions. You do not need to put on an act to keep things sweet – be yourself and the rest of us can like it or lump it! Finances may be a bit 'iffy', but expect the unexpected. Something is destined to creep up

behind you. Don't worry – you will like this surprise.
Black for protection.
Cancer is a bit of a 'chancer'.
Lucky Numbers: 31.4.24.33.26.7.

Sagittarius: You can get by on a wing and a prayer this
week. Don't panic – things are not what they seem. There
is a reason for the challenges facing you and you are able to
pass this test. Hop on the magic carpet and glide over everything that troubles you. The more you get entangled, the
worse it will be. So detach, smile and move on. Trust me
you are the winner on this one. Love is bringing passion and
delight – maybe Turkish!
Green for matters of the heart.
Leo is hot and heavy going, but in the best way possible.
Lucky Numbers: 4.28.19.30.31.24.

Capricorn: Capricorn goats are sure-footed creatures, but
when you are scaling mountainous heights this week do
keep things in perspective. Do not lose the run of yourself,
or you just might topple into the cavern. If that's the local
pub, fine! But if you are trying to impress and have had one
too many, don't be surprised if you are shown the door.
Capricorn sometimes forgets to look behind. Check out
your fishy tail intermittently and go with the flow of your
emotions. Time to be honest and up front, but don't rely on
Dutch courage or get too big for your boots –hoofs!
Purple for spirituality.
Aquarius is your match.
Lucky Numbers: 42.13.15.27.18.29.

Aquarius: Take 'stock' this week, Aquarius, and reflect on your good fortune. You may not be exactly flying without wings but at least you are headed in the right direction. Love tantalises and teases, so enjoy the flirt and be quietly confident that a deeper connection will develop. Some of you need personal space and privacy at the moment. Don't be afraid to tell it like it is. People respect your honesty and direct line. Stay grounded on a matter close to your heart. Aqua brightens vision.

Pisces is very psychic – listen!

Lucky Numbers: 29.33.34.15.17.4.

Pisces: Don't put your foot in it, Pisces, but do speak from the heart of your bottom – sorry, the bottom of your heart! Be prepared to display genuine emotion and follow your instincts. The likelihood of an intense connection is high. Choose to leave stressful situations behind, and do not allow someone suspect to worm their way into your affections. Take a well-deserved break and relax. Unwind and uncurl everything – a bit of preening is called for!

Yellow/gold attract sunshine vibes.

Scorpio may get tricky.

Lucky Numbers: 3.6.9.30.31.40.

Aries: Make the most of your business acumen as there are good opportunities on the horizon. Wait a while for a change of vehicle and you will get better value for money if you buy the newer model. Don't be 'backwards about coming forwards' as it is a great time to sell yourself. Love brings a twinkle to your eye and the desire to breed may become an issue.

Live in the moment and enjoy the company of loved ones.
A message from abroad brings a smile to your face.
Red enhances identity and survival.
Cancer hits the right spot.
Lucky Numbers: 32.13.16.27.18.39.

Taurus: Play your cards close to your chest this week, Taurus – nothing new there then! If you feel in a rut and your heart's desire eludes you, try a different approach. You can charm the birds off the trees so have more confidence when it counts. Move away from a love match that doesn't work anymore. Pastures new beckon the old bull, so plod along and see what the next field tastes like . . .
Violet for healing.
Gemini keeps you enchanted.
Lucky Numbers: 4.25.33.36.17.19.

Gemini: Don't count your chickens this week. Make sure your investments and finances are in order before you commit to a new project. Destiny plays a hand in affairs of the heart – expect a soul mate to materialise. In established relationships, room to breathe is important. Don't make mountains out of molehills or molehills out of mountains. Get real with the big issues and don't get sidetracked by a load of old nonsense. Balance is your key to success.
Yellow to support thinking.
Libra brings good luck.
Lucky Numbers: 14.19.28.34.25.16.

Cancer: Things are scuttling along nicely for many crabs at the moment. Make sure that you are not seduced unless you want to be. There are many schemers who will use a kind heart, so keep your eyes open. At times your good nature is abused and you wind up feeling manipulated. Don't forget you set yourself up, and take advantage of the positive energy this week. Move onwards and upwards and away from everything that weighs you down.

Sea green for tranquillity.

Scorpio brings intense challenges.

Lucky Numbers: 3.12.5.26.17.19.

VIRGO Time:
August 24th – September 23rd

WEEK THIRTY-FOUR
August 20th - August 26th

Virgo: There is a major career boost on the horizon. Get your priorities right and assess both your motivation and integrity. A delayed prediction will come right. Do not be down-hearted about family difficulty. If you muddle through in good faith, things will turn out for the best. Temptation manifests and looks like fun. However, do not jump in with two big feet if circumstances have you tied. Certain bonds cannot be broken so do not deny the inevitable.

Green for heart issues.

Aquarius may lead you astray.

Lucky Numbers: 5.6.11.26.38.40.

Libra: Be thoughtful this week, Libra, and keep your balance. All things come to him/her who waits, so be patient with a difficult situation. Smile through your pain and you will have the last laugh. Be determined and playful to win the heart you desire. There is no point battling with something that no longer works. You will be surprised what is lurking around the next corner, so remain confident. Financial investments will serve you well.

Pink for unconditional love.

Capricorn could prove difficult.

Lucky Numbers: 12.13.17.19.30.33.

Scorpio: Yes, well, um…! There is no room for embarrassment in matters of the heart this week. A sweet face will catch your attention – don't be backwards about coming forwards. Try to rest, work and play in equal measure, as you need an outlet for tension. Trust your intuition and don't doubt what you see. A major risk will pay off and far exceed your expectations. Destiny has a great sense of humour and what takes shape will have you smiling to yourself for a long time.

Black for seduction.

Fellow Scorpio will rock your world.

Lucky Numbers: 6.23.16.27.18.29.

Sagittarius: Broaden your horizons this week and adopt a different approach to a long-standing problem. Lateral thinking should change the dynamic of a situation. Do not be afraid to try reverse psychology with a loved one. Make sure practical arrangements are in place. Certainly do not move location if you have any doubts. Lightning may strike twice; love could get complicated. Be cautious financially. Red boosts for energy.

Pisces will do your head in!

Lucky Numbers: 24.33.22.12.35.26.

Capricorn: Don't leave any stone unturned this week. The Universe is leaving you with a riddle to solve, and it is a tricky one. Look before you leap financially or you will have a bigger mess to clear up. You need to think on your feet - be smart, not stupid. Tell it like it is or not at all. Love might muddle you up, but it's a delicious confusion. Discipline at work is important.

Purple for healing.

Virgo turns your world upside down.

Lucky Numbers: 13.24.35.26.17.19.

Aquarius: Don't fall out with family about a conception. Allow life to take its natural order and do not force things along. Even ideas in their embryonic stage should be allowed to develop at their own pace. Be at peace about a trip abroad and let someone go. Learn to give up control now and again. Others have a different approach that works —don't knock it!

Aqua lightens vision.

Gemini offers interesting insights.

Lucky Numbers: 10.20.30.12.16.40.

Pisces: Watch your temper and don't give into dramatic displays of anger. Being the drama queen does not suit you! Try to respect other people's boundaries and give up banging your head off the wall. Life has a different solution to your problems. You do not need to design an elaborate plan, as the simplest approach works best. Look right under your nose for the answers.

Green for money.

Libra may bring some balance into your life.

Lucky Numbers: 12.26.37.19.20.21.

Aries: A match made in heaven could quickly descend into a hellish connection if you are not careful. Do not take loved ones for granted. Bide your time in an emotive situation and do not push for answers. Use your independent mind to good effect. Cast a spell over someone you want to impress, as flattery will get you everywhere this week! You are someone's rock – just make sure you don't cause a shipwreck. Softly, softly, Aries . . .

Gold boosts riches.

Taurus is up to old tricks.

Lucky Numbers: 4.14.34.10.19.5.

Taurus: Are you hitchin' a ride on life's highway or perhaps asleep at the wheel? There is a need to take control, so get back in the driving seat or at least pull in for a rest. If you continue in the present groove there is crash potential in a mile or two. Watch for unforeseen events and people who are determined to step in your way. Be careful, Taurus, or you will regret your complacency. Recharge your batteries, look at the map, and keep your eyes on the road.

Browns for grounding.

Virgo is highly seductive.
Lucky Numbers: 24.15.16.28.39.5.

Gemini: Step lightly this week, Gemini, as an easy relaxed mind will take you further. Watch that motor mouth tendency – sometimes you talk but don't listen. Stop thinking of the next thing and focus on the moment. You may throw caution to the wind in matters of the heart. But be careful whom you confide in. Fly free in confidence of the Divine plan; controlling others is not an option. Focus and don't worry about what anyone else has in the pipeline.
Yellow to de-stress.
Sagittarius may get under your skin.
Lucky Numbers: 28.13.15.26.39.4.

Cancer: Stop fretting and get real with love. Security is important but so is freedom of expression. Allow others to simply be. Try tapping into your individuality and you may be surprised by renewed confidence. More trust is needed and a leap of faith won't go amiss. Do not be afraid to follow intuitions, as these are your radar signals. Some crabs have eyes on stalks so their antennae are primed to cover all angles. Tap into this sensitivity or you might miss important information.
Blue for peace.
Fellow Cancer offers understanding.
Lucky Numbers: 3.6.9.19.20.21.

Leo: Keep major decisions at arm's length and stall for time. The penny will drop eventually and love knocks unexpectedly. Open your heart to the good things and lose any fear or negativity about this connection. A financial surprise is looming – make hay while the sun shines…Be not afraid of the blessings coming your way. Strange as it may sound, there is a deep fear of success lurking in your psyche. Lose it once and for all!

Yellow for stress.

Gemini is on the ball.

Lucky Numbers: 33.21.25.14.17.39.

WEEK THIRTY-FIVE
August 27th – September 2nd

Virgo: Try to hold yourself together. Unexpected stress may be testing you to the limit. Be objective, philosophical and stay centred to get through this test. Learn to be vulnerable and allow other people to look after you for a change. Reserve judgement in all things and don't be hasty. Listen to body, mind and heart – your answers lie within.

Turquoise assists liberation.

Capricorn is a challenge.

Lucky Numbers: 23.14.16.27.38.22.

Libra: Try to see the funny side of challenging events this week. If you don't keep a sense of humour, no one else will. You have a potential role as co-ordinator and peacemaker. Set a realistic timetable or demanding schedules may knock you for six! As an elegant Libran, you may want to preen, pamper and generally make-over your appearance. Be thoughtful and try to empathise with someone who is annoying you. Wait until you can see the whole picture before making an important decision.

Russet enhances warmth and texture.

Aries may do your head in.

Lucky Numbers: 24.15.16.27.38.9.

Scorpio: Bravery is needed in matters of the heart – do not be afraid of rejection. Confidence may be boosted by flattery but watch out for agendas. Have the courage of your own convictions. There is no need to be quite so 'edgy', though do keep your style that way. Someone is interested, don't doubt it. Will you return the favour? It is important not to let something slip away. Out of sight is not necessarily out of mind.

Blue enhances peaceful vibes.

Virgo is seductive.

Lucky Numbers: 11.14.15.26.36.22.

Sagittarius: Shoot your fiery arrow into the heavens and expect it to land on target. First decide on your goal then focus to reel in what you want. It is not a time to tread on toes but do blow your own trumpet just a little. Arrogance is not pretty but healthy self-confidence is very attractive. Keep that in mind to impress your romantic interest. Speak plainly and from the heart, as persuasive talk will get you everywhere.

Green for freedom.

Fire signs will drive you mad, in a good way.

Lucky Numbers: 33.11.27.37.18.29.

Capricorn: Time to frolic and play…let the good times roll! Spice your life up a little. Watching paint dry is an analogy that comes to mind. Don't you think tedium loses its appeal after a while? I know you are patient and thorough but why not live dangerously and escape whatever it is that stifles you! Go after your heart's desire to avoid the boredom of waiting.

Purple for Divine help.

Take on Virgo at your own risk.

Lucky Numbers: 29.30.14.15.26.3.

Aquarius: You may feel that your time is running out. Certainly a confrontation or letting off steam is highly likely. Once the air is clear calm will descend. Room to breathe is important for everyone. Do honour someone's boundaries and make sure your own are respected. Relief is a buzzword this week, so sigh away to good effect! Help to put a mind at rest so that sanity prevails.

Aqua enables high-octane protection.

Watch out for Pisces.

Lucky Numbers: 13.25.16.37.40.20.

Pisces: You are a great support, but do make sure that you attend to your own needs. Lively chats and sexy giggles are set to spice up your romantic life. Do not be alarmed at developments. Great change is afoot. Keep the tempo upbeat to get through a testing phase and ignore nasty details. Time is the supreme healer, so allow time to pass. Dare to be different, why not!

Yellow to de-stress.

Leo will make you smile.
Lucky Numbers: 14.26.37.18.8.20.

Aries: Be cautious and be practical. The end of the runway is in sight, so glide into land elegantly. There is no need to fall short or overshoot the mark. Balance is the key to success. Avoid smugness at all times, even though you have reason to be. Surrender one issue or you will run to ground. If you remain philosophical about recent events you will be guided to a calm oasis. Sizzle socially to make an impression. Red enhances energy.
Keep an eye on Taurus.
Lucky Numbers: 3.31.23.37.19.30.

Taurus: Crocodile tears and false, empty gestures don't do it for me, Taurus . . . Will you try a different approach? You are more powerful and impressive than you realise. Carry yourself with dignity at all times. There is no need to win approval and, in fact, if you try too hard you might blow it! Just be you and the rest will unfold in its own good time. Watch your tendency to control and manoeuvre other people. It will all come out in the wash!
Orange boosts joy.
Aries is too pushy.
Lucky Numbers: 4.14.25.36.17.29.

Gemini: Try to give loved ones more room. Quizzing will not encourage confidences. Adopt a relaxed approach and you will get further, and access the info you need. Someone needs your support so take up the slack. Altruistic gestures will be rewarded. Communication gives love its best chance. What you don't know can't hurt you, so leave controversy alone.

Olive enhances feminine leadership.

Sagittarius is interesting.

Lucky Numbers: 26.37.18.29.30.4.

Cancer: Stop being so hard on everything – yourself, others, and life in general! Are you very 'crabby' at the moment? This can be amusing to watch, but do be careful you don't become the butt of too many jokes. Access healthy self-esteem and a sense of humour to get through challenges. Few are as clever and intuitive as you, so make the most of your natural abilities. Take control in love but don't permit possessiveness in yourself or others.

Sea green for tranquillity.

Aquarius may cause problems.

Lucky Numbers: 23.14.15.17.29.24.

Leo: Be proud and 'strut' your stuff to good effect! Many doors will open for you if you gently push your way through. Not much can hamper your progress and certain people will bend over backwards to help you. Fret not about finances. All good things will come to you in a timely way. Perform to the best of your ability. Socially you will be the centre of attention and sexually there is no competition! Spicy colours to turn on the heat.

Cancer may 'niggle' you.

Lucky Numbers: 13.14.26.37.9.30.

WEEK THIRTY-SIX
September 3rd – September 9th

Virgo: Try to stick to a recent decision and hold onto your integrity. People may resent or distrust you. Never mind the 'begrudgers' . . . do your own thing and smile sweetly. Love remains complex but exciting. Anything can happen now, so be prepared for surprises. A 'bridge over troubled water' becomes the 'rainbow bridge' to a new life.
Use yellow to de-stress.
Taurus is winding you up.
Lucky Numbers: 21.33.24.15.19.30.

Libra: Your natural charm and '*joie de vivre*' will win people over this week. Display flare and ability in an interview or meeting. Work to good effect to impress the right person. In matters of the heart don't kid yourself any longer. It is time to be honest, and lose the plot . . . just a little! A ghost from the past may return to haunt you, but never mind the skeletons in your closet. Relax and be philosophical.
Use purple for spirituality.
Fire signs may annoy you.
Lucky Numbers: 10.19.28.37.4.33.

Scorpio: Be prepared for a barrage of questions that would be funny if the situation weren't so serious! Keep your privacy intact and hold precious secrets in your heart. Love is in the air, and you will live to fight another day. Yes, there's truth in these clichés, Scorpio. Follow your instincts at the moment and be aware that you do not have to toe the line in every fine detail. Take up a surprise invite, even if it looks risky.

Use blue for peace of mind.

Virgo is seductive.

Lucky Numbers: 23.14.25.16.28.30.

Sagittarius: You may need to solve a riddle this week, and unlock the reasons for your discontent. A key is a vital tool which lets you walk into somewhere previously locked. Look within as you carry your own answers. Open your heart and push all doors, as they may only be ajar. Never say never as another chapter of life begins. Think carefully, make your decisions, then go for it. Put no restrictions upon what may unfold . . . the sky is the limit.

Use green for personal space.

Pisces is a challenge

Lucky Numbers: 13.24.35.26.37.9.

Capricorn: Mountain goats are courageous, foolhardy creatures. Be aware of the treacherous or dangerous areas you walk, but be brave and determined. You are destined to succeed in whatever you put your energy into. However, you must be careful not to tread on toes in the process. Remember that what goes around, comes around. Do not take shortcuts at the expense of your competition, as this will backfire. Love looks soft, light and energising.

Use turquoise for creativity.

Fellow Capricorn may lock horns.

Lucky Numbers: 13.25.26.17.9.33.

Aquarius: Have you caught yourself out with something, Aquarius? Sometimes, your need to control or manoeuvre people can catch up with you. I'm sure you can charm your way out of a sticky situation, but be prepared to learn a lesson. Love is wonderfully comfortable and relaxing. Follow an exciting lead that takes you to where you want to go.
Use silver for clarity.
Leo knows a thing or two.
Lucky Numbers: 22.11.31.24.36.8.

Pisces: Are you a flatfish at the moment, Pisces, or one of those 'guppies' that look as if they are about to explode? Something is not quite right with the sea you swim in. You could migrate or change location, but really what is needed is a de-pollution programme. Detox your life on all levels to reduce the pressure and enliven your energies. Then you will neither 'peter out', nor blow your top. Tackle problems head on, as running away will not help.
Use magenta for depth of vision.
Earth signs will ground you.
Lucky Numbers: 31.25.36.17.8.14.

Aries: You may think you have it made, Aries, and in many ways you do. Your clever, wily nature and tenacity have earned you an esoteric pat on the back. Do not be complacent in matters of the mind or heart. A storm is brewing, but you will enjoy the excitement it brings. Stay centred and in control. Your circumstances are about to change. New and dynamic challenges abound. Love is good.
Use peach/coral for unrequited feelings.

Aquarius speaks the truth.
Lucky Numbers: 12.13.34.25.36.17.

Taurus: Are you being devious, unkind or unfair in an attempt to cover your tracks, Taurus? Clever you certainly are, but are you always true to yourself and others? Take stock of recent events and try to unravel a tricky situation. Past embarrassments may surface and catch you out. Love is uncomfortably relaxed. This unease could prove to be the spanner in the works. Prepare to be blown away, as someone enters your life to shake things up!
Use gold to boost riches.
Capricorn is helpful financially.
Lucky Numbers: 23.14.15.36.28.39.

Gemini: Try to keep your feet on the ground, Gemini. A lot of activity will keep you busy. Make sure you have covered your tracks and expect to be pulled up about something. Keep communications honest and clear. Love looks interesting, and opportunities are many and varied. Close encounters are likely. Just make sure you are not waylaid by an alien life form! Flirtatious behaviour will get you everywhere.
Use olive for your feminine aspect.
Scorpio speaks home truths.
Lucky Numbers: 29.30.31.32.14.3.

Cancer: Depressed you may be, but don't make things worse for yourself. The grass is not always greener. The far-off rockpool may look enticing to a crab but really it's no different. Work with what you have or you will undermine your achievements to date. Do not sabotage the future by digging too deep. Be prepared to live without answers for the moment. Love is under your nose. Just allow things to develop.

Use lilac for protection.

Virgo is clever.

Lucky Numbers: 16.23.4.15.29.34.

Leo: Do not allow your pride to destroy a good thing. Relaxation is important, but laziness is inexcusable. Sounds dramatic? Life is set to become very busy indeed, and it would be a crime to pass up the opportunities that are about to present themselves. Take it easy, pace yourself and then learn to fly. Leo, you do not have wings, of course, but before too long you will feel as if you do. Find time for love. Frenetic activity brings delight and confusion.

Use red for passion.

Taurus is a pain.

Lucky Numbers: 2.33.21.25.16.17.

WEEK THIRTY-SEVEN
September 10th – September 16th

Virgo: Love, gentleness and all things pink . . . Use this time for intelligent soul-searching. Try not to feel sorry for yourself. Plans have gone awry for good reason. There is something (and someone) better on the way. A challenging, dynamic and exciting phase is around the corner. Hang in there and remain philosophical. Do not be tempted to sell your soul. It will pay you more in the long term to hold onto your integrity at this point. Be duly warned. But enjoy the feeling of power you have!

Rose pink for magic and conception.

Be cautious re Aquarius.

Lucky Numbers: 22.35.5.41.9.20.

Libra: Libra should be on top form at the moment: top of the class, top of the ladder, top of the world. No? Well, then, I'm baffled. You have everything going for you. If it hasn't happened yet, I suggest you get out there and make it work. Most of you are looking gorgeous, but for those who need added confidence, spend some time and money on your appearance. The face you present to the world is your key to future advancement and luck.

Yellow/purple in combination enables karmic resolution.

Scorpio may both assist and hinder you.

Lucky Numbers: 10.25.26.37.4.19.

Scorpio: The suspense is killing me…are you going to make that move or not? Try to avoid stringing people along. It may be part of your charm not to want to hurt others, but be aware that your vagueness could also cause damage. The wheel of fortune is bringing great things your way. Be generous and kind, and never take anything for granted. Major love thrills are on the horizon. Be bold, brave and unusual in matters of the heart.

Green for luck.

Virgo is sexy.

Lucky Numbers: 21.32.34.4.5.16.

Sagittarius: Hot air balloons are…full of hot air! Be careful someone does not burst your bubble this week. Make sure that the 'words of your mouth are the meditation of your heart'. Do not be tempted to talk angrily, nonsensically, or aimlessly. Make every word and gesture count for something. If I sound like a killjoy, or less than fun, it is because you should be taking your life a bit more seriously than you have of late. Keep your sense of humour, of course, but shift up a gear when it counts.

Blue brings a bolt out of the blue!

Capricorn may be annoying.

Lucky Numbers: 3.21.14.25.26.17.

Capricorn: Expect the unexpected and be prepared to think on your feet. Try to surrender control on an important matter. The outcome of certain events is out of your hands. Trust and faith are needed. A shift in the balance of power is important and you will have to adjust. Love links and family ties deserve attention. Good communication and gestures from the heart can turn anything around. Don't panic.

Gold and silver bring riches and rewards.

Aries is a challenge.

Lucky Numbers: 21.33.14.15.26.17.

Aquarius: Try to adopt a less rigid perspective. Sometimes you are so fixed and immovable, that an elephant would be easier to shove into touch. Faith moves mountains, so reserve judgement and allow the magic to happen. Learn that control issues need to be surrendered to the bigger picture. Clever as you are with yourself and others, you sometimes misfire and get the wrong end of the stick. Right as you can be, it is highly dangerous to gloss over your mistakes.

Green/white combinations enhance transition and change.

Listen to Taurus.

Lucky Numbers: 14.23.19.4.36.24.

Pisces: Deep breaths are needed to avoid panic and the gulping of too much water. Slow down a bit, and certainly don't be hasty with important decisions. You may be a bit wide-eyed and delirious – perhaps someone has waltzed off with your heart without permission. Hopefully the delirium derives from heavenly happiness rather than the drowning of sorrows. Remember fish can swim, so make sure you stay buoyant through good times and bad.

Red enables grounding.

Aquarius talks sense.

Lucky Numbers: 29.14.35.26.17.8.

Aries: Sunny times and celebrations may turn into a challenge. You will rise to the occasion as always, but be alert for those who bring unexpected surprises. 'Nowt so strange as folk', will be a phrase to keep in mind for the foreseeable future. Expect both anguish and laughter, and the depths and heights of our worldly experience. Support and favours abound, so relinquish the need to be so damned independent!

White for karmic reward and clarity.

Leo is a laugh.

Lucky Numbers: 1.3.14.25.26.17.

Taurus: You may be on an emotional rollercoaster with no easy way to step off the ride. Hopefully you are strapped in and don't lose your head with all the screaming. Life is supposed to be fun, so how come this pleasure trip went off the rails? Well, maybe it didn't – it's just entered the spooky tunnel for a nail-biting stretch. Taurus loves risky moments but also quakes amidst any threat to security. Go with it. There is no other option. But don't expect to land in the same place you started.

Vivid dark green attracts the wheel of fortune.

Aries is bluffing.

Lucky Numbers: 24.35.16.27.18.9.

Gemini: Elvis is a rock-and-roll legend…what will you be remembered for? Be careful of those who have 'left the building' carrying your secrets. Review your priorities and your approach to life. Irresponsibility usually has a payback clause. Be wary of what you sign and whom you commit to. You are destined to make an impact; make sure it is a good one. Love looks promising so don't promise what you cannot deliver. Find your correct direction and all will be well.

Deep purple enhances magic.

Taurus is putting on an act.

Lucky Numbers: 23.14.25.36.7.12.

Cancer: To scale the oceanic heights, you must put in the work, Cancer. It is not a time to sink into the sand or sunbathe on a rock. Get out there and 'scuttle' to good effect. Make sure that you pace yourself and recharge your batteries intermittently. A juggling act makes an impact only if the balls stay in the air. Reduce the number of elements that vie for your attention, or pay the price – delegate and segregate. Give love a fighting chance.

Deep reds for impact, and a bold statement.

Scorpio is sexy.

Lucky Numbers: 4.25.36.17.28.9.

Leo: You may be on the prowl this week. Look around, survey the landscape, spot your prey, then pounce. Oh, and don't forget the chase. The thrill of hunting down a loved one is very much in the air. Enjoy the excitement of new or renewed love. Pay attention to the detail of legal documents. Too much of a good thing may leave you satiated but content. Get back into a disciplined regime, but only once you have taken a decadent break.

Yellow/gold combinations attract sunny success.

Sagittarius is good fun.

Lucky Numbers: 31.24.25.16.27.8.

WEEK THIRTY-EIGHT
September 17th – September 23rd

Virgo: Get back into gear, Virgo. You need more fun and laughter in your life, so go out and get you some! Leave stress and heartache in a corner and spread your wings. At the same time pay attention to detail and be careful not to make a molehill out of a mountain. In other words, don't get caught out by your new relaxed demeanour. Gloss over important documents at your peril . . .

Green to support your heart.
Scorpio has a sting in their tail.
Lucky Numbers: 1.2.3.14.15.16.

Libra: Be sure to honour all your commitments this week. Serious matters will keep you on your toes. Yes, going out to play is much more appealing. However, a pressing itinerary will get on top of you if you don't pace yourself. Light-hearted flirtation and a sense of fun will keep you buoyant. Just be careful it does not cast you adrift at the same time. Blue for peace of mind.
Aquarius may rock your world.
Lucky Numbers: 3.6.9.29.21.30.

Scorpio: Are you being unfair, nasty or unnecessarily secretive? Withholding information to avoid hurting someone can actually cause more damage. Keep things 'pure and simple'. Be true to yourself and shoot from the hip to clear up a mess! This will confirm your decisions and strengthen you. Someone is madly in love with you, well very passionate anyway – why ignore it? Reassess your priorities and give a feisty female the benefit of the doubt.
Red enhances passion.
Go for earthiness with earth signs…
Lucky Numbers: 24.34.6.17.19.20.

Sagittarius: There is every reason to expect success. A flaming and intense Cupid's arrow is winging its way towards you. If you can't handle the heat . . . RUN! Family matters can be settled if you all give each other a chance. Learn to listen and try to be more accepting and tolerant. Make an important phone call. Things will pass you by if you wait too long. Be more assertive and follow your aims through. Find the target, flex the bow . . . and fire!

Yellow for intelligence.

Watch out for Gemini.

Lucky Numbers: 23.14.16.17.28.10.

Capricorn: Someone holds a lot of bitterness and resentment towards you. Clear up this negativity and look for ways to redress a balance. Try not to lose your spirituality in material concerns. There is more to life and a new set of priorities is needed. Finish what you started and be careful not to leave a loved one dangling. If you follow things through and sort out a muddle, you can look forward to a fresh start. A new chapter...

Turquoise boosts creativity.

Pisces needs attention.

Lucky Numbers: 13.15.17.26.3.4.

Aquarius: You have the knack of a 'spin-doctor' and can turn the bleakest scenario on its head. If you have to convince someone that black is white you can do it. Don't be too complacent though as the truth will out, whatever complexion you try to put on it. Your 'cleverness' could be your downfall. This is not a time to wriggle, but a time to admit mistakes and say sorry.

Pale blue for protection.

Scorpio sees you.

Lucky Numbers: 33.30.31.9.27.4.

Pisces: Are you're a little overfed, or fed up? Both perhaps. You look a bit like you are about to roll over and float to the top of the tank! Too much attention or lack of it is starting to affect your balance. It is time for diet, discipline and denial. Well, maybe not, but at least swim away from everything that curtails your creativity and freedom. All things fishy need to be gutted and cleaned.

Lilac brings transmutation.

Aquarius is light and airy.

Lucky Numbers: 21.31.41.5.26.7.

Aries: Shout to be heard, Aries! This is not a time to be stuck in the corner sulking. If someone is not with you perhaps it is good to be without them – move on. Equality is important, and you need to feel cherished and loved. Do not settle for less than the best, never mind the rest. To be short-changed is very debilitating and unnerving. Avoid the attempt to make something out of nothing and value your independence.

Orange boosts vitality.

Gemini is sweet.

Lucky Numbers: 33.31.24.25.27.3.

Taurus: Tuck into that steak now, Taurus. You need to boost the red bloodflow pumping through those veins. Added oomph and oodles of 'X factor' will attract admirers like a moth to the flame. Your legendary staying power is an added bonus. When you come up for a breather, I'll tell you what's next – later! No, I mean it . . . you need the rest. Watch your energy levels. And be careful to guard your secrets, past and present, carefully.

Black for mystery.

Virgo is full of mischief...

Lucky Numbers: 34.12.6.27.18.29.

Gemini: Up at the crack of dawn, Gemini? You do seem to have a lot on your plate. Offload and delegate or you may feel yourself 'flagging'. Try not to be so supercilious with certain people. You command respect so do not chase it away with flippancy. Smugness won't work either. I'm not exactly talking humble pie here, but you will retain your position only if you eat some – never mind the diet!

Gold attracts treasure.

Capricorn is a handful.

Lucky Numbers: 3.13.26.37.18.39.

Cancer: Wean yourself off anything that challenges your system. Never mind the stamina drinks or ginseng. Try to isolate the real cause of your weariness. Emotional issues need to be faced. You can bury yourself in the sand only for so long. The tide is still going to come in and expose you, however much you hide. Put the feelers out in love matters and remember you have the pincers in case things get rough. Get on the move and in the groove!

Bright blue to cheer you.

Leo has home truths.

Lucky Numbers: 23.24.25.17.39.4.

Leo: Tighten your belt and hold in that tummy, Leo! You seriously need to curb your expenses. Save it up for a rainy day, which, of course, will never come. Be prepared so that you don't get caught out and you won't. Life's rhyme and reason will reveal itself. In the meantime be cautious and canny, considering all scenarios. Preen your appearance for encounters of the close kind. A smart turnout ensures success.

Libra is objective and kind.

Purple for a regal heart.

Lucky Numbers: 24.15.36.27.18.29.

LIBRA Time
September 24th – October 23rd

WEEK THIRTY-NINE
September 24th - September 30th

Libra: Keep balanced in challenging situations and rely on your common sense to pull you through. Enjoy a well-deserved rest, even if it is only 5 minutes at lunchtime! It is important to make an extra effort at this point with loved ones. So watch out for laziness in love relationships. A job offer or promotion looks good – do go ahead in confidence. Be at peace about finances and monitor your stress levels. A leap of faith will get you out of a tight spot. Consider a new health regime . . .

Yellow for brightness.

Cancer is attractive.

Lucky Numbers: 33.21.4.25.36.7.

Scorpio: You can be a complex character, Scorpio, but you are intrinsically sweet. Be careful that you don't miss the boat with a love entanglement. Still waters run deep, but sometimes you are like a deep, dark well that can't be fathomed. Make sure you do not alienate people by being too unavailable. You need to reciprocate or you will lose interest, and so will they. Get stuck into work commitments. Your ship will come in as luck is on your side at the moment. Get on the move and in the groove!

Blue for peace.

Pisces is good fun.

Lucky Numbers: 33.31.25.36.17.28.

Sagittarius: There are fun times ahead, but get the practical things done first. You will connect with someone important very soon. Work on your appearance so that you make the best possible impression. Charm and humour are your keys to success. Brave financial choices will pay off and speculation will indeed swell your coffers. Maintain your equilibrium and do not succumb to unreasonable demands. If the price is right...pay the price!

Green for money.

Capricorn assists investment.

Lucky Numbers: 21.33.24.35.26.7.

Capricorn: Never say never! You may find yourself dragged into a situation that is so not you. And yet . . . There are no accidents. Unusual scenarios will test and develop you, so enjoy the challenge. An intricate knowledge of geometry would help you manoeuvre out of a corner. But if this is not your forte, draw on the resources of honesty and integrity to break free. Think intelligently and laterally, and the riddle of life will solve itself. Love becomes unexpectedly beguiling. Purple for all things regal.

Aquarius sees through you.

Lucky Numbers: 3.21.36.35.10.13.

Aquarius: A time of taking stock may be in order. You need to sort out your priorities and disengage from some of your commitments. Cool customer you may be, but make sure you are there for those who count. Admitting to a mistake may free you up in more ways than one. Do not ignore a dangerous situation or person. If you carry on regardless, you may fall foul of your own confidence. Technical hitches may do your head in! Shine on . . .

Turquoise boosts creativity.

Cancer is sweet.

Lucky Numbers: 12.33.25.4.6.19.

Pisces: Be strong in your resolve to leave the past behind. Your clean slate looks good and will bring you renewed zest for life. Do not allow negative people or situations to drag you down. Be proud of who you have become, and look towards the future full of hope. Positive expectations will take you further than bad thoughts ever would. Leave all ghosts, skeletons, and monsters in the closet, then shut the door and turn the key!

Magenta restores thinking.

Libra provides balance.

Lucky Numbers: 3.16.17.26.40.39.

Aries: You should be fighting fit and ready to go. Make the most of your vibrant energy and get outstanding tasks finished. The time has come to say no to nonsense. You don't suffer fools gladly, but lately you have relaxed your standards. Give loved ones a gentle kick if necessary. Tolerance is good, but blind stupidity is . . . just that! Be on your guard and preserve your territory. You will reign victorious and be delighted with your achievements.

Red enables grounding.

Virgo is honest.

Lucky Numbers: 34.25.17.29.40.5.

Taurus: Be courageous and finally lay something to rest. The opposite sex does not bite; well, not all the time! If someone is pushing your buttons, avoid them until they stop. You may be sad about your situation, but don't wallow. Be aware that something can always be done. Take the bull by the horns and get busy. If anyone can clear up a mess, it's you. Good energy and sheer determination will pull you through.

Grey for grey areas.

Fellow Taurus will clash.

Lucky Numbers: 12.21.22.11.33.41.

Gemini: Trial and error may be key words in matters of the heart. Keep experimenting and you will gain and maintain interest. It is important to focus on your goals. Do not neglect your career at the expense of frivolity. Have good times, yes, but make sure the work is done first. Watch stress levels. Parents or people in authority may be demanding. Patience is a virtue and will be rewarded.

Sea green for flow.

Virgo holds the key.

Lucky Numbers: 32.16.27.38.19.30.

Cancer: Hold onto your hat and season your protective outer layers. There is a chill wind brewing and winter is upon us. Well…not quite, but you will need to wrap things up and look after your own interests. Ditch anything that no longer works. Remember that if someone is not for you they may not be worthy of your time. Commitment is important and you need evidence of support. Expect the best and it will surely arrive. Love has some surprises up its sleeve.

Emerald green for heart stuff.

Pisces is cute.

Lucky Numbers: 30.4.1.15.16.28.

Leo: Spellbinding and spellbound? Your powers to captivate and be captivated are high. Enjoy the intrigue but make sure your tracks are covered. Don't be caught on the hop and be prepared for questions. Charming as you are, remember that not everyone will be wooed. Be persistent and bide your time and things will come good. Variety and loyalty are possible bedfellows. Be bold and brave with a work decision.

Indigo for head rest.

Aquarius is smart.

Lucky Numbers: 21.36.37.28.19.30.

Virgo: It is an understatement to say that you are up against

it. In many respects you face one of the most difficult challenges ever. Hang in there. Remember past successes, and do
not be dismayed. Time is on your side and you will pull it
all together at the last minute. You have a way of coming
good however bleak your circumstances. Love will brighten
your day. Smile amidst adversity and eventually the Universe
will smile back.

Pink for unconditional love.

Scorpio is an enigma.

Lucky Numbers: 4.31.27.38.41.22.

WEEK FORTY
October 1st - October 7th

Libra: It's time to celebrate your success and move forward
with a spring in your step. Do be careful not to hold yourself back with destructive thought patterns, for your future
is as good as you want to make it! This is your moment, so
capitalise on your chances and expect to reap a good reward.
Sunny climes beckon. Monitor your fluid intake, as your
levels of hydration may not be quite right.

Pale blue for Divine guidance.

Fellow Libra brings peace.

Lucky Numbers: 1.14.40.19.18.8.

Scorpio: Remain cool and circumspect about finances. Be
realistic and grateful for what you have already achieved.
Love is very important and the powerful decisions that you
are about to make will surprise even you! Stop resisting the

inevitable. A tidal wave of good feeling is winging its way towards you. So, lie back and enjoy your great fortune. A positive attitude will attract everything you wish for, and then some . . .

Beige/muted colours for subtle sophistication.

Virgo is compelling.

Lucky Numbers: 23.14.25.36.17.8.

Sagittarius: Family matters are well starred. Do bury the hatchet and make your peace with an important person. A sense of feeling hard done by should diminish, but you need to make good decisions. Moving onwards and upwards is the noble aim to strive for – reach for the stars. Give no thought to failure, and go for gold...Be independent and determined. Your destiny is in your own hands so make it count. Red assists energetic action.

Pisces may dampen your spirits.

Lucky Numbers: 12.33.26.17.19.40.

Capricorn: Once upon a time...well we could all live in fairytale land but it wouldn't get us very far. Unusually you have your head in the clouds over an issue. See the real picture or a tale of woe will find you, never mind the fantasy. Pull yourself through a tight spot and victory is yours. Be careful not to hoodwink people. They are smarter than you give them credit for.

Purple for spiritual perspective.

Earth signs are supportive.

Lucky Numbers: 2.12.14.25.36.17.

Aquarius: Are you being bold and rude to someone to make a point? This really isn't the way to go…Admit the *faux pas* you have made and stop trying to throw it back in the face of another. Silence is golden in many respects, but a bit of common courtesy or some kind of explanation would not go amiss either. Love needs input, not the cold shoulder! Communication is the key, not mystery.

Green for finances.

Sagittarius is a blessing.

Lucky Numbers: 23.4.15.26.37.3.

Pisces: Here, fishy, fishy . . . never mind the cat, what about you? Garbled and mad this may seem, but it does reflect your state of mind at the moment. Zany, twisted and jumbled thoughts are saving you from convention. Madness is not an option, but at times you feel as if you have lost the plot. Don't panic, and enjoy your quirky, eccentric way of being. A sense of offbeat humour is your salvation! Remember rules are made to be broken.

Blue for peace.

Cancer is calming.

Lucky Numbers: 2.33.25.36.27.18.

Aries: Everyone thinks you are heroic, but you know better. Or you would if you analysed your motivations. Try to be as real as you have a mind to be. The rest of the world will catch up eventually. Diversion tactics are effective but misleading. Channel your energies into projects worthy of your full attention. A sweet smile hides a vicious temper. Take your time . . . it is not a good idea to lose your cool.

Orange enlivens vitality.
Leo is a handful.
Lucky Numbers: 23.41.25.19.37.5.

Taurus: Do you feel like an illegal alien in your own home? The capacity for you to be misunderstood is high. Try to curb petulant behaviour and don't be bold out of perversity. Part of your psyche is stifled. You believe you are on track, doing the right thing, but your better self feels uncomfortable – something is amiss. It is impossible to be all things to all people. Your attempts are commendable, but don't ignore the real thing.
Green for a healing heart.
Avoid fire signs 24/7.
Lucky Numbers: 3.14.28.17.36.4.

Gemini: Turbulence in the sky overhead makes you uneasy. You sense 'grumblings' on the horizon and uncertainty does not an easy bedfellow make. Peace will descend when you isolate the rough spots. Ironing, smoothing, and pressing are all needed to improve the appearance of things! Being well turned out is nearly as good as a real achievement. Starching may be purgatory but its rigorous discipline is necessary.
White for clarity.
Aquarius tells the truth.
Lucky Numbers: 13.26.37.18.39.4.

Cancer: Did you get pipped at the post by a mightier apple? Sometimes bigger and better temptations come along which are hard to resist. Be philosophical and magnanimous.

Whoever stole your cherry will pay the price. Rely on karmic resolution to placate the balance. Retaliatory action would not look good. Sour grapes make vinegar, and you must keep the resonance of fine wine. The path of dignity is the best route to follow.

Burgundy for claret!

Virgo is cute.

Lucky Numbers: 31.13.17.19.16.15.

Leo: The wrong end of the stick is easy to pick up, particularly when your life is strewn with more dead wood than the forest floor. Take the log challenge, and sift through the rotten aspects of those who profess to be friendly. Be gentle in your judgements, but at least be shrewd. Take no prisoners. You don't need hangers-on or people with agendas. Listen to your heart and fight your way out of this thicket. Dense undergrowth makes way for pastures new.

Olive inspires leadership.

Air signs have reasons.

Lucky Numbers: 31.14.36.27.38.10.

Virgo: The grand finale is looming and victory will be yours. Often you get overlooked and underestimated. People should be careful not to tread on your toes. 'No more Mr Nice Guy' is an appropriate decision to make. Don't be paranoid amidst disappointment. You have done your best, but backed the wrong horse. Accept your loss, and make sure you can trust the tipster next time you gamble. Misinformed, you pay the price and the perpetrator runs home free.

Magenta helps grounding.

Expect a Capricorn clash.
Lucky Numbers: 29.36.40.21.3.15.

WEEK FORTY-ONE
October 8th – October 14th

Libra: Get to grips with a tricky situation. You can make the most of things as they are. Try to placate awkward people with a smile and charmed tongue. It is important to leave any residue embarrassment to one side. Now is not the time for regrets, so build on strong foundations and go for gold. Be as serene and calm as you know you can be. This is the time to speak clearly, truthfully and from the heart. No one will be able to fault your integrity. It is a magical moment if you resist the temptation to hurry something through.
Black for trousers!
Virgo is enticing.
Lucky Numbers: 3.31.22.36.17.29.

Scorpio: Wooah . . . Put the brakes on! You are about to jump to a very hasty conclusion that could turn things nasty. Get your facts straight and give an exciting person a chance. Control is important but so is the thrill of 'going with the flow'. Don't overestimate your ability to read a situation. You are missing one vital clue – there's a free ride waiting. Take every opportunity that presents itself. It is impossible to please all of the people all of the time. So make sure that you at least are happy. It could be costly to lose the grip, but at least it will be fun!

White for clarity.

Cancer has a message.

Lucky Numbers: 14.15.16.27.38.4.

Sagittarius: Nothing is set in stone, Sagittarius. Just remember that and keep ahead of things. This is not a good time to take any one or anything for granted. Love will make you feel both challenged and appreciated. Mixed blessings abound. Take the best things in life, for they are free. Make sure that accounts and records match up . . . but don't get unnecessarily bogged down with details. There is no panic! The Universe will always attend to your needs, just not quite in the way you expect.

Green for money matters.

Virgo brings joy.

Lucky Numbers: 10.9.8.7.6.15.

Capricorn: Keep your cloven hoofs on the ground, Capricorn. Pride comes before a fall, so make your footing sound and true. This is not a good time to trip yourself up over a detail. Double-check the small print of documents and make statements clearly. There is no room to manoeuvre out of a tight spot. If you are boxed in, be patient, kind and tolerant. Refine your commitments and reassess priorities. Finding love in the little things is the best way forward. Accept your limitations and move through the line of least resistance.

Blue for peace.

Aries is a head wreck!

Lucky Numbers: 2.4.6.8.12.42.

Aquarius: Ever onwards and upwards! Things can only get better . . . recharge your batteries if necessary. Then re-engage in the battle. Life does not have to be a struggle, so detach yourself from difficulty. Never make things more complicated than they have to be. Take people at face value, and lose any tendency towards paranoia. Love will see you through and strengthen your resolve. Pay attention only to what really matters and sift out people and places that no longer work for you.

Sea green for tranquillity.

Earth signs ground you.

Lucky Numbers: 3.25.36.17.19.20.

Pisces: Detoxification is necessary to restore balance in body, mind and spirit. Tackle everything head on and then nothing will hold you back. Sweeping things under the carpet never works for long. So get out the Dyson/vacuum and rigorously cleanse your environment. Restructuring your life will take as long as it takes. So pace yourself, show willing, and remain philosophical at all times. Life will present you with challenges, but it is nothing you can't handle.

Turquoise boosts creativity.

Scorpio is a challenge.

Lucky Numbers: 21.13.17.28.39.4.

Aries: Clear your head and get on with the next thing. Not everyone has your drive and determination. Be careful you do not push one connection to its limit. Step back and keep your distance or you may sabotage your future. Patience is needed. Sometimes you race ahead and catch yourself out.

Calmness and poise will boost your demeanour to good effect. The planets are working in your favour so expect to make a lasting impression.

Purple for healing.

Gemini is an effort.

Lucky Numbers: 30.20.41.16.37.4.

Taurus: You may think you have all the time in the world. But do not take anything for granted at the moment. Other people put you under a lot of pressure. Remain as gracious as humanly possible and bow out on the rest. Remember your humanity and everyone else's. Running your life at fever pitch used to be OK. Now you must knuckle down and accept your responsibilities. Pace yourself.

Green for money.

Air signs know best?

Lucky Numbers: 23.21.42.15.6.7.

Gemini: Are you running out of time with a project close to your heart? Be not downcast as the Universe may have other plans. The heavenly host often has a different agenda from our human concerns. Surrender some control and exercise trust. When things are out of our hands, indeed it's all we can do. Smile in the face of adversity, but realise that things are not as bad as they seem. Down the road this stretch will make sense. So reserve judgement and be philosophical.

Pale blue for Divine guidance.

Virgo may help.

Lucky Numbers: 14.35.26.17.28.10.

Cancer: Time marches on and the changes you are waiting for never happen. Take charge of your destiny, Cancer. Stop the rot and get on with it. Hitching a ride is not an option. Knock your laziness on the head and be prepared to take responsibility for the next phase. You are in this for the long haul, so need to focus on the road ahead. Remember that when dynamic shifts occur, dust settles slowly. So, be patient and the landscape that emerges over the hill will be all the sweeter.

Lilac for clearing debris.

Leo is reassuring.

Lucky Numbers: 12.23.25.30.29.18.

Leo: Move magnificently into your own power. Do not let anyone hold you back. The time is now and you need to make the most of the current planetary alignments. If you want something . . . ask and you will receive. There is no stopping you at the moment. Leave behind those who 'diss' you or make you feel uncomfortable. Life is too short for silly games. Accept people on merit or not at all. Listen fully to your inner voice and you will gain the guidance you need. All the answers lie within your own energy field.

Orange assists dynamic activity.

Air signs hover round you.

Lucky Numbers: 12.13.15.27.38.10.

Virgo: Take the challenge and unlock the box. Do not be afraid to release the skeletons from the closet. You may feel you are opening a can of worms . . . but this honesty will be liberating for you. What a relief it will be to be rid of everything that holds you back. Lay negativity finally to rest, and once the work is done leave it be. Some situations no longer work for you. Recognise this and lose the people who undermine you. Embrace the future as the master of your own destiny.

Yellow for brainpower.

Capricorn is stubborn.

Lucky Numbers: 24.15.37.20.14.21.

WEEK FORTY-TWO
October 15th – October 21st

Libra: Checks and balances will lessen the sense of deflation you feel. A bit of personal discipline will put you back on track. Things are not quite right in a work situation, but hang in there and don't lose your nerve. Love will find a way, and even save the day! Remain hopeful and optimistic of the breakthrough you are looking for. More haste less speed. Trust the Universe to provide, as and when you need enlightenment. There is no point in trying to bargain with God at this point. He hears you, and has a cunning edifying plan for you. All will be revealed!

Vivid blue makes an impact.

Aquarius has useful insights.

Lucky Numbers: 25.36.15.20.21.4.

Scorpio: Wishing on a star won't get you very far . . . but making a safe bet will. Your dreams may get a bit trampled on by reality this week. Take the safe route and stick with what you know. Give new love a look in, or a good opportunity could go awry. There are three steps to heaven: find, woo and keep your loved one. Yes, it really is that simple. So don't complicate matters by looking for hidden agendas or traps. Expect the best and the rest will follow.

Charcoal grey suits you . . . sir!

Phone Virgo.

Lucky Numbers: 26.11.5.9.42.30.

Sagittarius: Be careful not to spread yourself too thinly – you are more Nutella than Bovril. For once less is not more! So layer it on and spread yourself around to good effect. You need the complete experience of your fulsome flavour to make an impact. Prime those taste buds for lashings of indulgence. It is time to enjoy the good things in life, and to rid yourself of the guilt of so doing. Pamper and look after number one this week. Make decadence your 'buzz word' . . . at least for the weekend!

Red for passion

Fire signs light your fire.

Lucky Numbers: 2.14.16.29.40.31.

Capricorn: A twinkle in your eye may develop into something more. But you must harness the full power of your creativity. Focus on a pipe dream and it just may become a reality. Grounding of visions comes naturally to Capricorn. So do not undermine your gut feeling with doubts. Maintain your perspective and balance. Weigh everything up, then follow an intelligent risk through to its conclusion. Your luck and charm will wins hearts.

Purple for regal vibes.
Scorpio may lash out.
Lucky Numbers: 32.11.25.36.27.18.

Aquarius: Well intentioned you may be, but be careful not to put your foot in it! Sometimes people are best left to their own devices. You cannot be responsible for the whole world. Know when to step back and surrender control. Your belief that you are always right needs to be tempered with caution. Indeed you usually are spot on. But watch out for the times when you're not...they are dangerous. Lose decisions and statements that are ego-based. Love will take you to a better place and lift you higher.
Turquoise inspires creativity.
Gemini may run rings around you.
Lucky Numbers: 21.33.41.36.28.37.

Pisces: Get out and about. Explore things physically, emotionally and spiritually. If you have neglected some aspect of your life, now is the time to step out bravely. Take things further in matters of the heart. New experiences await but you have to go out there and find them. A new dietary and fitness regime is also important. Follow through and you will be feeling a new man or woman before you know it! First impressions count so listen to your extra-sensory perception. Develop your spiritual antennae and learn to discern the truth.
Lilac transmutes negativity.
Leo is fun.
Lucky Numbers: 1.2.33.40.24.35.

Aries: Expect big changes, Aries. The world as you know it is about to be blown apart in a very dynamic way. Time to play the drama queen to good effect and enlist the sympathy vote. Call in favours and find support in unexpected places. Excitement is your middle name and dramatic events will follow you. So don't run away or anticipate how things will pan out. No plans can be set in stone and whatever you count on will be challenged and shaken. Make the most of this energy and live fully in each moment.

Black for protection.

Virgo has the answers.

Lucky Numbers: 27.28.29.20.31.2.

Taurus: Someone is missing you more than words can express. Pick up the phone and sort out a disagreement. Life is too short for silly games . . . so stop playing them! Bend the rules a little bit to accommodate some healthy mischief. But don't overstep the boundaries. Your life is characterised by a juggling act . . . can you keep all the balls in the air? In the long run something will give way. But you will be delighted with the outcome. You have misunderstood someone really special.

Pink for unconditional love.

Fellow Taurus has an agenda.

Lucky Numbers: 32.13.25.36.17.19.

Gemini: This is my second attempt to write your stars this week, Gemini! So do not be surprised if you miss things, forget things or generally trip up. Mercury, your ruler, is retrograde. Double-check all documents, e-mails and appointments. Little surprises may be sprung upon you. Stay cool and tolerant of those who wind you up. Expect hard work to be overlooked or ignored, at least for the moment . . . Patience is needed re the breaks you hope for. Love should keep you sweet and sour in equal measure. Add spice to boost the flavour and don't overindulge . . . less is more. Turquoise boosts communication.

Virgo may let you down . . . well, she forgot to write your stars!

Lucky Numbers: 33.41.25.36.17.39.

Cancer: Pop stars, pop tarts, pop in, pop out . . . is everything instant but fleeting these days? You need to build towards a grounded future. Make the most of ephemeral things, by all means, but do aim for something you can ultimately rely on. Since 9/11 you would rightly question what if anything provides 100% security. In our times nothing can be taken for granted, but your life needs attention. Go for substance rather than the quick fix. Superficial answers fill a hole, but they leave an even wider gap once the thrill is gone. Persistence and commitment in your emotional and working life will unravel the riddle.

Green for space.

Libra is sexy.

Lucky Numbers: 24.35.26.37.40.1.

Leo: Shake your thick 'Leonine' mane to good effect this week. You have the power to make friends and influence people. Your confidence and energies should be at their peak. So perform to the max and reap due attention. Ignore jealousy and resentment – some 'begrudgers' have nothing better to be going on with. Inspire those who love you, and forget the rest. Negative thinking is like a curse. Leave it alone and develop positivity as a protection. Don't buy into doubts or fears. Trust in your abilities and character to steer you through.

Red enhances fiery determination.

Scorpio is mad!

Lucky Numbers: 33.16.27.38.20.4.

Virgo: Love will finally turn a corner and you will get the answer you are looking for. Don't fret if things are not going according to plan. Sometimes the tensions of stress and uncertainty deliver a result just when you are giving up. Bide your time and detach a little from your situation. The more you try to make things happen the further away they get. Relax and don't tamper with people or events. Have faith in the bigger picture, and be assured that everything will make sense in the long term.

Yellow to de stress.

Avoid Capricorn.

Lucky Numbers: 23.14.26.38.7.9.

SCORPIO Time:
October 24th – November 22nd

WEEK FORTY-THREE
October 22nd - October 28th

Scorpio: Many sets of important eyes are looking in your direction . . . enjoy the unprecedented attention! Expect to shine in very unlikely circumstances. Things that fall apart may be rebuilt. But don't tackle the impossible. Accept the end of a situation and try to be dignified amidst disappointment. Love is waiting in the wings. Try not to be too conventional in an attempt to impress the right people. They are already on your side. Just be your good self and the rest will follow.

Magenta enriches you.

Earth signs excite.

Lucky Numbers: 13.16.1.31.6.19.

Sagittarius: Pace yourself with work commitments. You may find your mind wandering towards 'what might have been'. Be focused and controlled. It is important to keep your priorities clear. New additions to the family bring delight but stretch your patience. Watch your diet and consider a new fitness regime. An unexpected windfall is a possibility. Accept all job offers or promotions with an open heart. Passions will stir . . . keep emotions loving rather than angry.

Green for space issues.

Cancer makes you think.

Lucky Numbers: 13.24.35.27.18.19.

Capricorn: Weigh up your options carefully this week. Others may let you down, so reassess your expectations. People are only human and not everyone can live up to your high standards. Make an effort to rebuild fraught relationships. Don't be too proud. If you show willingness to change and adapt, loved ones may follow your example. Make love the order of the day and be as unconditional about it as possible!

Blue for peace.

Virgo knows best.

Lucky Numbers: 13.31.24.42.35.15.

Aquarius: Step out of your time warp and catch up with new trends. Things have changed and you should modify your expectations. Pose an intelligent question and you will get the answer you look for…It's all in the asking. Passion and romance are on the horizon so keep your eyes peeled. New contracts and a work choice look worthwhile. Do not beat yourself up about a foot you put wrong. The Universe will sort the situation out, so reserve judgement and don't panic.

Aqua enhances freshness.

Taurus is sensible.

Lucky Numbers: 31.24.35.27.19.40.

Pisces: Uncertainty will give way to peace of mind. It's all about perspective. Engage in the positive and disconnect from the negative. More of what you expect is on the way. So make conditions good for yourself. Oxygen and the freedom to breathe freely under water is essential for fish. So verbalise emotions and express yourself fully. That way you won't drown in a quagmire of your own making. Economise for a while and rely on your own resources. Love is a miracle that doesn't cost anything.

Purple for spiritual healing.

Water signs support you.

Lucky Numbers: 31.24.26.37.3.17.

Aries: Time is money and money is time. Release yourself from this pressure or you just might explode. A cheerful grin will refresh your memory and brighten your day. Don't give way to smugness over a personal victory. Value every minute with loved ones and cherish the moment. Change is inevitable but exhilarating. To be kept on your toes is a way of being you require. Whether or not you realise it, life will present you with self-made challenges. Enjoy solving the puzzles and leave any mischief time to play out.

Red/gold boosts Aries' identity.

Cracks appear in earth signs.

Lucky Numbers: 4.25.16.37.9.10.

Taurus: Listen to your inner child this week. Fun is there for the taking but also be responsible. You need to be studied and nurtured. Spell out your wishes and make sure you are understood. Misinterpretation of body signals and misplaced words are highly likely this week. A new timeframe is important. Prioritise your commitments and leave triviality out of the picture. Accept credit and blame where it is due. An honest assessment of your heart is important.

Mud colours for homeliness.

Fire signs leave you gasping.
Lucky Numbers: 14.26.37.18.29.4.

Gemini: A one-horse race is easy to win, but surely some competition is healthy! Be confident in your abilities and don't worry if there's a new kid on the block. Look after your own standards and let others fend for themselves. Love will run rings around you – enjoy the ride. Victory is yours if you look to the future and forget past failure. The point of no return gives you a definite framework in which to function. Accept the challenge and prove yourself a winner.
Yellow to de-stress.
Water signs perplex you.
Lucky Numbers: 24.15.36.17.8.33.

Cancer: Your instincts are at a premium, so take advantage of the headstart you naturally possess. Stand up for yourself in a work situation. Life is more wonderful than you realise. Lose the grumpy streak and open your eyes to what you have achieved. Your business has you scuttling from one place to another. Take time to reflect and give yourself a break. Others may resent you, but take this in your stride. A winning streak will come into play…so expect a good return on a gamble or investment.
Copper for autumn vibes.
Virgo makes sense.
Lucky Numbers: 4.21.32.36.17.6.

Leo: Your patience and tolerance may have run out. Hang on a little longer before you wreak havoc! Something you were banking on may yet come about. Reserve judgement before you point the finger. Someone you doubt will prove to be correct and trustworthy. Watch that your generous heart does not fall prey to prowlers. Healthy cynicism is needed where some people are concerned. Unravelling who is for you or against you should prove to be complex but interesting. Love will pounce when you least expect it. Orange boosts vitality.

Aquarius is intolerant.

Lucky Numbers: 31.24.35.40.9.2.

Virgo: If you could unravel and rewind your life, I'm sure at this point you would be tempted. Certain friends and advisors have been serving their own purposes. At least you now have a better idea of whom to trust. Be philosophical about where you have landed. Life still has major shifts and turns to play out. Future surprises will be both stimulating and challenging. A chance to replay events and decisions may seem desirable, but in the long run you will appreciate the current changes taking place. Go with the flow and trust the outcome.

Lilac shades enhance beauty.

Gemini is an opportunist.

Lucky Numbers: 32.14.26.38.40.19.

Libra: The chance to stick up for someone should be taken. You owe a few favours and should champion justice wherever possible. Try not to get so wound up though. Discernment is needed about when to speak and when to remain silent. Positive attitudes are important to boost your

progress. Both work and romance benefit from persistence.
A situation may be dragging its heels and patience is crucial
to the survival of a project.

Lemon and lime for fruitiness.

Scorpio is sweet.

Lucky Numbers: 16.27.38.41.20.31.

WEEK FORTY-FOUR
October 29th - November 4th

Scorpio: Time-out to reflect may be necessary. You are
under pressure. Make sure that people are not taking you for
granted. Love is light and fluffy. At least warmth and understanding will cheer you up. 'Take stock' and reassess your
future. Determination and focus will get you to where you
want to be. But things won't pan out in quite the way you
expect. Everything is cool nonetheless!

Blue for peace.

Earth signs unlock your heart.

Lucky Numbers: 6.23.14.29.40.31.

Sagittarius: Fun and frolics should put a smile on your face.
If someone is missing the point, you might want to give
them a miss. Your sense of humour is second-to-none. So if
someone else doesn't get it or has the inability to laugh at
themselves . . . well that says it all! Don't overstep your
boundaries, and make sure that people respect your personal space. You have a lot to offer, so be loud and proud to
good effect.

Red for passion — aim true!
Air signs fan the flames.
Lucky Numbers: 31.42.15.25.36.17.

Capricorn: Expect to pass a test of faith, and to gain recognition for so doing. You are a formidable mountain of strength when you want to be. I do hope you appreciate fully your value and worth. Don't be afraid to step out into the limelight. You must learn to present yourself effectively with confidence. This won't be an arrogant statement. False humility is pointless when there is work to be done. Love trials come through and Lady Luck smiles upon you.
Blue greens for the heart.
Potential clash with Taurus — be careful.
Lucky Numbers: 32.41.25.36.37.18.

Aquarius: Your plans to prosper and develop may fall upon deaf ears. Be determined to succeed, come what may. Things are not as bad as they seem, so stick to sorting out the molehills. The mountains will look after themselves. Concentrate on the next thing and pace yourself. Modest confident steps will take you further than big blind leaps of faith. Now is not the time to gamble. Build your profile on a sure thing and leave hazard arrangements to the tricksters.
Lemon and lime for freshness.
Earth signs unravel the pieces.
Lucky Numbers: 30.11.17.18.19.29.

Pisces: Swimming against the tide was never your cup of tea. Yet there is something of the maverick about you these days. Not one to stand on ceremony, you no longer give 'two hoots' what people think! Salmon swim upstream then conk out when they reach their destination. You have no time for such pointless fishy behaviour. You intend to trawl the oceans until what you are looking for manifests in front of you. With the greatest of ease you face your destiny. Plum the depths and expect to make a catch.

Aqua enhances all things watery.

Water signs are kindred spirits.

Lucky Numbers: 21.24.36.17.29.10.

Aries: Don't make promises that you can't keep, Aries. You may be overreaching yourself when it comes to commitments. Rely on your own tenacity and determination to win through, but do reassess your priorities. God helps those who accept responsibility for themselves. Most things you do under your own steam, but don't be too proud to delegate. Ask for Divine guidance, as certain puzzles are beyond your ken. You may wish upon a star, but God knows who you are!

Papal colours for Divine protection.

Sagittarius is interesting.

Lucky Numbers: 31.24.36.17.39.4.

Taurus: Was it the chicken or the egg . . . or the chicken? You need to lose the analysis, as you won't be able to unravel the complicated situation you find yourself in. Rhyme has no reason, remember? Something has a grip of you, but you wouldn't want it any other way . . . I think it's called love! Accept everything that happens now with an open mind and an open heart. The most logical route is not necessarily correct. Life has a way of turning things upside down and inside out. Expect to be beaten by circumstances, even while you love every minute of it!

Warm colours.

Does Virgo need a dressing-down or dressing-gown!

Lucky Numbers: 31.26.37.18.39.10.

Gemini: Fight for your rights, Gemini . . . be they animal, vegetable or mineral. You must stick to your own style and own way of doing things. It is your independence and intelligence that separate you from the rest. So do not be dictated to. When you are good, you are very good, and when you're bad . . . well, we know the rest! Pull your socks up, as you don't want to be caught out. The face you present to the world has to shine at the moment. Opportunities abound. Be open to where they are coming from.

Green for financial affairs.

Taurus may corner you . . . but it's fun!

Lucky Numbers: 21.15.36.27.18.19.

Cancer: Get all the 'niggly' things completed and have some fun. You deserve a rest, so get as far away from the 'madding crowd' as possible. Retreat into your own space as a survival policy. Preserve your energies and don't be so damned helpful all the time! Learn when to say 'no'. Certain people are inclined to take advantage. This drains you and saps your willpower. Give your inner child a treat and look after yourself. Winning is inevitable in some shape or form . . . you can't go wrong.

Lilac boosts tranquillity.
Libra is easy-going.
Lucky Numbers: 31.34.25.16.28.30.

Leo: You may be ruffling more than a few feathers. Sometimes you inspire jealousy and complicated reactions in people. This is not deliberate on your part…simply be, and others will have a problem. These folk have got you wrong. They look at your life and think you have everything on a plate. If only they would scratch beneath the surface and see the real you. Undoubtedly you are a survivor and life has been tough enough. Those who matter know the truth…the rest you may ignore. Be selective and discerning. Orange brings zest and joy.
Cancer is sweet.
Lucky Numbers: 21.14.17.19.30.23.

Virgo: Your workload is incredible…and so are you if you can keep up with everything you have to do! Watch out for those who wish to trip you up. Not everyone likes to hear a success story. Your loyalties will be challenged and tested. Be patient and kind. But run a mile from those who are keeping tabs. Only genuine people are worthy of your time. Value yourself more highly and make yourself heard when it's important. Order will at last descend upon your financial situation. Love will spring a few surprises…enjoy!
Black for protection.
Gemini has agendas…what's new?
Lucky Numbers: 22.26.17.37.14.38.

Libra: Keep cool amidst adversity. If you hold onto your goals and smile sweetly, the rumours and gossip won't affect you. People can be quick to point the finger. Just ignore all the nonsense. Maintain balance and be rational about what you have already achieved. Great things lie ahead. Plans may indeed change, but you will ultimately be very pleased with yourself. Trust in the Divine plan. What more can you do? There is no point denying the truth. Things will come out in the wash as always. A clean slate and fresh vision brings peace of mind.

Coral helps unrequited feelings.

Cancer is cute and clever.

Lucky Numbers: 25.36.40.19.28.3.

WEEK FORTY-FIVE
November 5th – November 11th

Scorpio: Take it to the bridge, beach, or wherever you feel most groovy, Scorpio! It's time to let your inhibitions fly. Grab your opportunities and don't miss out. Surrender control and find confidence in a relaxed frame of mind. Life can be more mellow and fulfilling. But you have to 'give it up'! Love is liable to get complex. But what is new! Attract your mate as you will– you know that no one does it like you! Making time for the right priorities is always a great idea.

Berry colours excite.

Filial feelings re Libra.

Lucky Numbers: 23.24.15.36.27.18.

Sagittarius: The time is now, so don't be backwards in coming forwards, Sagittarius. Being the Archer of the Zodiac, you can light the way ahead. Use your dynamic fiery nature to full effect. As your arrow blazes through the heavens expect good things to descend. Obey the safety rules, however, or there really will be fireworks! Projects will bear fruit, but wait until the harvest is ready. Before too long you will have a big smile on your face courtesy of universal goodwill. Sky blue for Divine focus.

Air signs fan the flames.

Lucky Numbers: 3.21.16.27.38.10.

Capricorn: Autumn is upon us so make sure your seasonal moods reflect external events. Gather, assimilate, and prepare for the winter ahead. This should be a joyful, cosy and reflective time. So why are you so depressed? Turn things around. You know it's all about perception. At the end of the day you have done well. Take credit and a well-deserved rest!

Purple for richness and royal blue for deep peace.

Aries is a challenge.

Lucky Numbers: 31.24.26.37.19.20.

Aquarius: Deck the halls . . . well, it's not quite that time yet, but it's fast approaching. Calm down though. There's no need to rush around quite so much as things will take care of themselves. Hang loose and enjoy life – it's a joyride! Obey the rules of the road and not much can go wrong. Just make sure you're legal and allowed to drive the route you have chosen. The traffic warden in the sky may have other plans . . .

Green for heart space.

Taurus is self-sufficient.

Lucky Numbers: 14.18.19.21.32.4.

Pisces: A pout is an unusual breed of fish. Make sure it remains a rarity. There's no need to sulk or behave out of turn. All you fishy folk out there can thank their lucky stars. New heavenly constellations herald dynamic change for Pisces. There is certainly no reason to panic. So wipe all traces of discontent from your demeanour! And prepare for festivities and fun.

Magenta presents the real picture.

Virgo is watching.

Lucky Numbers: 32.14.26.37.7.33.

Aries: Who will rock the boat first? Because if you don't, someone else will! Is it chicken and egg or time and money? What takes precedence in the scheme of things? Reassess your preferences and rethink your expectations. Don't expect the obvious to take place. Some things are pre-dictable and eternal – the rest is up for grabs. This autumnal stretch is a challenge to all things decaying, mulching and disintegrating. Do not expect to hold onto what no longer works.

Red/gold supports identity.

Earth signs are leaving.

Lucky Numbers: 31.27.38.40.21.35.

Taurus: Shift into gear and rev up the engine. It's time to take the plunge and be brave. I would say we have only one life and this is not a dress rehearsal, but you feel as if you have all the time in the world. 'Plod' is sometimes your middle name . . . Go on. Live dangerously! You could always wait until the next time around, but you don't really want to. In your heart of hearts you know that delay of the inevitable has taken its toll. Resign yourself to fresh pastures . . . they look tranquil and lush.

Black for protection.

Earth signs hold destiny secrets.

Lucky Numbers: 31.24.36.40.19.3.

Gemini: Keep your feet on the ground, Gemini . . . You are hovering and uneasy! Use humour to get your way. When you focus, you are quite determined to win people over – relentless we might say. No harm, just don't tread on too many toes to get to where you're going. Destination 'out of bounds' may become less compelling and more worrying. Tedium and tension will stress your energy field if you push too many boundaries. Watch your step.

Lemon to ease bitterness.

Libra will raise the stakes.

Lucky Numbers: 23.34.25.16.18.19.

Cancer: Your 'crabby' nature is really grating the nerves of loved ones. Do try to ease up or else go hide in the nearest rockpool! Your natural petulance often reflects indefinable frustration or boredom. If you could isolate the problem, you would feel much better. So adopt this mission and the world will be a happier place. Humour means you are charming and fun to be with. Rediscover your lighter side…please!

Sea green for tranquillity.

Pisces may do your head in.

Lucky Numbers: 26.25.15.24.14.2.

Leo: Love will have you preening and pruning like there's no tomorrow! Make sure you are sending all those positive vibes in a worthy direction. You cannot help the stirrings of your heart, but you can protect yourself just a little bit. Sometimes you are too open and generous. Never change, but don't be taken for a fool either. Forewarned is fore-armed. Watch a tendency to splash out and overspend.

Red helps grounding and passion.

Taurus is interesting.

Lucky Numbers: 13.15.17.19.30.5.

Virgo: Excitement is in the air…I hope you are ready! A creature of habit you can be, but now is not the time to stand on ceremony. This is not a case of act in haste, repent at leisure – quite the opposite. You may actually regret not taking the bull by the horns if he charges in your direction. Go on, hold on and enjoy the ride. Tempting fate is sometimes a good idea. Certainly it is more stimulating than a lifetime of work . . . work . . . more work . . . and did I say . . . work! Pink for romance and red for play.

Taurus, of course . . .

Lucky Numbers: 14.26.17.19.21.29.

Libra: Your lovely nature means that you can sometimes be too nice for your own good. Be on guard! Use your looks to good effect as they can take you straight to the top . . . no

need for the casting couch. Your charm will get you everywhere and everyone else will follow you. You tend to inspire
loyalty and support rather than resentment and jealousy. So
distrust people who dislike you. Friendly and amenable as
you are, there is something very suspect about the person
who riles you.

White for clarity.

Scorpio is a chancer!

Lucky Numbers: 12.16.17.39.20.21.

WEEK FORTY-SIX
November 12th – November 18th

Scorpio: Serious challenges and changes haunt the air
around you, Scorpio. Breathe deeply and rise to the occasion!
Your time is now, so make the most of this stretch. Don't bat-
ter your head off the wall in a personal situation. A slow
steady pace will take you further than a mad panic! Give up
the ghost and stop being spooked by someone who can read
your mind. They see more than you – just admit it . . .

Deep red helps grounding.

Virgo fathoms the depths and mystery of your soul.

Lucky Numbers: 31.24.35.26.7.1.

Sagittarius: Expect a Montague/Capulet type clash or feud
of the domestic kind. In-laws or family members may have
a rather large bee in their bonnet at the moment. So unless
you want to get severely stung, allow Romeo and Juliet a bit
of personal space and airtime. Give love, star-crossed or not,

the freedom to run its course. Nothing beats the value of self-expression. Let others make their mistakes and avoid a row, or pistols at dawn may make a comeback!

Crystal aids clarity.

Pisces is a head–banger!

Lucky Numbers: 15.16.17.18.29.31.

Capricorn: Single someone out . . . they need a talking to or a dressing-down. Put an 'onlooker' firmly in their place. It's your life and you don't need unnecessary interference from others. Control freak you may be, but this time it's appropriate to scan the horizon for trouble. Your in–built antennae make you hyper sensitive to the faintest whiff of insincerity. Pay attention to this psychic 'raider' or repent at leisure.

Purple for rich serenity.

Taurus will clash horns.

Lucky Numbers: 31.26.27.39.40.21.

Aquarius: Time is of the essence, Aquarius. Don't miss a golden opportunity leading up to Christmas. You will be 'quids in'…but you have to be in to win! At the risk of con-tradicting myself…try not to be so fixated on material goods. Security is important and all very well, but approach life from a different angle, and new perspectives will change you. The Universal flow of abundance has more manifestations than just hard cash. Check that your balance is not off the scale!

Turquoise helps creative flow.

Capricorn has a plan.

Lucky Numbers: 32.26.37.28.19.3.

Pisces: A recent disappointment will turn itself around in an unexpected way. The less tampering you do the better. Destiny has a very definite plan, but you don't see it yet. Perhaps it is time to give someone a second chance. Times have changed more than you appreciate. Move forward and don't look over your shoulder, but you may be surprised to see the past catching up on you in a positive way. Integration of events past and present is necessary for a happy future. Sea colours, greys and greens.
Earth signs annoy you!
Lucky Numbers: 29.30.14.25.36.17.

Aries: Restore your equilibrium with serious pampering. If you don't look after yourself…who will? Resume control in a personal situation, but don't get complacent. A surprise is set to catch you out. React not and retain your cool exterior. You may rage inside but don't let it show. No one crosses you and gets away with it, so. Serve the dish cold – it's tastier that way. Love will mature or die. There is no halfway house in which to put your feet up!
A red rag to a bull?
Avoid Taurus.
Lucky Numbers: 13.25.37.40.5.15.

Taurus: Take the plunge – go on! You won't be disappointed and that's a promise. Stop worrying so much about what other people think. At the end of the day you have to live with yourself. Guilt feelings can be a poor excuse for cowardice. Honesty is the best policy. And that means clearing things up so that you can have a life…or your life back, as the case may be. Be a devil…there's an angel waiting in the wings!

Pastels or browns help you.

Earth on earth *ad infinitum* makes mountains – scale the heights.

Lucky Numbers: 12.13.15.16.27.3.

Gemini: Strip the light fantastic. Normally it's 'trip' I know. But let's not repeat things. Life is camp and gay! Well why not . . . anything goes at the moment. If you can't beat 'em join 'em. For if you don't your tolerance levels will be severely tested. Good news will put a spring in your step, just don't trip yourself up! Riddles abound – get your thinking cap on . . .

Yellow to de-stress.

Fellow air signs help you fly.

Lucky Numbers: 25.16.27.39.21.4.

Cancer: Trust your intuition at all times, Cancer. Something does not add up. You can't put your finger on the reason for your malaise, but you know it's there, like an annoying itch waiting to be scratched. Get beneath the surface of your dilemma and lay the truth bare. Something right under your nose will register. Then everything falls into place. The moral of the story is…whatever you want it to be!

Blue for peace.

Pisces is watery company.

Lucky Numbers: 19.30.25.34.19.23.

Leo: Take the money and run? You think a quick fix is the answer! Think again…Sad and shady dealings will come to light. Be temperate and measured in your response. You can't fool all the people all of the time. After a while someone is bound to notice…How wonderful you are! Overlooked, ignored, taken for granted you may feel. But this won't last. The object of your affections will catch up eventually. Will you be waiting, wanting, hoping for much longer? I don't think so!

Cerise for passion mixed with kindness.

Taurus is enigmatic.

Lucky Numbers: 31.24.35.28.19.30.

Virgo: Take the leap of faith with new opportunities that come your way. Stressed and unnerved by recent events you may be. But do relax, reassured that your star is in ascension. The rate of your accelerated luck may be difficult to cope with. Fear not! Nothing untoward will happen. Every event, however bizarre, has purpose and direction. You are being propelled towards your destiny at a rate of knots. Go with it . . . resistance is futile.

Black for protection.

Avoid smug air signs.

Lucky Numbers: 18.27.30.31.4.5.

Libra: Quality is what matters now. In work, love and family matters, you need to put in a good performance. Stick with what counts and ditch the rest. There is no room for compromise or nonsense. So give wasters no time. Those who work with you will understand. Those who work against you are not worthy of your energy. Peacemaker, remember sometimes bridges won't be built. Leave a wide chasm rather than 'mend' grief, heartache and betrayal. Not everything can or should be fixed…damage limitation time! Red/pinks for letting go.

Walk away from earth signs.

Lucky Numbers: 5.3.15.16.38.39.

SAGITTARIUS Time:
November 23rd – December 21st

WEEK FORTY-SEVEN
November 19th - November 25th

Scorpio: Hang in 'there', Scorpio! Sit loose to people who try to manipulate you. There's no need to buy into their agenda. Stay independent and impervious to nonsense. The machinations of others are tedious. So avoid rising to the bait and don't get caught in sticky webs spun by the opposite sex!

Black is sexy.

Don't get stung by fellow Scorpio…nasty!

Lucky Numbers: 23.14.16.28.39.3.

Sagittarius: Megabucks, mega-star, or mega-mess! It's up to you…Which do you want to be looking at in years to come? Don't overshoot, but reach for the stars by all means. Just take your time to discern what presents you with the best chance. Your humour and instincts won't let you down, but be patient in matters of the heart. A leisurely approach will build long-term connections. Lasting links are more satisfying than short sharp shocks!

Green for heart stuff and finances.

Libra may give you the runaround.

Lucky Numbers: 32.12.15.26.37.28.

Capricorn: Preserve your energies. You will need all your resources on tap for the juices to flow. Creativity is at a premium, so nurture it rather than burn out. Intelligent decisions are set to take you further than ego-based frantic panics! Stay measured and calm. Let the powers-that-be come to you. Know your worth and be proud of your achievements, but be balanced. Availability and willingness to improve are also important.

Blue for peaceful times.

Virgo is smart and canny!

Lucky Numbers: 12.24.36.41.33.2.

Aquarius: They say live life to the full, Aquarius, but do watch expenditure. Money is an energy that needs to flow. Just make sure it flows towards you rather than away from! Luxurious indulgence is expensive. However, loss of identity and real values is a huge price to pay. Follow through your dreams, but not at the expense of love, honour and integrity − remember there's no credit card for these! The most costly things cannot be replaced. Discern what counts . . . finances are the least of your worries.

Yellow to de-stress.

Gemini means business.

Lucky Numbers: 29.30.31.24.35.27.

Pisces: I'm emphatic – the emphasis you need to place on priorities cannot be emphasised enough! Tautology comes easy to the word-player but don't mince yours this week. Speak plainly and from the heart. Swim free and chart new waters rather than get caught in the nets with the shoal. Slippery fish get away with it. You may not. Make sure the risks you take are watertight. What you decide now…matters!
Receive a veil of protection from purple.
Aries is scary!
Lucky Numbers: 42.15.27.18.39.32.

Aries: 'It ain't what you do/it's the way that you do it – that's what gets results!' Sorry, I never did warm to the sentiments of Bananarama! What you do now is crucial to the shape of your future. Make sure you are not investing in futile diversions. Every second counts and the clock is ticking. Your measure of input will directly reflect the return, so choose a sure thing. Watch your step with love. The old waltz is set to change into a mad tango – unavoidable I'm afraid. Reds to floor the opposition.
Earth signs are up for it.
Lucky Numbers: 2.31.14.26.5.11.

Taurus: I don't know what to say…you've stumped me! I'm lost for words. Makes a change, so! Taurus can have this effect on the unwitting. Do remember this and have mercy on us lesser mortals. All the charm and charisma at your disposal may just retrieve the situation. Think quickly and act on impulse. If not, the most precious thing that ever presented itself will be gone. Plod on if you will, but times change. What you thought was for keeps will disintegrate. Pink for love.

Listen to male Taurus (not female).

Lucky Numbers: 10.22.41.23.4.21.

Gemini: 'Words don't come easy', Gemini. Not true in your case! No matter how complex things get, you have an answer for everything. Don't be too complacent though, as you don't want to trip up. Be circumspect and cautious. Keep your winged feet firmly in those shoes, or your Achilles heel may be exposed and floor you. Flying high is all very well, but reality bites and you are due an early wake up call! Turquoise inspires creativity.

Taurus is on your tail!

Lucky Numbers: 24.31.27.19.33.4.

Cancer: Stop all that dithering, Cancer. You may be reeling from shock but the time is now. Be brave and make lightning instinctive decisions. Many twists and turns to the plot are likely. So take centre stage for your finest performance. Heroic behaviour will stand you in good stead. Remember 'the show is not over 'til the fat lady sings'. As far as I'm aware she hasn't entered the auditorium yet! Panic not: loosen up and give it your best shot.

Lilac assists transmutation.

Leo is waiting.

Lucky Numbers: 21.28.39.42.3.4.

Leo: 'Hopalong Cassidy' or 'Strollalong Bill', which are you? The ease with which you move through life is an issue. Are you on safari or aimlessly wandering the plains of the Midwest? Leonine prowling is on the agenda. Just make sure you are focused and know who you are and where you're heading! Stay out in the open in full view. This is not the time for lurking. Let your prey see you coming. That way the victory is all the more impressive! Pounce when they are complacent in your company.

Green for money clarity.

Air signs hover, watching.

Lucky Numbers: 2.4.6.18.32.19.

Virgo: Are you losing patience with your impatience? It's time for a different approach. Turn up the volume – pump it up (even if you don't really mean it!). Draw attention to yourself for all the wrong reasons and you just might get noticed. Kick and scream down the corridors of power and demand to see the manager! Yeah, I'm joking…such undignified behaviour doesn't suit you. Relax and let life happen. Destiny will seek you out. Surrender control, and prepare for some surprises! Be seriously cool…

Black protects.

Avoid dithering air signs.

Lucky Numbers: 13.24.26.37.19.4.

Libra: Checks and balances are all part of the Libran experience. Do yours tip the scale nicely or weigh in beneath your requirements? A mere feather or niggling annoyance can upset your equilibrium. Don't reduce your standards, but remember the rest of us are human, so cut us some slack. Now is not the time for prissy fussiness. Get those feet firmly into the mud and have some earthy fun! Count your blessings and stop looking for that pound of flesh. Vengeance, resentment and frustration don't suit your normally refined temperament.

Violet awakens you.

Get stuck in with earth signs!

Lucky Numbers: 13.24.35.26.17.18.

WEEK FORTY-EIGHT
November 26th – December 2nd

Sagittarius: Hey, Sagittarius, 'keeping up with the Joneses' may be on your agenda, but think again! Count your many blessings and review what you have achieved. There is no point looking over your shoulder at the prosperity of others, particularly if it is just for show. Move away from such superficiality and have confidence in your own identity. Ironically, when you idolise the things money can't buy, the Universe will provide!

Gold heightens wisdom.

Leo adds to the fun.

Lucky Numbers: 2.33.24.15.27.11.

Capricorn: Use humour to lighten your spirits and those who 'block' you should fall over backwards. I guess it's better to die laughing than to keel over from stress. Get 'niggles' and troubles into perspective. You will be the stronger for a new outlook and more than ready to take on your detractors. Use 'reverse' psychology to floor the opposition with your charm. That way you are the winner and your conscience is clear. Present the world a smile – it may just smile back!

Black for protection.

Gemini for a laugh!

Lucky Numbers: 23.14.25.37.40.19.

Aquarius: Try to avoid tapping into others' energy. Be as self-sufficient as you know you can be. You are determined to achieve a personal goal at all costs, but hold onto your integrity…and your hat! Any funny business will backfire. The Universe does not take kindly to being forced along. Indeed resistance to your plans is inevitable if you remain stubborn. Your way through the maze is to relinquish control. 'Impossible' you say…'unavoidable', I say! You are being challenged to trust, so surrender to Divine Will.

Pale blue for a Divine connection.

Apologise to Virgo.

Lucky Numbers: 21.24.35.27.18.39.

Pisces: Kissing fish often become glued together. Do you have room to breathe or is someone asphyxiating you? Fish need full use of their lung/gill capacity, so swim off if you feel stifled. Boundaries are so important to Pisces. Too much leeway and you go bananas; not enough and you go quietly insane. Different expressions of the same thing, so! Make sure you are balanced and keep your equilibrium intact.

Insist on your freedom, but also realise you need connections to flourish. When the river bursts its banks or the flow is reduced to a trickle expect a fight for survival.
Yellow for stress.
Capricorn brings structure.
Lucky Numbers: 13.25.37.38.19.10.

Aries: You have only yourself to blame, Aries! No that's not strictly correct, but it doesn't help to see it any other way. Take responsibility for your part in a complex situation. Blame the monsters in someone's head by all means, but don't be oblivious to the fact that you own a few too! Investigate your blind spots. As near perfection as you are, sometimes your hot head needs a shower! Take a 'rain check' on your future with a particular person. Delay of the inevitable never helped anyone. Muster your best resources and claim victory with your head held high!
Purple for courage.
Listen to Gemini.
Lucky Numbers: 1.7.14.15.23.40.

Taurus: 'When the going gets tough'…you run for the hills! Whatever happened to the rest of the song Taurus? Remain 'with it' and have the courage of your convictions. It's time to be brave, stick your neck out and fly. Stop protecting your interests quite so desperately. By the time you have worked out what really counts, the opportunity for freedom may be long gone. Do you want to languish in a sense of failure? You already know what could happen. So go out there and take the bull by the horns. Don't be weakened by circumstances or imaginary obligation.

Red helps grounding.

Fire holds the key to your heart – run!

Lucky Numbers: 7.14.21.33.42.1.

Gemini: Have more confidence in your sweet poetic soul! Don't you recognise that description, Gemini? Dig deeper! You have unfathomable depths at your disposal. Although not immediately obvious, you have profound imagination and sensitivity. People who love and know you experience your softer side, but access gentleness and consideration on a broader scale and you will have the rest of us eating out of your hand! The world awaits your input and pearls of wisdom. Tap in and monopolise on the 'feel good' factor…you won't regret it!

Green for heart stuff.

Aries fans the flames.

Lucky Numbers: 3.6.9.37.27.18.

Cancer: A bit of a wandering minstrel you are! You jolly along, with your head in the clouds, leaving your dependants wondering. There's nothing wrong with being a law unto yourself or giving vent to your maverick nature, but do keep your feet on the ground. It's OK to enjoy your own little world, but open your eyes long enough to see what's going on around you, sometimes at least! If you feel like an alien in a strange land – connect. Come out of your shell and land on *terra firma*. The next high tide will sweep you away, of course, but at least we'll have seen something of you!

Blue for tranquillity.

Scorpio understands you.
Lucky Numbers: 3.33.9.27.38.24.

Leo: Munchkins of the world unite! There's a sense of mischief about you at the moment. Cause mayhem, havoc and be a general nuisance. Why not! This feeling of abandon doesn't happen often, so make the most of the high jinks…pay later. I'm only partly serious, of course. This advice doesn't sanction robbery, assault and battery, but it does sanction a damned good time – enjoy!
Leprechaun green … definitely.
Gemini to add to the nonsense.
Lucky Numbers: 31.24.35.27.38.1.

Virgo: You may be the main culprit or the prime target. Either way there's a set-up in the air – don't buy into it. Stay away from your enemies, never mind that nonsense about keeping them close. Your pure nature, full of good intention, lays you open to abominable treatment sometimes. Albeit quite subtle, it's abuse nonetheless. So stay centred and in control of your world. Run things your way and avoid those who 'tap' in and drain you.
Deep blue brings deep peace.
Air throws you off track.
Lucky Numbers: 13.25.16.41.7.27.

Libra: An event will tip the scales in your favour at long last. You may have felt imprisoned lately or constricted by your commitments. Your stretch behind bars is drawing to a close. Unfetter yourself from the ties that bind and the chains that hold you. Simply turn the key that's been staring you in the face for a long time. The answer is right under your nose. Have a look!

Red/orange boosts bravery…once the shock has worn off. Scorpio is a pain.

Lucky Numbers: 4.14.32.5.11.16.

Scorpio: Mysteries captivate and enthral you. Scorpio love all kinds of extremism as long as they feel in control (No, I won't mention serial killers!). Be careful you don't get in too deep. It wouldn't do to create riddles and entanglements beyond your capabilities. Walk into the maze and you can expect to get lost. What seems like a challenge could lead to frustration. Make clear and precise plans for retreat. Keep many balls in the air if you're able…but juggling and game playing doesn't suit you!

Deep red offers protection.

Libra is annoying.

Lucky Numbers: 30.21.27.38.4.5.

WEEK FORTY-NINE
December 3rd - December 9th

Sagittarius: Quit that spoon-rubbing for just one second! True magic is not that simple. You can't contrive it, demonstrate it or conjure it, unless you're a magician, of course. But trickery is one thing . . . magic is another. Many magicians resort to deviant moves to pull the wool over your eyes. Impressive as it is, illusion does not satisfy . . . you need real

events to put the spring in your step. So 'get jiggy with it'
... get out there and make it happen – all by yourself!
Purple hues raise spirits.
Virgo proves exciting, given half a chance.
Lucky Numbers: 13.14.25.17.38.17.

Capricorn: Take stock, clean out cupboards and generally
scour the pantry. No there's not a war on (not yet anyway);
but you do need to be practical and check over your
resources. There is a test of duration, stamina and stick-abil-
ity on the horizon. Count your blessings and work to mul-
tiply your impact using the rations at your disposal. It's
amazing what you can achieve when push comes to shove!
You don't mind 'roughing it' as long as it means you scale
the heights eventually and gain recognition. All power to
you...
Green for finances.
Mischievous Gemini is up to tricks.
Lucky Numbers: 3.14.27.37.18.9.

Aquarius: It's about time you accepted responsibility for
being wrong about something. There are a few 'blind spots'
on the highway of your life. Be fair and don't hog the main
lane, especially not when others need a break. Pull in for a
rest, have a fry up, strong coffee, wee nap...anything so long
as you stop hogging the limelight! Modesty becomes you far
more than arrogance. Revving up your engine won't get
you noticed; it will just annoy people. Watch out for a severe
case of road rage if you don't start toeing the line!
Blue to calm you down.

Fire signs get romantic and wind you down.
Lucky Numbers: 2.3.4.15.16.38.

Pisces: A spot of fishing will help you adjust to imminent changes, Pisces. Cast out a line and see what you catch. There are plenty more fish in the sea, and being the Zodiac fish your understanding of the waterways is second-to-none. Use your intuitive antennae to fathom uncharted waters. The more mysterious your options the better. You need some magic and intrigue in your life . . . something to look forward to. Trust me . . . it's coming!
Sea Green for peaceful fishing.
Scorpio makes loaded suggestions.
Lucky Numbers: 14.15.36.27.38.4.

Aries: The mercurial Freddie has words of wisdom…thunderbolts and lightning…very, very frightening! Magnificent as Bohemian's Rhapsody can be, do make sure you can still hear at the end of the blast! Don't repeat mistakes. There is a price to pay for pushing the boat out and living beyond the extremes of your endurance. Look after yourself! Excess is all very well but it doesn't leave you very well at the end of the day. Moderation in all things please. I may be a killjoy…but life is precious, no?
Red boosts fiery determination.
Leo will take you on.
Lucky Numbers: 12.41.32.14.25.3.

Taurus: Have you become a bit of a joke? Has someone had the last laugh? Prepare for fun and games, Taurus. What you dish out, be it amusing, witty, or rather unkind, will come back to haunt you. The tables can turn and unless you think quickly, embarrassment will be your bedfellow! It's all very well making a point, but don't set your good self up in the process. Someone is on your tail with a set of ready-made answers. Take a familiar stranger seriously. Your charm can get you out of most things, but not this…!

Green and blue support an honest heart.

Gemini keeps you in place.

Lucky Numbers: 16.17.28.19.30.1.

Gemini: Laborious, tedious and routine life may be, but don't let it bug you! Very shortly you will be swept off your feet in a highly unlikely manner. Gossip or scandal will catch your attention. Do keep your elegant nose out of it. 'Something' is set to hit the proverbial fan soon. Interesting and entertaining – yes! Messy – yes! Sad – definitely not! Justice is served and someone receives his/her comeuppance. Communicate your wishes, and focus on your long-term dreams. There's only one person who can make it all happen…YOU!

Vibrant colours to cheer you up.

Be nice to Virgo.

Lucky Numbers: 13.32.21.24.25.16.

Cancer: The grass is always greener? Why believe this deception? Don't buy into illusion or you will reach the wrong conclusion. Be more observant - distant pastures are paler. And the lush greenery is right under your nose! Far horizons may be tempting, but they are a poor substitute for the real thing. Do stop looking over your shoulder at the deep distant past and surrender your dreams to heaven. Divine inspiration can be yours. So turn your attention to seascapes and ignore the grassy verge! Crabs feel more at home exploring the ocean depths. Relish every present emotion and the various shades of green become irrelevant. Colour: NOT green for the moment!

Pisces understands you.

Lucky Numbers: 13.24.35.26.17.19.

Leo: You may feel shredded and frayed at the edges. Don't worry. You still look pretty! Present a positive image to the world regardless of your inner turmoil. You will thus impress the faces that can bring you peace of mind. Hold onto your composure and hope for the best, as you are still on track to receive it! Keep the faith and surrender your little will to the guidance of the Divine Will. Life has a happy way of teaching us the lessons we signed up for. So don't fret if things are going pear-shaped. The bigger picture looks great.

Pale blue for God's way.

Sagittarius will lift your spirits.

Lucky Numbers: 3.21.40.29.38.14.

Virgo: I smell a rat! Someone has pulled the wool over your eyes, Virgo – a most unusual state of affairs. Don't get paranoid or distrustful. Angry you may be but do continue to take people at face value. This is difficult when you can read motivations and souls but desirable nonetheless! So what happened? You already have a sense of the deception – you're sitting right in it! Justice will be done, but it's not up to you to serve the sentence. Clear up your situation as best you can and accept responsibility. It's the only thing to do. Keep your dignity at all costs.

Deep red protects.

Taurus has decided.

Lucky Numbers: 13.15.16.27.38.9.

Libra: Are you tired of the razzamatazz? Unlikely, as your sociability is high, but you are getting tired– a night's sleep wouldn't go amiss! Don't pin all your hopes on the career you thought would take you higher. It will, but not quite in the way you expect. Destiny has a trick or two up its sleeve. Surprises will be merrily sprung when you least expect them. Forewarned is not forearmed. Prepare to be disarmed, swept sideways and off your feet altogether! Panic, shock and delight will hit you simultaneously. Get ready for weird sensations.

Deep blue brings deep peace.

Gemini is a laugh.

Lucky Numbers: 14.16.37.27.32.41.

Scorpio: If you have any secrets I hope they are swept well and truly under the carpet. Mysteries, scandal and gossip will be revealed in very sensational ways. Make sure you're not part of it. A sharp-clawed fat cat will cause havoc amongst the pigeons…feathers will fly and it could get nasty! People who were previously charming could suddenly about-turn…Typical! Don't let it eat you up. Keep your cool and your independence. You will have the last laugh, but you need to be free of those who undermine you with a smile on their face.

Black and white keep you clear.

Cancer is seriously funny!

Lucky Numbers: 31.10.20.30.16.4.

WEEK FIFTY
December 10th – December 16th

Sagittarius: Keep a handle on your temper and use humour to defuse a situation. Your instincts pull you through a tricky scenario. Take credit, and give yourself a pat on the back. Money can buy you items, possessions, trinkets, but not anything of real value. Assess your priorities and don't blow a good thing. Folly isn't a pretty sight.

Blue and pink combined for inner healing.

Leo is a contender for your heart.

Lucky Numbers: 14.24.34.25.36.2.

Capricorn: If events are not quite going to plan – don't panic! There's a rhyme and a reason for most things under the sun. As for the rest, a philosophical approach will keep you sane. Our vulnerability and mortality are important factors we often overlook. Accept that it's not possible to demystify life totally. Not everything can be cut, shaped and tailored to fit our requirements. Lessons of trust and surrender are potent but necessary. Be courageous and ask for guidance. A sense of enlightenment will descend but you must do the work first.

Deep royal blue links to Archangel Raphael.

Expect a battle of wills with Aquarius.
Lucky Numbers: 14.25.6.36.3.24.

Aquarius: Surprisingly, someone is running rings around you – makes a change! There's something to be said for being kept on your toes, but ballet routines leave you cold. Stop pirouetting for a minute and survey the landscape. You may find you have more leeway than you thought. Stop trying to accommodate 'all and sundry'. Not everyone can be helped. Give up circular arguments as you are expending a lot of energy in the wrong direction. The treadmill should soon become the Ferris wheel…full of colourful promise. Shimmering silver for moon power.
Earthy company…Taurus/Virgo.
Lucky Numbers: 31.25.36.37.28.19.

Pisces: Sign on the proverbial 'dotted line' by all means, but go in with your eyes wide open…Leave the rose-tinted specs well hidden! Realise what it means to sign your life away as issues of commitment surface. If in doubt –DON'T! Selling out for a quiet time is perilous behaviour. Keep your soul intact. Any paperwork that ties you to a binding contract needs careful scrutiny. Be sensible, cool and follow your instincts. If you feel that inner wobble…RUN!
Pink for unconditional acceptance.
Taurus lights your fire.
Lucky Numbers: 30.16.37.26.14.25.

Aries: A welcome event is upon you – the stirring of the thick soup that is your life. Liquefy, water down and season!

This makes things more palatable, tasty and digestible. Drastic measures will help the redistribution of heat, and lukewarm parts can savour the glow of new intensity! Use economics and good sense. Most chefs are too proud to serve up bland broth. So go 'cordon bleu' with your expectations and rev yourself up to Michelin star level! Oh and give those last remaining lumps a good pummelling too (or vigorous workout).

Deep red helps grounding.

Aquarius is cuddly.

Lucky Numbers: 23.41.14.25.16.17.

Taurus: Has something upset your balance, or co-ordination? Are you absolutely sure you are not to blame for this? Only in part perhaps! There's a cosmic reshuffle taking place – for very good reason. Don't look back in anger, but do look forward to new blessings. A distortion of what you had been expecting will come about. But your destination is at this point a bit hazy. Trust the navigator in the sky. The stars are bright, but planetary activity is mysterious. Enjoy the suspense…it won't kill you!

Magenta/turquoise: 'go with the flow'.

Virgo/Capricorn are in the wings.

Lucky Numbers: 19.20.34.25.36.1.

Gemini: Your plane is coming into land. But do be aware there may be a few aborted attempts before touchdown. You can expect a bit of turbulence and clouded vision. Traffic control has more urgent priorities at present. Be prepared to stay up in the air for a time to come. Relax and enjoy the ride. There's no point resisting the current conditions. Things are beyond your control. Burn off excess fuel/energy and intermittently check with the tower for instructions. Look after what you can attend to and trust for the rest. When you get the 'all clear', the runway will of course be CLEAR!

Navy helps aerodynamics.

Air signs will help you along.

Lucky Numbers: 24.16.37.40.19.5.

Cancer: Cruise control may need to alert the stealth bombers! Get surveillance to keep a close check on the enemy. After all there may be a surprise plot to take you out! If this is a hot but dangerous date…go for it. On the other hand you may just be overly paranoid. Relax a smidgin. Don't buy into intimidation or conspiracy theories. Try to keep a handle on your negative thinking – you are undermining your strong position. Your reality reflects your beliefs. So create a healthy environment to scuttle around in. Purple/orange help spiritual shock/deception.

Virgo is a comfort.

Lucky Numbers: 13.14.15.17.29.5.

Leo: Be at your roaring riotous best! You have something to shout about. So make a BIG noise! Whether it be good (joy) or bad (anger)…let off steam. You're like a pressure cooker ready to blow. Twiddle the knob quickly or there will be a messy explosion. An eruption at this stage will be a short sharp shock. Leave it much longer and you'll be cleaning gunk off the ceiling, or we will be scraping you up off the floor. Say your piece, celebrate, or have a good old ball. You'll feel better in the morning!

Magenta grounds you.

Sagittarius gets you going.

Lucky Numbers: 24.15.26.37.29.10.

Virgo: 'The times they are a-changin.' So hold onto your hat, brolly, or whatever else you use to keep the rain from your eyes. 'Love and theft' may have become a reality. You need a bob or several to sort it out. Be careful you don't have your most precious commodity robbed from under your nose. Your freedom counts for something. So value and respect it, even if no one else does. Be gentle with a battered and bruised heart. And get ready to meet your soul mate.

Turquoise helps creative flow.

Air signs are deceptive – be careful.

Lucky Numbers: 20.34.25.36.17.2.

Libra: For heaven's sake, look skywards! You have become bogged down in mundanity at the expense of the bigger picture. Practical considerations are all very well. But material concerns are no substitute for soulful communication. Speak from the heart…don't lose touch with what's important. Circumstances do not have to dictate your reality. Become master of your destiny and co-ordinate the action. Take up the reins of the chariot that nearly went off the track. And steer yourself through the riot…don't surrender!

Yellow to de-stress.

Gemini is fun.

Lucky Numbers: 4.3.17.19.11.3.

Scorpio: Untangle that sticky web, or your spidery behaviour could entrap you. Never mind the prey, or target. Leave your machinations on the shelf. If someone is meant to wander into your lair or 'trap' it will happen organically. The more you try to twist events, the more they will work against you. Give into 'Murphy's law'…a pint of the Black Stuff should see you right. The Yin Yang effect is a non-negotiable Universal concept. The blacker things get (negativity)…the more they will be balanced by the light. So don't lose the head…the frothy bit is important!

Black and white helps clarity.

Virgo is sexy underneath the cool exterior.

Lucky Numbers: 1.2.13.14.25.36.

WEEK FIFTY-ONE
December 17th - December 23rd

Sagittarius: The countdown to Christmas is well under way. Try to sound excited! Treat yourself for added cheer. Then at least you have some control over what Santa puts in that stocking. Don't let the tedium of what's expected get to you. Actions speak louder than words…though at this time of year the reverse is true. So beware of Greeks bearing gifts…don't trust anything gift-wrapped! Listen to what people SAY, not what they present. For the moment they just might mean it…

Fiery reds for oomph!

Gemini really cares.

Lucky Numbers: 1.6.25.32.14.3.

Capricorn:Think about what you really want and need this Christmas. Make a wish list and ACT upon it (so wish!). Don't fret about the things you cannot change. But make damned sure you sort out the things you can! Be responsible for your decisions. Take this seasonal time to prioritise your future and mull over the wine. Intimate chats and special presents make for an important moment. Be of good cheer – 'tis the season to be jolly after all! Put misery aside and lock Scrooge in the cupboard – he's not useful when extravagance is called for.

Green for lavish spending.

Virgo is canny and smart.

Lucky Numbers: 25.34.16.17.28.19.

Aquarius: Rummage in the attic for all the tinsel, fairy lights, glitter balls you can lay your hands on. Deck the tree and lay out the presents. Show willing to embrace 'the love in the room'! If everything is in the right place, then maybe the right things will start to happen. Create your own magic. On the other hand, if the trappings of Christmas leave you cold, use your imagination and creativity to prepare another way. You don't need to buy into the clichés. . . But do get involved. Let there be no signs up this year which say 'cancelled due to lack of interest'!

Blue for peace.

Fellow air signs see the other side.

Lucky Numbers: 14.5.27.31.17.21.

Pisces: Do you feel like there's a 'slow train coming'? Something is in the air, but you can't put your finger on it!

With the geese fattening up by the minute, you need to get into gear. So stoke the engine and keep a steady pace. If you're chugging along in the right direction, you will make the destination…eventually. Relax a bit and enjoy the view. Frenetic activity causes derailment, so avoid the big rush. However, if you're stuck on the platform waiting, be assured and listen for the distant whistle. Patience is a station that is tedious but necessary!

Aqua boosts freshness.

Taurus is tempting.

Lucky Numbers: 14.15.17.29.34.12.

Aries: Fret not! Your 'Mission Impossible' will be accomplished. The delectable Tom may not be in your corner, but cruise along trusting the bigger picture. Gather all the resources at your disposal. Nifty tactics are needed to traverse the rocky terrain up ahead. The more premeditated your decisions are, the better. So co-ordinate a strategy and follow it with military precision. The discipline will pay off and you will reach your target, blazing a trail behind you!

Gold assists wise action.

Gemini pays up.

Lucky Numbers: 12.11.17.26.36.3.

Taurus: To all hobbits and littletons…There's a dangerous journey that needs to be completed carefully, responsibly, and bravely. Don't be daunted by the goblins, ogres, and gremlins that line the route. Steer a steady course towards Mount Doom and dispose of your burden. Big Brother is watching you. Keep your eye on the way ahead and hold onto your dignity. Ring bearing has its price. Your task is placed upon you for a reason. So watch, listen and learn. SEE clearly and no challenge will defeat you.

Deep red provides protection.

Earth signs bring passion.

Lucky Numbers: 34.25.16.27.8.19.

Gemini: Harry Potter has plenty of tricks up his sleeve. Do you? Tap into some natural wizardry and make your own magic this Christmas. You can create, manifest and concoct some seasonal surprises. If life has become a little stale, freshen things up. Be the magician who channels energies wisely and potently. The Universe allows a bit of dabbling on occasion. Just make sure your integrity and spirit are WHITE. Then nothing can come back to haunt you.

Yellow to de-stress (again).

Fire signs rally round.

Lucky Numbers: 28.38.19.20.33.24.

Cancer: Nestle into your home environment and make it comfortable. Enjoy the festivities – there are big changes afoot. Santa may unintentionally put his big Wellington in it! Laugh off any embarrassment and keep things in perspective. 'Sliding Doors' syndrome means that however complex your circumstances become, you end up with the same result. You may think you know what you want, but the Universe will show you an alternative. Open Sesame…!

Pink for love things.

Scorpio entices.

Lucky Numbers: 11.21.32.14.25.36.

Leo: Don't get too full (of yourself) amidst the festivities. You love a party, so do attend everything in sight. Plenty of envelopes are opened at this time of year! Give and receive graciously- it's all in the wrapping. So present a good face to the world...you may just feel better deep inside. Your popularity is at a premium. But remember the Beatles' adage 'money can't buy me love'. Keep a reign on the purse strings and don't overextend your credit. Do unwind and have fun, though stay wise to hangers-on and liggers!
Gold attracts riches.
Capricorn understands.
Lucky Numbers: 23.14.25.17.38.9.

Virgo: Although your spirits may be down, there's no need to raise them artificially. OK, so the liquor cabinet looks tempting, colourful and tantalising, but leave high levels of abuse to the experts. The indulgence of 'drowning your sorrows' doesn't suits you. Find other ways to get high...like cheering up, counting your blessings and laughter! Pick yourself up – ah, go on! Justice will be served, but not in the way you expect. Let the Big Man in the sky fight your corner and defend your rights.
Silver for moon shadow.
Healing from Scorpio.
Lucky Numbers: 13.25.14.37.6.28.

Libra: Balance is everything for you, Libra. So don't torment your soul with extremes of behaviour. The pendulum can swing either way...just let it sway with its own momentum. Reserve big judgements for later. Energies will shift naturally and effortlessly if you detach and remain impartial. The problems that wreck your head at present will dissipate of their own accord. Enjoy the craic and keep warm to fend off chills…what better medicine!

Purple for healing.

Fly with Gemini.

Lucky Numbers: 12.34.15.26.9.18.

Scorpio: Leave control, composure and consistency in a corner. Wrap it up for another time. Now is the season to let it rip! 'Tis the season to be jolly, so get out and about and spend some lolly! Never mind the corny rhyme. Clichés serve a purpose, especially at Christmas. Enjoy all the glam and glitz. Frivolity and fun will spark up your mood, and clear fogginess from ze head! Unite with friends and family to go the whole hog. Make up for lost moments and consider the real meaning of Yuletide (when you have a minute).

Turquoise boosts communication.

Libra is a distraction.

Lucky Numbers: 23.14.25.37.8.29.

WEEK FIFTY-TWO
December 24th – December 31st

Capricorn: Happy Christmas, Capricorn. Have a good one! Things will settle nicely, so relax and have some fun. Switch off to routine, pressure and stress as much as possible. If you have to work, get things done A.S.A.P…then chill.

Delayed plans will come good, so stick to arrangements. Your patience will be rewarded. Smile and laugh with the rest of them. And when you can't perform, your best 'fixed' grin will suffice. If you're stuffing the turkey, make sure it doesn't get stuck on your head!

Christmas colours for cheery thoughts.

Virgo will support you.

Lucky Numbers: 6.17.25.34.17.38.

Aquarius: Merry Christmas, Aquarius…may it be bright and light! You could find there's one too many crackers on the table. So make sure everyone is included in the fun. Absent guests will be there in spirit. Celebrate and decide to enjoy yourself. The novelty of food, presents and drink may have worn a bit thin. So use your imagination and connect with people on a deeper level. If all else fails, remembering the TRUE message of Christmas should shake you into shape! Santa will warm the cockles of your heart…Hot toddy's at the ready.

Gold, frankincense and myrrh…Be wise!

Quiet times with Aries.

Lucky Numbers: 21.32.4.15.36.27.

Pisces: *Joyeux Noël*, Pisces! There's an international flavour to festivities this year. Embrace the world with your fine spirit and good resolution. Fish can feel a bit misplaced…'at sea', if you like. Engage in the fun and be part of a scene you can relate to. Be true to yourself and don't be under pressure to come up with 'expected' behaviour. This is the time to let your hair down and be YOU! Don't fall out over the pudding though. There's enough nonsense in the air. So don't squabble over who gets the ring! Be gracious enough to wear the paper hat for once...

Plum, figgy colours ooze richness.

Cancer is comforting.

Lucky Numbers: 31.24.35.17.20.2.

Aries: Family fun, frolics and plenty of sherry should guarantee a good Christmas. You love all the fuss and warmth of the season. So have a great time and steer clear of killjoys. After all your hard work, you deserve to be treated like royalty. Find your throne and lord it over the proceedings...no one minds you running the show...for once! When you have a moment, sit quiet and reflect on Silent Night. Blessings are highlighted and emotions run close to the surface. Count the good things and be grateful for the rest!

Green and red help loneliness.

Taurus talks too much!

Lucky Numbers: 16.17.34.21.6.5.

Taurus: Seasonal Greetings to all bulls! You love the sensual opportunities of Christmas: log fires, family times, plenty to eat and drink...Taurean heaven! Spare a thought for those who don't have these comforts or who are lonely. Your charm and humour will brighten many a gathering. Watch that the mistletoe doesn't get misplaced...there's a potential embarrassment waiting to pounce...Enjoy! Affairs of heart and mind get deliciously complex. Go with the flow and follow your instincts. Events have been a long time coming...

Red boosts energy.
Don't resist earth signs.
Lucky Numbers: 19.20.30.42.21.2.

Gemini: What a buzz, Gemini…Merry Christmas! Your feet will hardly touch the ground. The Big Santa in the sky has many gifts and presents for you. But some blessings will come in disguise. Think on your feet this time. All the toys, trinkets and treasures under the tree make an important statement. Give from the heart or not at all. Do an 'MOT' on your spirit and willingness to participate. Free yourself from conditions and expectations. Acceptance is crucial, and unconditional love is the best gift of all.
Turquoise boosts communication.
Get grounded by earth signs.
Lucky Numbers: 33.31.6.16.27.8.

Cancer: *Gute Nacht*…sorry, wrong sentiment! You may feel like kissing 'goodnight' to all the festive fun, Cancer. But hang in there! There's plenty of scope for entertainment. Events will engage your interest. So remain open and well disposed. You don't like phoney or clichéd expression, so certain aspects of Christmas turn your stomach. Too much turkey perhaps? 'Sit loose' to all the nonsense and enjoy yourself in your own sweet way. Avoid sentimentality and 'deck the halls' in whatever way you choose.
Lilac transmutes negativity.
Fellow Cancer understands.
Lucky Numbers: 21.33.24.34.2.4.

Leo: Hey, Leo…no need to wish you well this season. It's a given you'll enjoy yourself- you always do! Watch Christmas doesn't go to your waistline though. The extra tyre may not be a welcome sight come January. But do have fun. You have been working extra hard and deserve a break – a bit of self-indulgence won't go amiss. Carrying a 'spare' is an important safety measure anyway, so…! Breakdown is highly unlikely, but you should be prepared. In fact you need the buffer of an extra layer, so coming events don't overwhelm you. Protect your heart and keep a clear head.

Reds and orange attract fiery passion.

Sagittarius lights your fire.

Lucky Numbers: 17.38.29.4.32.6.

Virgo: Camaraderie (bonhommie) brings good feelings to the fore. So supposedly does a romantic partner (*bon homme*)! As you will see there's not much difference (in spelling)- where's a good man when you need him? Get out there and embrace him/her /them…whoever! I'm not saying anyone will do, but make your connections count. Whether party-ing with a crowd or in the company of a 'good fellow', wear a smile. Let happy vibes carry you, wherever they come from. Loneliness is criminal at Christmas – you don't want to get locked (up) now do you!

Pink for unconditional love.

Leo is generous.

Lucky Numbers: 31.2.4.6.17.19.

Libra: A Joyous Chrimbo to you, Libra! Your carpet will be swimming in gift-wrap and rubbish by the end of it all.

Enjoy the exchange of gifts and good feeling. There's a lot of excitement in the air. It's a magical time…so get inspired by film land. Many profound clues and messages lurk in the script and scenarios of events you witness. Listen and learn. Synchronicity is working overtime. So be open and receptive to what the Universe provides. The best presents are intangible and immaterial (look up the other meaning!).

Pale blue for Divine Will.

Gemini is funny.

Lucky Numbers: 22.17.19.5.11.24.

Scorpio: Get the mistletoe ready! Merry Christmas Scorpio! You're even more in demand than usual. So expect lots of attention and good vibes. 'Do you feel the love in the room?' You are well loved, to the point of confusion. So many offers – such little time. Be rebellious and follow your heart, but don't expect to keep up with everyone. Do your best and suit yourself. You will get everything you wish for 'and some' this Christmas! Be bold, brave and beautiful, as only you know how.

Black for cool.

Virgo is good for you.

Lucky Numbers: 31.33.24.25.36.17.

Sagittarius: This is your season to be jolly, Sagittarius. Have fun! Keep your sense of humour as potent rumour and scandal does the rounds. It all adds to the spice of life. Variety is the key to your fulfilment, or so you believe. Calm down a bit and concentrate on those who give you their undivided attention. You love a challenge, but you do need a rest from looking over the fence. Look skywards for inspiration. Listen to your better self and follow your heart. A quality present is a declaration of love. Don't be afraid to express your feelings, so!

Bright blues for good vibes.

Leo is good company.

Lucky Numbers: 14.25.36.27.18.9.